WARLORDS RISING

WARLORDS RISING
Confronting Violent Non-State Actors

Troy S. Thomas, Stephen D. Kiser,
and William D. Casebeer

LEXINGTON BOOKS

A DIVISION OF
ROWMAN & LITTLEFIELD PUBLISHERS, INC.
Lanham • Boulder • New York • Toronto • Oxford

LEXINGTON BOOKS

A division of Rowman & Littlefield Publishers, Inc.
A wholly owned subsidary of The Rowman & Littlefield Publishing Group, Inc.
4501 Forbes Boulevard, Suite 200
Lanham, MD 20706

PO Box 317
Oxford
OX2 9RU, UK

British Library Cataloguing in Publication Information Available

Library of Congress Cataloging-in-Publication Data

Thomas, Troy S.
  Warlords rising : confronting violent non-state actors / Troy S.
Thomas, Stephen D. Kiser, and William D. Casebeer.
      p. cm.
  Includes bibliographical references and index.
  ISBN 0-7391-1189-2 (cloth : alk. paper) — ISBN 0-7391-1190-6
(pbk. : alk. paper)
  1. Political violence. 2. Terrorists. I. Kiser, Stephen D. II. Casebeer,
William D. III. Title.
JC328.6.T56 2005
303.6'25—dc22   2005006761

Printed in the United States of America

∞™ The paper used in this publication meets the minimum requirements of American
National Standard for Information Sciences—Permanence of Paper for Printed Library
Materials, ANSI/NISO Z39.48-1992.

Contents

List of Figures and Tables

Acknowledgments

N O BOOK IS AN ISLAND. Over the past several years, numerous individuals and organizations have provided the intellectual, financial, and emotional support required to bring this manuscript to completion. The following list is by no means exhaustive, and to those who remain (by accident) unmentioned, we offer our apologies.

Institutionally, we thank the Institute for National Security Studies (INSS) and the Institute for Information Technology Applications (IITA), both located at the United States Air Force Academy. Dr. James Smith, the director of INSS, and his sponsors have generously provided both seed capital (in the form of research grants) and a venue (in the form of conferences and occasional papers) for exploring ideas. We thank him and his staff for their efforts; we are gratified that royalties from this book will be used to support INSS initiatives. General James McCarthy, the director of IITA, along with his staff has provided insight into how to frame our ideas to make them operationally salient. Their generous support of our modeling work during its infancy was critical. Colonel Russell Howard at West Point Combating Terrorism Center provided moral and financial support for area familiarization and conference presentations. Our graduate and fellowship institutions, including the Pardee-RAND Graduate School, the Council on Foreign Relations, the University of California at San Diego, the University of Hawai'i at Manoa, the United States Air Force Academy, the Joint Military Intelligence College, and the Naval Postgraduate School, all did their best to equip us with the intellectual rigor and creativity needed for analyzing violent non-state actors.

Individually, multiple scholars, family members and friends provided corrections, insight, and encouragement. In particular, Donald Hanle, Timothy

Kane, James Russell, James Cook, Bill Rhodes, Carl Ficarrotta, Peter Chalk, Rohan Gunaratna, Read Montague, Thomas Coakley, Russell Swenson, Patrick Flood, Jason Bartolomei, and Paul and Patricia Churchland provided useful feedback and academic mentoring. Paula Thomas, Shelley Taniguchi, and Adrianne, Jonah, Mara, Linnae, and Mason Casebeer not only served as excellent "in-house editors," but were tolerant of the frequent travel. Our families shared their minds and time to make this work possible.

Much of what is true and good in this book we owe to these organizations and individuals. As for the rest, we take full responsibility. Our best and only hope is that the ideas presented here can be fruitfully developed so as to make the world we all inhabit a more safe and secure place in which to live, learn, and grow.

Preface

THE SECURITY ENVIRONMENT OF the twenty-first century will be characterized by two important trends. First, global integration and connectivity will increase. The world's trajectory toward the free exchange of goods, capital, people, and information will continue. The second trend both results from and is a cause of connectivity: the increasing influence and power of non-state actors. Moreover, non-state actors that use violence to achieve their goals will add uncertainty to an already turbulent world security situation. As we write, foundational national security documents of the United States identify international terrorist organizations—a type of violent non-state actor—as the foremost security threat. Despite these trends, the relationship between nascent non-state organizations and the environments that create and nurture them remains largely unexplored. Indeed, theoretical frameworks that comprehensively delineate the inputs, processes, and outputs necessary to cause the genesis, growth, maturation, and possible transformation of violent non-state actors (VNSA) are difficult to come by. This is unfortunate, as such a framework is a necessity if we are to formulate a comprehensive, consistent, and workable strategy for confronting malignant armed groups. Deterring, disrupting, and defeating organizations such as terrorist groups requires an empirically defensible approach.

One very promising paradigm for framing the violent non-state actor challenge is open systems theory. What environments give rise to VNSA? What environmental inputs sustain VNSA throughout their developmental cycles? How can we change the environment or intervene in the functionality of a VNSA so that it develops a less threatening organizational structure or ideology? How can we confront these warlords rising in a manner that channels their development into more fruitful political spaces or, if that fails, that actually succeeds in disrupting and defeating them? This line of thinking about these issues owes much to the pioneering work of systems theorists such as Ludwig von Bertalanffy among others. However, the systems approach on offer here is not merely an application of the original; it is sensitive to the failures and shortcomings of past attempts to apply systems thinking to political and social realities. As such, our approach is pragmatic, informed by contemporary research in organizational theory, ecology, individual and group psychology, and political science.

While it may be thought that systems theory has already had its heyday in political science, we hope this freshly framed systemic approach can reinvigorate the study of violent non-state actors and can serve as a "walk-in closet" in which can be hung the pioneering work of political scientists ranging from Martha Crenshaw to Charles Tilly. It is not an attack on ideas proffered by those engaged in the serious study of terrorism and violent social movements so much as homage to the invaluable work already accomplished. Moreover, our approach frames violent systems in such a way that it is relatively easy to translate important qualitative insights into the behavior of the system into quantitative models and simulations which can be used to stress-test ideas and to flesh out such foundational work.

The bulk of this book was written before the invasions of Afghanistan and Iraq; the framework offered herein, though, is generalizable (as it was developed both inductively from myriad examples and case studies and deductively from existing theoretical approaches). While we do not address these two conflicts in as much detail as we would like, our framework can usefully provide advice regarding how to proceed (indeed, we are happy to report that it is currently in use by those involved in formulating counter-insurgency strategy in Iraq). We hope that by the end of the book the strategic upshot of our analytical vision will be apparent.

Two important caveats: First, our framework is not a panacea; we fully expect ourselves and other investigators to describe its limits in the future and that many of its insights will merely confirm received wisdom rather than innovatively undermine it. Even where theoretical clarity is possible, practical action ("What do I do *now?*") may remain a murky affair. However, this cannot be helped, and it should not be used as a rationale for abandoning attempts to examine security problems systematically and comprehensively. Second, interdisciplinary projects like this are difficult; our academic backgrounds are in political science, policy analysis, cognitive science, management theory, systems engineering, and philosophy; our work, however, touches on fields ranging from sociology to ecology. No doubt we have skated over details that practitioners of any particular field justifiably find to be critically important. Our brevity, and in some cases our outright "informed ignorance," was necessary if we were to begin to make progress at all. We hope those whose work we have adapted will be inspired to explore how these various fields can contribute to the formulation of a comprehensive strategy for confronting violent non-state actors.

1

Warlords Rising

Despite the scorch marks on his hindquarters, the donkey is standing re-markably still while the American soldiers decouple the tri-colored, four-wheel cart. With agricultural produce stacked high, this donkey gives all appearances of heading to market, which is in no way surprising since today is a Friday in Baghdad, Iraq. Except today is not any Friday; it is November 21, 2003, and this donkey has just played an inglorious role in an insurgency being waged by former elements of Saddam Hussein's regime and foreign fighters, some linked to the al Qaida terrorist net-work, against the United States and its coalition allies. Underneath the dusty heads of lettuce, this cart and at least three others are carrying up to twenty-one rockets. Minutes before, two to three rockets strike the Palestine Hotel, temporary home to western journalists and contractors. Two civilians are injured at the Palestine, and in a case of extreme mis-fortune, one rocket bounces off the sixteenth floor and lands in front of the Sheraton, killing the bell boy. A seven to ten rocket salvo against the Iraqi Oil Ministry hurts no one, and two additional weapons-heavy carts are found near a Kurdish party headquarters and a law school.[1] While clever in their economy of design, the attack of the donkey carts is un-likely to have any significant operational or strategic impact on its own; but when combined with ten to twenty other attacks throughout central Iraq, involving improvised explosive devices, surface-to-air missiles and coordinated guerrilla tactics, the cumulative effect grows. The perpetra-tors are known generally, but the specifics of their organization remain shrouded in the fog of war. They may have been of a state, but now they are without. They may reflect the nuances of the struggle for control of post-Saddam Iraq, but they are characteristic of the contemporary face of collective violence.

DONKEY CARTS LADEN WITH rocket-propelled grenades, teenage girls wrapped in nails and explosives, and civilian airliners filled with fuel and travelers: these are the weapons found in the arsenal of today's most ubiquitous adversary—the violent non-state actor (VNSA). With few exceptions, VNSA play a prominent, often destabilizing role in nearly every humanitarian and political crisis faced by the international community. A sample from across today's geo-political landscape reveals a Hamas suicide bomber haunting the streets of Jerusalem, Nepalese Maoists launching another round of bombings in Kathmandu, and Indonesian terrorist groups and human traffickers exploiting the horrific aftermath of the December 2004 tsunami. As non-state armed groups gain greater access to resources and networks through global interconnectivity, they have also come to dominate the terrain of illegal trade in drugs, guns, and humans. The broad spectrum of objectives and asymmetric methods of these contemporary assassins and Barbary pirates fractures our traditional conceptions of war and peace. Whether concerned about national security or human security, the warlords of the modern era pose a pressing challenge for which the nation-state is ill-equipped.

This book aspires to equip those charged with confronting this mounting challenge by *delivering a framework of analysis designed to improve understanding of VNSA in order to affect their development and performance.* To achieve the first half of this goal we introduce and employ an inter-disciplinary framework, rooted in open systems theory and guided by modern organization theory. Our analytical framework represents an alternative paradigm for diagnosing armed non-state organizations as *open systems* on three inter-related levels. At the environmental level, it provides more powerful insight into the conditions and dynamics that shape VNSA formation and development. At the organizational level, it directs our inquiry toward holistic characteristics and relationships that enable VNSA to prosper, adapt, and achieve goals. Conversely, the open systems methodology exposes weakness—vulnerabilities directly related to developmental phasing, environmental dynamics, and internal mechanisms. The internal workings of the VNSA represent the third level of analysis, which focuses our attention on the organization's functions and their contribution to overall performance during periods of uncontested growth and, more importantly, in the context of a turbulent environment. The open systems methodology is a universal framework for a global problem set. As a flexible tool, it allows for structured analysis across regions and functions, which is increasingly important given the transnational character of VNSA. Recognizing the uniqueness of groups like Hezbollah, the levels of analysis also provide common scaffolding on which the signatures of specific groups can be built.

Thus equipped, the other half of our goal, affecting VNSA development and performance, is tackled. Whether the policy maker's goal is preventing, coercing, or conquering, we offer an innovative strategy for countering VNSA. We examine the utility of traditional theories of deterrence and warfighting in light of the insight gained through open systems analysis. In so doing, we elevate and sketch out the role of environmental shaping in VNSA development, recast deterrence in ecological terms that incorporate emotional as well as rational factors, and proffer principles for crafting strategy and operations to ultimately defeat the adversary. The result is an integrated approach that marries diagnosis to strategy, and optimistically enables forecasting future organizational behavior and assessing the effects of a counter-VNSA campaign. At the end of the day, we establish a comprehensive framework that links analysis to action and action to analysis.

Our integrated approach is informed by literature on the subject but is also distinct from it. This book certainly does not represent the first effort to address violence outside the state. The surge in terrorism literature in the last decade and revolutionary warfare three decades ago produced extensive inquiry into the subject. Anarchists, communists, philosophers, and a variety of other thinkers were writing on the subject at least two centuries ago.[2] It is the increase in non-state violence in the last generation, however, that moves the subject from a minor interest to a significant subject of research.

While a thorough categorization is well beyond the scope of this book, literature on VNSA is largely compartmentalized. Work on "terrorist organizations" is extensive, owing largely to the sea change in scope and lethality of terrorist activity from the 1960s to the 1980s, the increasing notoriety of al Qaida in the 1990s, the horror of the September 11 attacks, and the ensuing global war on terrorism (GWOT). Writing on transnational criminal organizations, mafias, drug cartels, and smuggling operations is less frequent and less developed, but it exists in small circles we enter later. Serious inquiry into emerging warlords, environmental terrorists, modern-day anarchists, and violent anti-globalization organizations is sparse. Missing from all these efforts is a unifying framework. In fact, the term "violent non-state actor" is not yet popular in the international security lexicon, as most analytic efforts reach a level of specificity that preclude such a general term.

Existing VNSA literature is further compartmentalized into three categories. In descending order of scope, these categories are (1) environment, (2) organization, and (3) individual. The first category seeks contextual explanation, scanning the political, economic, and social landscape to find empirical commonalities or a theoretical basis for violent organizations to emerge. A second body of literature generally looks at the violent organization itself, searching for internal dynamics that lend explanatory power to why a group eventually (or initially) turns to violence in pursuit of its goals. The last category examines the individual. It is a more psychological and philosophical effort, searching for common traits or beliefs among the individual purveyors of violence. The lines between these three general approaches to violent organizations are not clear and certainly not mutually exclusive, but neither is there an effort to develop linkages among them. The result of this intellectual compartmentalization is a level of granularity and specificity in knowledge that is without question valuable but leaves the impression that no commonalities or "category-crossing" explanations exist. We leverage the existing literature, applying it within a unifying framework to draw out the commonalities that are relevant to policy.

In the remainder of this chapter, we outline the broad contours of a changing international security environment, set forth a basic definition for VNSA, clarify the core elements of our interdisciplinary approach, and preview the chapters and key concepts of the book. As a final introductory note, the tone of this work suggests that all VNSA are bad. They are not. Examples abound, including America's own revolutionary history, of armed groups contesting the state for enlightened purposes. Bearing this in mind, and recognizing that our work is emerging during a period defined by a GWOT, our efforts are intentionally geared toward understanding non-state actors in order to preclude their selection of violence. Where this fails, and assuming that their use of violence is a threat to security in its many forms, this work is intended to mitigate and eliminate the threat.

Whither the State?

"There never was in the world two opinions alike, no more than two hairs or two grains; the most universal quality is diversity."[3] This observation by Michel de Montaigne—over 500 years ago, when the world's population was about one-twelfth of what it is today—only begins to capture the political kaleidoscope of our world. Thousands of different colors, creeds, religions, practices, cultures, actors, ideologies, and myriad other categorizations make up the composite of humanity. While this richness is something often celebrated in the pages of National Geographic, it has also been the source of much human misery throughout the ages. Tribes fought tribes, clan conquered clan, believers slaughtered heathens, those who have plenty are attacked by those with little; indeed, brutality is a common feature throughout the relatively brief history of homo sapiens. Whereas de Montaigne was celebrating the diversity of the world, another famous social commentator one hundred years later suggested that same world was a place where everyone lived with "continual fear, and danger of violent death; and the life of man, solitary, poor, nasty, brutal, and short."[4]

Different groups of humanity have always tried to do something to bring order to this chaotic tapestry, primarily in order to protect themselves and their means of eking out life. Owners of flocks in Central Asia and Mongolia didn't try to defend borders—a foreign concept to a nomadic culture anyway—but simply tried to protect their flocks and families as they roamed the vast steppe. The Qin Dynasty built a Great Wall to keep out raiding Xiongnu tribes while Hadrian built a smaller wall to keep out the raiding barbarians. Others simply walled their cities rather than their frontiers to keep out those who would do them harm. Warrior classes were created and tasked to defend interests, usually the lives of the privileged. More than one powerful figure attempted to bring order to their world through conquest. Despite the various creative manners peoples attempted to protect themselves, in the absence of an international system of order, might made right.

Not until the 1648 Treaty of Westphalia formally codified the state, however, was security and order based on territory and an absolute sovereignty. While this new political creation helped create order and safety within their borders, relations between states still proved to be anarchic. Relations were based on unequally distributed power, and the system was deficient in supranational authority and international law. Independent sovereign states were forever threatened by stronger states; most continued to exist precariously through a balance-of-power system while some failed to survive. Just as all political entities formed alliances and power blocs, these new states found it in their interests to create collective security arrangements through treaties and alliances with other states. States participated in ever-more elegant political balancing acts, as they believed that was the best inoculation against international lawlessness. The world became less and less multi-polar through time; only two power blocs existed during the Cold War, and in the post–Cold War, a unipolar power emerged with a possible return to a multi-polar system may be on the horizon. Thus, the relations among humanity historically have tended to move upward toward greater and larger organizations and away from the basic, irreducible unit of security—the individual.

But there is a fundamental tension between the greater organization that states represent and human diversity. Early on, the peculiar unity and coherence of the modern state was largely based on its physical, corporeal characteristic: an expanse of territory with demarcated borders often marked with a "hard shell" of fortifications. These marked borders defended by the "hard shell" to some extent secured the state from foreign penetration, thus making the state the ultimate protector for those within its boundaries. Thus, the state became the primary focus for security, the impenetrable atom of political physics. It was assumed that people—the very entities that the state was designed to protect—in the long run, would recognize that the authority which possesses the power to protect is the authority with which their loyalty must lie.[5]

There was more than that. As states evolved from more than protected real estate and monarchies to entities encompassing loftier goals and ideals, individuals were more than potential soldiers awaiting their conscription or chattel of the state; they required more than mere protection. They needed a sense of identity. As direct rule expanded throughout Europe—the birthplace of the modern state—the culture, language, and daily routines of ordinary Europeans came to depend on their state or residence. Internally, states imposed national languages, educational systems, military service, and more. Externally, they began to control movement across frontiers, to use tariffs and customs as instruments of economic policy, and to treat foreigners as distinctive people deserving limited rights and closer surveillance. As a result, life homogenized within states and became more differentiated between states.[6] Thus, the idea of the state being an "impenetrable unit" and the primary element of security analyses appeared to be an increasingly safe assumption.

In an era of globalization, the "impenetrable unit" is becoming increasingly porous and its grip looser. Individuals have always been able to swear their loyalty to any idea, be it a religion, an ethnic group, family, or local power structure. However, the power of the state typically limited the implications of these non-state loyalties; once formally created, states were clearly the loudest and most powerful voice in the mix of shouting for attention from fickle individuals. As authority and legitimacy have been lodged with the state for the past several centuries, citizens of the state and actors external to it have been habituated to accept orders from and actions by the state as the final word. Their creation, however, did not sweep away all the other potential suitors vying for the individual's attention, acceptance, or loyalty—it merely overpowered them, and temporarily at that.

The success of the European states at homogenizing life at home led them to believe they could accomplish the same abroad. Colonial powers exported their own religious, economic, administrative, and political orders, efforts that essentially cloaked much of the non-European world for over five centuries. Tribes and clans, remarkable for their fluidity, were catalogued, given new identities, and otherwise rigidified by colonial governments. Traditional power structures, rarely as formal and delineated as European governance structures, were forced aside, and cultures perceived as inferior were suppressed. Imagined communities were created, wishful power arrangements made, and a temporary—and false—order and harmony were bestowed upon the savages.

Much has changed since the height of state power. Centuries passed, myriad wars were fought, territory traded hands, and empires crumbled. The global system of states continuously morphed as various shocks, large and small, changed the nature of international power. As technology led to greater and greater destruction in the ever-present conflict between states, the changes in the system became increasingly profound. The most system-shattering of these wars were World Wars I and II, which all but destroyed European states as global powers, leaving them unable to maintain their vast colonies in Asia, Africa, and the Middle East. In their place, new states were created, sometimes with sufficient thought given to the underlying geo-social realities, but often not. Collapse of the Soviet Union and violent destruction of the Federation of Yugoslavia followed decolonization by several years, adding even more new and progressively weaker states to the world's tally. The result of these trends is remarkable: The number of states in the world mushroomed from more than fifty after World War II to nearly two hundred at the beginning of the twenty-first century. In a geo-politically dizzying pace, vast empires were replaced with weak and dysfunctional states, often incapable of running their own bureaucracies, let alone defending themselves from threats from without—or within.

Other trends are eroding the state monopoly on international political power. Technology diffusion gnaws away the monopoly of power states once enjoyed by providing smaller and smaller groups with sufficient tools to elude, or sometimes even to challenge, state authority. Porous borders allow smugglers equipped with adequate vehicles to move sometimes even large groups of humans and materiel across political lines with impudence. Powerful non-state actors can provide more attractive incentives to key individuals within a state, making the state less effective at protecting itself, or in some cases harnessing the state's power for itself. Communication and coordination can occur across great distances, despite state efforts to prevent such activity. Money can electronically change hands across thousands of miles. Technology has made the angry young man nimble and loud, capable of interacting with elements both in and outside the "impenetrable" state. Conversely, the geriatric, ossified state sits befuddled as it slowly discovers that the forces of globalization render its "hard shell" into so much Swiss cheese. The result is burgeoning populations placing increasingly large demands on progressively incapable states around the world. A dog starved at his master's gate predicts the ruin of the state, indeed.[7]

The state always was and continues to be less than a perfect mechanism to express, enable, or contain the diversity of the world. Initially, this defect didn't matter; as long as the state was the most powerful actor, the world's texture of disorder and discord could easily be spackled over with the broad knife of state authority and the coercion it could bring to bear. But with the trends described above—more, smaller, and weaker states coupled with increasingly powerful and capable individuals—competing loyalties in the world matter more and more. The relative power disparity between states and individuals is shrinking. Thus, when an individual decides to swear loyalty to a religion, a family, or a local power broker instead of a state, it matters a great deal.

Today, the Dutch are no longer exporting teak wood from the East Indies, but the not-entirely-loyal Indonesian Army is fighting ethnic separatists on the island of Aceh. Spain no longer mines silver out of the Kingdom of New Grenada, but the government of Colombia is fighting an intractable war against the Revolutionary Armed Forces of Colombia (FARC), a group that controls stretches of the Colombian hinterland. The Czars no longer play the Great Game with Great Britain in the Caucusus, but Chechen separatist rebels have taken over theaters, bombed apartment buildings in Moscow, and held hundreds of school children hostage. The U.S. Army is no longer putting down rebellions on the island of Jolo in its former colony in the southern Phillipines, but is sending advisors to the to help fight the Abu Sayyaf and the Moro Islamic Liberation Front. Portuguese diamond merchants no longer are supplied from their former colonies in present-day Angola, Sierra Leone, and Liberia, but multiple rebel groups with links to transnational criminal organizations and militant religious groups fight for control of diamond mines in the region, as sales of these "conflict diamonds" fund additional recruitment and weapons purchases. Chinese Triads control flows of goods and cash in Asia worth possibly over $30 billion a year; indeed, some estimates suggest the Triads earn $3 billion a year smuggling humans.[8] Indeed, even in the motherlands of the former colonial powers, the Basque Fatherland and Liberty Party (ETA) continues to fight Madrid from the Pyrenees, planting bombs near police stations and assassinating Spanish authorities, while the Irish Republican Army (IRA) has splintered multiple times and appears to be more interested in drugs than in democracy. And in a sign of the times, governments are hiring private corporations to field mercenary armies to fight internal rebellions on their behalf—modernity's own Buffalo Soldier perversion. *Untrue, there have always been private armies*

Welcome to the world of violent non-state actors (VNSA)—a world of chaos where warlords are rising and states have yet to formulate a coherent strategy to deal with the anarchy they bring. In what could reasonably be called an understatement, United Nations General Secretary Kofi Annan stated, "Not all effects of globalization are positive; not all non-state actors are good."[9] He was commenting on what many sociologists refer to as the "dark side of globalization," a term referring to how the links and connectivity that bring the world closer together can quickly transmit crises around the globe, as the Asian financial crisis and the SARS epidemic so balefully illustrated. Prominent political scientist James Rosenau comments on what he refers to as a "skill revolution," whereby technology has not only made the individual vastly more aware of macro events around the world, but also empowers the individual to perform increasingly important micro events. A population undergoing a skill revolution is simultaneously less likely to blindly follow the orders and authority of their own state, and more likely observe and feel compelled to interact with activities around the world.[10] For good or for bad, both tendencies undermine the state system.

But these linkages are even more subtle and far-reaching. Diaspora communities, often more loyal to their identity than those who live in the motherland, can use modern and legitimate means to transfer goods and resources to support illicit and deadly activities. No longer is the Sri Lankan military simply battling a local, powerful rebellion, but they are battling the Tamil Tigers of Elan (LTTE) in Sri Lanka and the Tamil communities in Europe, Canada, and Australia that provide extensive support to the movement. The British were not only battling angry Dubliners, but had to contend with Libyan support and a sizable IRA support base in Boston as well. Al Qaida appeals not just to young Afghan men fresh from the refugee camps in Pakistan, but has evolved into an ideology with a global message. Networked VNSAs who are not hobbled by the political restrictions of states nevertheless benefit and exploit those things states created, which led to globalization in the first place. Indeed, globalization seems to be a tri-edged sword. It is globalization that is bringing all of us closer together—the first step to greater understanding. But that new proximity is highlighting our differences as well, which can be manipulated to shape conflict. Additionally, the technologies of globalization enable those groups who wish to prevent further shrinking of the globe to attack countries anywhere in the world. Globalization has given reason for and enabled the Luddites to attack the globalizers—an ironic and cruel twist.

Violent Non-State Actors

Providing a single definition for nearly any violent organization is difficult at best. For example, well over one hundred different definitions for "terrorism" (a single form of violence used by non-state actors) exist, and nearly that many exist for "criminal organizations" (a single type of VNSA organization). Given these difficulties, we offer a broad definition coupled with general attributes as a baseline for analysis: a *non-state organization that uses collective violence.*

While simple, the key terms of *non-state organization* and *collective violence* are the entry points to a far more complex reality. VNSA are much more than individuals armed with small weapons, more than recorded tapes released to media outlets around the world, and more than drug kingpins living lavish lives in broad daylight. These are merely the most visible elements of the organizations. VNSA have many functions and patterns of activities that may be mundane but are still important for their existence and operations. These organizations exist in an environment that influences them and is influenced by them. The VNSA themselves all have different characteristics, goals, sizes, and methods. A much richer discussion of VNSA attributes is therefore possible, and in fact, a book is required.

VNSA are a distinct form of non-state actor. Their purpose and method distinguishes them. VNSA resort not only to random or opportunistic aggression but to collective violence as a tool to achieve goals. Collective violence is really an extension of collective action, which is coordinated action by the members of the group in pursuit of common ends.[11] Usurping that unique role of a legitimate user of violence—an action that at least the members and sympathizers of VNSA see as justifiable and is tolerated by a significant portion of the rest of the world—puts them squarely at odds with the classical state system. This "relocation of authority" from the classical state system to the non-state system is not new in and of itself, but it is unprecedented in scope.[12] VNSA are also illegitimate as their goals typically put them at odds with states' goals. Challenging state authority, engaging in economic activity deemed inappropriate or conducted outside the white market, or pursuing goals generally deemed as socially undesirable make them targets of the state—or at least that part of the state system the VNSA has not been able to corrupt.

As social entities, VNSA have an "enduring membership and specifiable authority relationships."[13] Social movements, one-time demonstrations, and even some revolutions do not fit within the context of this non-state actor definition. Rather, those phenomena typify how the "leaderless public" emerges out of "the separate but convergent actions of many individuals who do not share organizational membership."[14] While such an amorphous grouping certainly has the potential to evolve into a VNSA, its lack of organization excludes it from our framework.

All VNSA exist within an environment that can create or prevent, can enable or inhibit, and can influence VNSA for good or for bad. The VNSA themselves are the actors in question; they act, operate, and pursue their goals. There are multiple ways to categorize VNSA: organization, identity, type of violence, goals, purpose, region, recruitment methods, etc. Depending on the context, the use of one categorization over another may be useful. For example, if an analyst is trying to understand the rapid growth of Sendero Luminoso membership in the late 1980s, comparing and contrasting their recruitment methods to other VNSA is useful. On the other hand, if a leader is trying to harden his or her facilities against possible attack from VNSA, the form of violence is the most appropriate categorization. Recognizing that various typologies of VNSA are possible and even valuable, we offer nested categorizations based on the group's primary purpose, or reason for being, and the nature of its core functions.

Analytical Approach

Open systems theory serves as the diagnostic framework for our interdisciplinary analysis of VNSA. We have deliberately used the term diagnosis several times already. As applied in modern organization theory, diagnosis is the process of employing conceptual models and methods to assess a target organization's condition in order to solve problems and increase performance.[15] We diagnose VNSA for a different but related purpose: assess the capabilities of threatening organizations in order to decrease and deny their performance. Our diagnosis is framed by open systems theory, meaning it is directed by an open systems—informed theoretical framework, which allows for analysis of key concepts and the relationships among them.[16]

The open systems framework springs from the general systems theory of Ludwig von Bertalanffy in the 1940s, but it did not catch hold in the social and organizational sciences until the 1960s and 1970s. Championed by Daniel Katz and Robert Kahn in their seminal work *The Social Psychology of Organizations*, open systems theory emerged as modern organization theory by the 1980s, replacing the more limiting structural approach. Among its many early benefits, the "adoption of a systems frame helped researchers in the social sciences to discover commonalities with fields such as biology and engineering, and it provided a basis for an interdisciplinary approach to organizations."[17] After over sixty years of applied and basic research, open systems theory has emerged as the principal approach to understanding organizations. Its language and methods have infused national security documents, war fighting strategies, and tradecraft of the intelligence community.

At its most basic, open systems theory views all organizations as systems, interacting with their environment in a dynamic manner. In the words of Bertalanffy, it conceptualizes a system as an "organized cohesive complex of elements standing in interaction."[18] The interaction refers to two generalized patterns of behavior that must keep our attention throughout: (1) the relationship between the organization and its environment, and (2) the relationships among the "complex elements" or parts of the organization. The latter constitute the transformational processes of the VNSA, while the former draws attention to the reality that organizations are exposed to the world, continually exchanging information and energy with the environment.

Too often organizations are analyzed in isolation from their environment with excess emphasis on internal structures, including organization charts, leadership, rules, formal communications, and process efficiency to name a few. While it is a useful aspect of organizational diagnosis, this *closed system* approach neglects the simple reality that an organization "must interact with the environment to survive; it both consumes resources and exports resources to the environment."[19] As put by Katz and Kahn, "living systems, whether biological organisms or social organizations, are acutely dependent upon their external environment."[20] The VNSA emerges as a response to environmental pressures, and it is in turn affected by contextual constraints and opportunities.

Thus, our approach lends itself more to an inter-disciplinary application based on ecology, engineering, social science, and cognitive science than it does to the Newtonian physics of closed systems.

It is an understatement to say that open systems are highly complex. As put by noted organizational theorist and practitioner Richard Daft, "the organization has to find and obtain needed resources, interpret and act on environmental changes, dispose of outputs, and control and coordinate internal activities in the face of environmental disturbances and uncertainty."[21] To simplify, which is essential to ensuring that our diagnostic framework is applicable on the street, we need to zero in on a common set of attributes. All organizations share the following basic components: (1) importation of energy and resources; (2) through-put (transformation of this energy and these resources); (3) export of product to the environment; and (4) dynamic pattern of activities and feedback. Organizational inputs are many but generally include the raw materials, money, people, equipment, and information.[22] Outputs can be objective and subjective but generally include products, services, ideas, and in the case of VNSA, collective violence. The transformations—the ways it converts inputs into outputs—are often the most difficult to diagnose, particularly given the shadowy character of VNSA. Finally, all relationships inside and outside the organization are dynamic; they involve feedback—VNSA are cybernetic systems. As put by Katz and Kahn, "Inputs are also informative in character and furnish signals to the structure about the environment and about its own functioning in relation to the environment."[23] Organizations learn.

An initial look inside the organization reveals a dizzying array of activities and behaviors whose overall contribution to performance seem beyond determination. Systems theory improves analysis by structuring these activities for us. Patterns of activity in all organizations are both formal and informal, and they reflect the most basic level of analysis. By examining how people interact with information and tools to accomplish tasks we can discern functions. Functions are *patterns of activity with a purpose that contribute to the whole.* For example, the function of a flashlight is to shine light. Even when the specific patterns of activity remain obscured, we can have confidence that most VNSA will perform functions that fall into one of several general categories known as sub-systems. Sub-systems "perform the specific functions required for organizational survival, such as production, boundary spanning, maintenance, adaptation, and management."[24] The four VNSA sub-systems—support, maintenance, cognitive, and conversion—and the associated eleven functions are introduced in the overview section and detailed in chapter 4. Rather than getting wrapped up in systems terminology, it is more important that we focus on the common set of functions that all organizations perform.

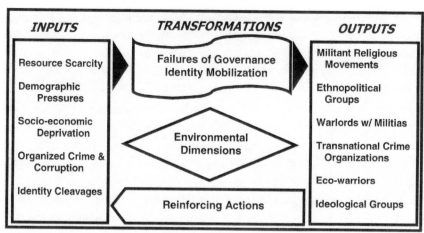

FIGURE 1.1
Open Systems Framework

Some functions acquire key resources, some control the organization itself, and some span the boundary between the organization and its environment.

To summarize, the open systems framework asks us to analyze all organizations, including VNSA, on three levels: environment (super-system), organization (system), and functions (grouped as sub-systems). Figure 1.1 depicts these three levels by showing a system, consisting of sub-systems, embedded in an environment with which it exchanges energy and information. In addition to stressing the importance of conducting analysis on relationships within and across levels, we are also left with these key ideas:

(1) An organization's effectiveness and success depends heavily on its ability to adapt to its environment, shape the environment, or find a favorable environment in which to operate;

(2) Organizations will use their products, services, and ideas as inputs to organizational maintenance and growth;

(3) An organization's effectiveness depends substantially on its ability to meet internal needs—including tying people to their roles in the organization, conducting transformative processes, and managing operations—as well as on adaptation to the environment; and

(4) Developments in and outside of the organization create pressures for change as well as forces for inertia and stability.[25]

With these key attributes in mind, we are left with a view of organizations as organic systems. That is, organizations bear more than metaphoric similarity to organisms. They grow, adapt, spawn, and in some cases die. An ecological view of VNSA is consistent with open systems theory and informs our analysis and strategy throughout.

Systems theory is not without its shortcomings, which we are obligated to state up front and address in the course of our analysis. The first and probably most important shortcoming is the temptation to rely on system principles that are simply too abstract to be useful to the policy maker and practitioner.[26] Second, an excessive focus on system theory's so-called "laws" can bias the analyst to an artificially narrow view of organizations that ignores other key characteristics. Finally, its value as a framework that provides a common means for analyzing all organizations is undercut by a tendency of researchers "to adopt a superficial approach that overlooks important details of organizational operations and ignores significant differences among organizations and among organizational contexts."[27] That is, we risk over-generalization.

We counter these shortcomings with a three-prong strategy. First, we thoroughly develop the key open systems theory concepts throughout the book, providing detailed explanations in common-sense terms. Second, we apply the framework to VNSA in real settings through the robust use of mini-case studies, empirical data, first-hand accounts, and other forms of evidence. Third, we draw on a variety of disciplines, particularly ecology and the social sciences, to explain and illustrate concepts. It is our hope that this robust analytical approach, backed by the rigorous marshalling of evidence, makes the case for open systems theory as a productive framework for integrating existing methods and developing new, ground-breaking ones.

Overview and Key Concepts

The systems approach also frames the book. In chapters 2 and 3 we treat the environment as a system, a system-of-systems with its own inputs, transformations, and outputs. In chapters 4, 5, and 6 we look at the organization as a system, peeling back holistic properties to look inside at functions, strengths, and weaknesses. The last of these, chapter 6, fixes on the organizational output of most concern—collective violence. Chapters 7 and 8 set forth a strategy for countering VNSA and broad recommendations for policy respectively. Each chapter contributes additional core concepts to our overall goal of diagnosing and achieving effects against VNSA.

Chapter 2 shines the spotlight on inputs to the environmental super-system. Environmental conditions, or roots of violence, cultivate communities ripe for mobilization into non-state groups. While every population contains individuals and communities at risk for recruitment (even U.S. citizens joined al

Qaida), we focus on those conditions most likely to create the environment in which VNSA emerge and prosper. While there are many dynamic forces impacting the environment, the roots of violence proffered here have explanatory power regarding the formation of an at-risk population, ripe for mobilization along existing identity lines known as cleavages. From among the varied sources of human insecurity, our analysis sets forth five conditions for violence: *resource scarcity, demographic pressures, socio-economic deprivation, organized crime and corruption,* and *pre-existing identity cleavages.* Each places significant stress on the individual, civil society, and the state. The roots of violence are highly interrelated and a greater stress in each has a synergistic effect on the whole. In regions where the impact is most acute, the environment is very likely to spawn VNSA. Grave stresses across the board are a reasonable indicator of impending group formation.

The roots of violence create optimal conditions for VNSA incubation; however, they are rarely sufficient to convert individual deprivation or communal dissatisfaction into organized violence. Chapter 3 explains the transformations, the engines of change that translate passivity into action—failures in governance, identity mobilization, and reinforcing behaviors. Current research focuses heavily on state failure as the primary catalyst. We agree that a weakened state is a key intervening variable; however, we amend the traditional view of state failure in terms of weakened capacity to include a broader conception of *failures in governance* to include illegitimacy due to ideological incompatibility, impotence in the ability to provide basic goods and services, and excessive coercion of the population. An often overlooked but equally important transformation process is *identity mobilization,* where members of the disaffected community begin to associate with other identity cleavages. The psychological process of identity formation is explored and related to forming or joining a VNSA. A key agent in this conversion is the *identity entrepreneur* or charismatic leader that leverages the conditions of violence and failures in governance to manipulate identity cleavages. The process is not linear since VNSA will also take *reinforcing actions* to perpetuate the cycle. Like organisms they seek out, adapt to, or expand the ecological niche in which they can prosper; it is a type of niche construction that deepens the roots of violence. The environmental "system of violence" framework shown in figure 1.2 captures divergent factors too often examined in isolation; it draws attention to the key relationships that amplify the cycle of violent collective action.

Chapter 4 builds on the environmental analysis and performs a diagnosis on the organization itself in terms of its overall properties and internal functions. In doing so, it not only explains how the VNSA works, but it exposes vulnerabilities related to its development. At the organizational level, we further explain and apply the key characteristics of all systems, including inputs, conversions, outputs, and feedback. More importantly, we premier three concepts

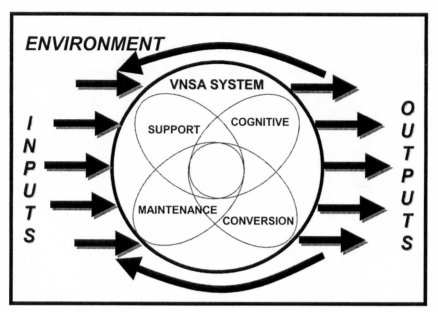

FIGURE 1.2
Violent Non-State Actor System

central to organizational theory: life cycle, negative entropy, and congruence. First, organizations do not magically appear on the scene. Rather, they pass through a series of *life cycle* phases during which they change in form and function. When the conditions of violence meet a weak state and identity mobilization, incubation occurs, and a VNSA enters the gestation phase. As the organization takes initial form, the VNSA will grow, adapting to its environment and becoming increasingly complex and differentiated. If allowed to prosper uncontested, or if highly adaptive even in a turbulent environment, the VNSA may reach maturity. The life cycle is certainly not linear; organizations can skip stages, move forward or backward, or splinter new groups that are placed elsewhere in the development chain.

The second major divergence from the biological metaphor is the VNSA's ability to flirt with death. Organizations can live forever. Of course, their ability to do so is contingent on many factors, not the least of which is its ability to avert the natural entropic process. The tendency toward disorder and decline—information is lost, people fail to uphold role behaviors, conditions worsen—is forestalled by building negative entropy. *Negative entropy* is the "store of fuel," and the "winter fat" on which the VNSA draws during periods of crisis. It is common and often appropriate to think of cash reserves, abundant recruits, and back-up sanctuaries as the forms of negative entropy relied upon by the VNSA. Through systems analysis, however, other more potent and less appreciated forms emerge, including culture, socialization, social services, intelligence gathering and command and control structures. Whatever it is, a counter-VNSA strategy must deplete the stores of negative entropy in order to keep the VNSA from reemerging in the future.

The third key system property, *congruence*, deals with the "fit" or "alignment" among the organization's parts and functions. A VNSA is most likely to prosper when it achieves reinforced working relationships among its functions and, also importantly, between the organization and its environment. Good fit works against entropy, optimizes performance, and propels the VNSA along its life-cycle path. Congruence analysis requires us to determine the factors that contribute most to harmonizing the collected functions, or sub-systems, of all VNSA—support, maintenance, cognitive, and conversion. The *support* sub-system manages boundary relations, acquiring resources, recruiting members, and attending to relationships with other key players, or stakeholders. The *maintenance* sub-system works on the people in the organization by socializing them to a set of values (culture) and enforcing role behaviors through a schedule of rewards and sanctions. The *cognitive* sub-system is responsible for decision-making through learning, strategy development, and exercising control over the organization. The *conversion* sub-system works on the energy brought into the organization. It trains recruits, produces goods, delivers services, and conducts operations, which do not always involve collective violence. Each sub-system and associated functions contribute to the VNSA as a whole and take leading roles during different phases in its life cycle.

Chapter 5 applies our methodology to several "types" of VNSA. Essentially, we put flesh on the three-level skeleton of systems analysis. Depending on the policy maker's requirements, open systems theory allows for deconstructing VNSA along multiple lines based on functions, cognitive style, culture, and several other categories. We lay out two inter-related typologies, which serve as a useful starting point for comparative analysis. The first typology is based on an organization's value system. It contrasts VNSA that reflect largely pragmatic or *transactional* values, with those that embrace a *transcendental* or supernatural world view. Each has implications for how the VNSA is most likely to build negative entropy, weather environmental storms, and relate to other actors in the international system. It is a critical initial distinction on the path to developing a comprehensive countering strategy. The second typology groups VNSA in terms of generally similar goals and functions, resulting in at least the following VNSA species: *warlords with private armies, transnational criminal organizations, militant religious organizations, ethno-nationalist groups,* [and] *an emergent set of eco-warriors, anti-globalizationists, and anarchists.* For each category we examine the environmental conditions most likely to contribute to their gestation as well as the dynamics that are most relevant to survival. Looking inside each species, we detail the patterns of activity most common to their functions, which reveals key insights regarding organizational performance and life cycle vulnerabilities. By also identifying the primary sources for each group's negative entropy, we set a foundation for a tailored strategy. The intent of this chapter is not only to advance our understanding of VNSA, but to illustrate the analytic usefulness of an applied open system framework.

Of all the system outputs, *collective violence* garners the spotlight even though it may be less critical to system performance than other sub-system functions. Nonetheless, collective violence is one of the two key definitional elements that distinguishes VNSA from other organizations, and its hard-hitting impact on security earns the full attention of chapter 6. The chapter opens with an examination of collective violence in relation to organizational development and the role violence plays in achieving VNSA objectives. At some point, VNSA violence verges on the threshold of war, and when it crosses over into this most dynamic of all environmental settings, it changes the face of battle.[28] Drawing on Carl von Clausewitz, a Prussian veteran of the Napoleonic wars and author of the influential book *On War* and other military theorists, we explore conflicts involving VNSA in terms of three decisive tests: *political purpose, engagement,* [and] *lethal force.* For each, we lay out the unique characteristics of conflict involving VNSA, beginning with a discussion of the disconnect between the received view of war as an instrument of rational policy and the more diverse "political" reasons for which VNSA fight. We follow an investigation into the *asymmetric* nature of the engagement between states and non-state actors, called "informal war," with a general discussion of the three main forms of warfare—conventional, guerilla, and terrorism. At the end of the day, we paint a picture of collective violence by VNSA that not only predates the state but has now escaped it.

In chapter 7, we trace out the implications for how we should coerce and ultimately destroy VNSA. Here, we introduce four critical concepts. First is the idea of *ecological deterrence*; if we accept expanded notions of both what deterrence consists in and what aspects of human psychology are pertinent to it, then we discover that it is possible (contrary to the contentions of some theorists) to deter VNSA throughout their life cycles. Second, we revisit the overarching counter-VNSA concepts of congruence and negative entropy— by focusing on disrupting the "fit" among all the parts of the organization we can cause organizational breakdown; in addition, attacking the "stores of fat" that VNSA accumulate will allow the direct attacks against a VNSA to have immediate and longer-term impact. Third is the notion of revised *operational art* for combating VNSA; while we should not abandon ideas such as "surprise" and "economy of force," there are other general principles that will aid us in our efforts to war-fight with VNSA, including attacking well-connected nodes, interdicting functions along boundaries, and inducing cascading effects across functions. Finally, for assessing the results of our counter-VNSA efforts, we offer the idea of *measures of performance* for attacking systems: we can measure how our efforts are affecting input-related issues (resource utilization), conversion-related issues (process efficiency), and output-related issues (goal attainment). Chapter 7 articulates how we effectively confront VNSA and assess the effects of our confrontation.

Chapter 8 summarizes of the book, outlining the main points of each chapter en route to big-picture guidance for policy makers dealing with VNSA and terrorism. As we confront VNSA, we should keep in mind that: force-on-force confrontations are only a small part of dealing with such organizations; VNSA are neither hermetically nor "hermeneutically" sealed; thinking like ecologists is critically important; effective confrontation takes many forms; and non-traditional intelligence is critical for the entire effort. While our systems scaffolding adds value to any comprehensive security framework, we also realize that it is in incubation but growing rapidly; so, in this chapter, we also offer an agenda to guide future research on VNSA in the systems vein. We conclude by noting that our approach can resolve anomalies and problems afflicting what sometimes appears to be a piecemeal approach to dealing with VNSA, including what are commonly called terrorist groups. In that sense, it is a paradigm shift we must take if we are to confront the grand security challenge of warlords rising.

Finally, in the appendix we provide a detailed case study illustrating how we might move from a qualitative descriptive narrative of VNSA to a quantitative heuristic of their nature via the use of computer models. We offer a repeatable methodology for initially modeling VNSA that leverages systems engineering tools in order to provide structure to how we begin thinking about VNSA. The tools we offer easily facilitate translating thoughts about the structure of organizations such as the Sendero Luminoso into workable computer models that enable us to gain insight into new policy options for dealing with them. They may even provide useful decision aids for policy makers and an efficient forecasting tool for VNSA growth and recruitment; put differently, the use of the quantitative heuristic can help bring the descriptive narrative to a new, more useful, level. The model we have constructed of the factors influencing Sendero growth and recruitment rates matches empirical data from the mid-1970s to the early 1990s. Ultimately, these systems-level computer models add computational bite to some of our qualitative theories, giving policy makers and analysts the ability to easily make revisions to and test foundational assumptions about how VNSA operate. While not a panacea, the process is relatively efficient and inexpensive and can provide guidance for more expensive higher-fidelity modeling and decision-aid methods. The systems engineering tools and processes we discuss in the appendix will be a useful part of our counter-VNSA toolkit.

Notes

1. Recount of the event is taken from two primary sources. British Broadcasting Company (BBC) world affairs correspondent Peter Biles, who was in the Palestine Hotel at the time of the attack, in "Terrifying Moment of Baghdad Blasts," 21 November 2003, provides a first-hand account. Available at BBC Online, news.bbc.co.uk/2/hi/middle_east/3226890.stm, as of 12 January 2003. The Cable News Network's (CNN) Jane Arraf, Matthew Chance, John King, Suzanne Malveaux, and Melissa Gray contributed to "U.S. general: Rocket strikes 'militarily insignificant,'" November 21, 2003. Available at www.cnn.com/2003/WORLD/meast/11/21/sprj.irq .main/index.html as of January 12, 2004.

2. Possibly the first systematic text for justifying violence outside the state came from the radical German publicst Karl Heinzen who authored a two-part essay entited *Der Mord* (*Murder*), published in 1849.

3. Michel Eyquem de Montaigne (1533–1592), a French courtier, wrote a series of essays. This particular quotation comes from chapter 37 of *Essais, livre 2*, by Michel Eyquem de Montaigne and Alexandre Micha (Paris, France: Flammarion, 1993).

4. Thomas Hobbes, *Leviathan* (Peguin Classics, 1968) 423.

5. See, for example, John Herz, *The Nation-State and the Crisis of World Politics* (Philadelphia, PA: David McKay Company Publishers, 1976).

6. Charles Tilly, *Coercion, Capital and European States AD 990–1990* (Oxford, UK: Blackwell Publishers, 1990) 116.

7. Adapted from William Blake, *Auguries of Innocence* (Burford, UK: Cygnet Press, 1975) 14.

8. See Marlowe Hood, "The Taiwan Connection," *Los Angeles Times*, October 9, 1994. See also "Transnational Criminal Activity" by the Canadian Security Intelligence Services, posted on the Federation of American Scientists website at www.fas.org/irp/threat/back10e.htm, as of October 14, 2003.

9. From text of a statement to the parliamentary group Parlatino in Sao Paulo, Brazil, July 14, 1998, by United Nations Secretary-General Kofi Annan on "The Emerging Power of Civil Society." Available at www.un.org/News/Press/docs/1998/19980714.sgsm6638.html as of January 12, 2004.

10. James Rosenau, "A New Dynamism in World Politics: Increasingly Skillful Individuals?" *International Studies Quarterly* 41, no. 4 (December 1997): 655–86.

11. Charles Tilly, *From Mobilization to Revolution* (New York: Random House, 1978), 55. See also Ted Robert Gurr, *Why Men Rebel* (Princeton, NJ: Princeton University Press, 1970).

12. This term was used by James Rosenau to help explain the changes in the international system after the collapse of the Soviet Union and the Eastern European revolutions. While Rosenau used this term as a way to explain how more conventional and non-violence changes took place, and did not write specifically about VNSA, his ideas are certainly germane to the discussion. See James N. Rosenau, "The Relocation of Authority in a Shrinking World," *Comparative Politics* 24, no. 3 (April 1992): 253–72.

13. Thomas Szayna, ed., *Identifying Potential Ethnic Conflict: Application of a Process Model* (Santa Monica, CA: RAND Corporation, 2000), 132.

14. James N. Rosenau, *Turbulence in World Politics: A Theory of Change and Continuity* (Princeton, NJ: Princeton University Press, 1990), 125.

15. For a primer on diagnosis, refer to Michael I. Harrison, *Diagnosing Organizations: Methods, Models, and Processes* (Thousand Oaks, CA: Sage Publications, Inc., 1994).

16. Ibid., 10.

17. Ibid., 39.

18. Thomas G. Cummings, quoting von Bertalanffy in *Systems Theory for Organization Development* (New York: John Wiley and Sons, 1980), 6.

19. Richard L. Daft, *Organization Theory and Design* (Mason, OH: Thomson South-western, 2004), 14.

20. Daniel Katz and Robert L. Kahn, "Organizations and the System Concept," *The Social Psychology of Organizations* (New York: John Wiley and Sons, 1978). Reprinted in *Classics of Organization Theory*, Jay M. Shafritz and J. Steven Ott, eds. (Fort Worth, TX: Harcourt College Publishers, 2001), 259.

21. Ibid., 14.

22. Michael I. Harrison and Arie Shirom, *Organizational Diagnosis and Assessment: Bridging Theory and Practice* (Thousand Oaks, CA: Sage Publications, 1999), 44.

23. Katz and Kahn, *Classics*, 262.

24. Daft, *Organization*, 15.

25. Harrison and Shirom, *Organizaitonal*, 47–48.

26. Ibid., 42.

27. Ibid., 43.

28. The phrase "face of battle" is a reference to the book of the same title by John Keegan, which confronts and illuminates the harsh reality of war on individual soldiers and units. *Face of Battle* (New York: Penguin Books, 1976).

2

Roots of Violence

A weary father joins a gathering crowd on the street corner, anticipating the collapse of a run-down apartment block. Anxious neighbors peer from windows as the steel chain cuts down the side of the adjoining building; a drab gray Soviet structure like their own. The father knows his building is next to fall in the remodeling plan for Ashgabat. As the capital of Turkmenistan continues its transition from Soviet outpost to turgid capital, the families of the inner city are being forcibly relocated to a sprawling periphery of equally squalid apartments or to outlying villages. In his new "community" he can expect acute levels of unemployment and derelict health care. If he can find work at all, maybe loading camels at the Tolkuchka Sunday Bazaar, a portion of his income will undoubtedly be needed to bribe his children's teachers for passing marks. Shortages of bread, which led to armed revolt in recent years, will undoubtedly add to his frustration. This father, from the politically marginalized and economically under-privileged Yohmud clan is part of a system producing the new Marxists, Maoists, and other violent radicals of the twenty-first century.

WE LIVE IN A DYNAMIC, RELIABLY violent world. Since World War II, each decade marked at least ten million people or more dead due to conflict. Two specific trends exist: first, those millions of combat deaths are increasingly non-combatants; second, they are increasingly at the hands of non-state actors.[1] One implication is that analysis of "security" ought not to be exclusively—perhaps not even primarily—state-centric. As the state is no longer an "impenetrable unit,"[2] security shifts across multiple levels of political interaction—individual, national, and international.[3] The political lumping together of large swaths of the population into states remains relevant; however, it no longer makes sense to analyze security from such a lumpy state-based approach alone. Rather, the landscape of contemporary organized violence has as much to do with the "tremendous stresses on human communities" as it does with geographically defined power struggles.[4] Therefore, security analysis must expand to encompass non-state organizations—a state-centric framework of security analysis not only provides incomplete answers, but it may prevent asking the right questions. Rather, *security analysis must go outside the state, below it to the individual and above it to the larger environment.*

What causes the individual to pursue goals outside the state using the means of collective violence? What is the true nature of power and influence of the state over its population in a globalized world? In addition to traditional security threats from other existing states, what security challenges do states now face from these empowered individuals? Exploring these questions, specifically those regarding the larger environment in which the individual exists and operates, is the purpose of this chapter. VNSA do not exist in a vacuum. Rather, they incubate in a primordial soup of ideas, histories and influences. Occasionally, this volatile mixture will be just the right "pre-VNSA" blend.

Importantly, just as appropriate environmental conditions are conducive to VNSA gestation, environmental factors positively and negatively affect existing VNSA. Environmental conditions, to use the term coined by psychologist J. J. Gibson, can be considered *affordances.* This term denotes the capacities offered to us by things present in our environments; for instance, in an office environment, a chair "affords" sitting. What is critical is the *relationship* between the organism and the thing in the organism's environment: some things will be affordances for us but not for other kinds of creatures (for instance, a telephone affords communication for an adult human, but it does not afford anything for an inarticulate entity, for example a dog). One way of preventing niche construction on the part of a developing VNSA would be to ask what affordances would this organization strive to make part of its environment? How can I detect those affordances and destroy them? Conversely, are there things you can place in the environment to provide affordances to the state but not to the VNSA?

This discussion highlights the key fact that the relationship works both ways—the environment can enable or inhibit. Should environmental conditions that initially led to VNSA creation continue unabated or become further entrenched, individuals affected by or concerned with those conditions may become increasingly sympathetic to VNSA goals or become members themselves.

The VNSA may find it easier to acquire financial resources, find greater levels of sanctuary, or exploit other conditions that enable it to gain strength. Conversely, should environmental conditions change in such a way that is adverse to the VNSA, the environment can act as a constraint on growth and operations. Taking away environmental grounds for existence, for example, can likewise decrease sympathy, remove potential recruits, increase the number of willing informants, increase the demands for covertness, and otherwise hinder its performance. However, the environmental dynamics do not work completely the same in reverse. While a modified environment may act as a constraint, it cannot put the genie back in the bottle. Once a VNSA is formed, just like most other organizations it is likely to pursue self-preservation–oriented goals regardless of its environment.[6] Those who remain in the VNSA will be the "true believers" who may refuse to believe the environment has taken away their *raison d'être* and exalt continued group existence over their original purpose.

A series of case studies by RAND terrorist experts Peter Chalk and Kim Cragin essentially arrived at the same conclusion: modifying the social and economic environments in which terrorist groups operate can influence those groups. Significantly, their study concluded that when done correctly, social and economic development policies can weaken local support for terrorist activities and can discourage potential terrorist recruits. Specifically, if such programs erase or ease the socio-economic differences between various groups who are in conflict, the environmental conditions cease to be as conducive for the general population to provide sympathy or material support to a terrorist group, and the pool of potential recruits shrinks. Furthermore, if such development programs help develop a middle class, that new group typically will act as both a brake on continued violence and as a facilitator or conflict mediator. The motivation for the middle class to take on these roles is economic stability.[7]

As policy, therefore, shaping the environment to prevent VNSA formation or to constrain existing VNSA activity is appropriate, but it is likely to be only partially successful for VNSA termination. The goal of this chapter in explaining the associations between VNSA and the environment is therefore twofold: explore what environmental conditions are conducive to VNSA formation and also how the environment affects VNSA once they are formed.

Environmental Conditions

VNSA emerge and prosper due to the interplay of environmental conditions, failures in governance, and identity mobilization. Environmental conditions are the focus of this chapter. Five specific conditions stand out in relation to VNSA formation and existence: resource scarcity, demographic pressures, socio-economic deprivation, organized crime and corruption, and pre-existing identity cleavages.[8] Each condition places stress on the individual and civil society and often demands a response from the state. Importantly, these conditions are unlikely to be sole causal factors in creating an at-risk population. There is no magic threshold of such factors that automatically lead to collective violence; however, mutually reinforcing factors coupled with failures of governance and identity mobilization are the most common set of conditions correlated with VNSA. A more effective response to the VNSA threat can be crafted only when an understanding of the environmental conditions examined here is linked to a study of transformational engines, which is addressed in the next chapter.

Not all the conditions that influence group formation are associated, let alone controlled, by states. Humans are exposed to a greater number of influences in the modern world than ever before, thanks largely to information technology and its globalizing influences. The state can control some of these influences but not all. To illustrate, most VNSA activities prior to World War II were aptly referred to as rebellions. The state and its rebels fought in fairly predictable ways in fairly predictable geographic areas. Today, the environment of the struggle is significantly different; instead of massive women's protests in Nigeria regarding oppressive colonial rule, there are massive protests over the actions of multinational corporate oil interests in the Niger Delta. While the Nigerian government relies essentially on the same tool set by colonial precedent—massive arrests and bloody crackdowns—the Ogoni tribe has expanded its tactics by utilizing world courts, the media, and the internet to find and exploit information about the multi-national corporations operating in the region. The tribe ensures that its sometimes-violent movement lives not only on the Niger Delta, but also in various chat rooms and human rights organizations around the world. Witness the asymmetric VNSA in action against the symmetric, erstwhile state.

The countries in Central Asia represent useful and appropriate case studies for examining the conditions, and we will refer to them extensively in the following chapters to illustrate our theory. The Central Asian republics suffer the distinction of the presence, to some degree, of all of the primary roots of violence, as well as multiple numbers and types of VNSA. Additionally, the region has the twin characteristics of being political entities artificially created by Josef Stalin and being very new states, achieving their independence only with the break-up of the Soviet Union a little over a decade ago. As such, citizens generally have a lower identification with their state than in many other regions of the world. Central Asia is thus the quintessential illustration of the environmental shaping influences on the creation and existence of VNSA. Finally, the author's direct experiences in Central Asia, Southeast Asia, Southwest Asia, sub-Saharan Africa, and South America affect our choice of examples.

Resource Scarcity

David Eastman offers a widely accepted definition of politics as "the authoritative allocation of resources."[9] Access to resources is a common reason many states have gone to war. Now, as the world population grows and resources dwindle, access to resources contributes to the individuals' entrance into collective violence. According to Thomas Homer-Dixon, a leading researcher on environmental degradation and conflict, resource scarcity can come from three different sources: (1) a decline in the quality and/or quantity of renewable or (especially) non-renewable resources, which can provoke resource scarcity conflict between states; (2) population growth, which reduces the per capita availability of resources; and (3) unequal resource distribution among a given population.[10] These conditions, influential in their own right, can be favorable for VNSA formation and also capable of creating second and third order facilitating effects. For example, should unequal resource distribution develop, questions about justice, fairness, and legitimacy of the state may arise.

The notion that environmental degradation or resource deprivation could have an impact on security issues, while having its roots as early as the 1960s, left the academic fringe in the late 1970s. Since then, political scientists, sociologists, environmentalists, and even prominent politicians have reflected their belief that resource scarcity and environmental degradation (which often go hand-in-hand) have a place in security discussions. These more modern analyses suggest that resource shortages are linked with stress, fracturing, and potentially the ultimate collapse of states. Theoretical works efforts include those of Lester Brown of the World Watch Institute who wrote extensively on an expanding notion of national security to include various components of resource scarcity.[11] This theoretical work is backed by empirical studies, which include the Failed States Project and various studies conducted using the Correlates of War databases.[12]

Thomas Homer-Dixon, who provided the working typology for resource scarcity, is the most accomplished researcher in the field of environmental degradation–based conflict. His research suggests how a variety of environmental issues, prominently resource scarcity, can impact social order and state stability. Through careful modeling and empirical observation, Homer-Dixon argues that resource scarcity can lead to conflict through three main routes, each with a unique type of conflict: (1) decreasing supplies of physically controllable resources can provoke interstate "simple scarcity" conflicts; (2) large population movements caused by environmental stress can precipitate "group-identity" conflicts, specifically ethnic clashes; and (3) severe environmental scarcity can increase economic deprivation and disrupt key social institutions, precipitating "deprivation" conflicts, such as civil strife and insurgency.[13]

Although the chain of events from resource scarcity to conflict is fairly clear, Homer-Dixon admits that resource scarcity is certainly not the primary source of conflict but rather a contributing cause; we extend this contention to the creation of VNSA. The world is full of people living in poverty, yet the entire world is not engulfed in conflicts of scarcity. Empirical evidence suggests, however, that various regions of the world—including Central Asia, parts of China, regions of Africa, the Middle East, and even parts of South America—have a variety of worsening environmental conditions that interact with political structures to trigger processes that heighten ethnic, communal, and class-based rivalries. This combination of forces encourages resource capture, the marginalization of the poor, rising economic hardship, and a progressive weakening of the state. These processes, in turn, culminate in increased group-identity and deprivation conflicts.

The dynamics of resource scarcity are at play in Central Asia. The supply of many basic resources (especially water and arable land) has always been historically low; rapid population growth, increasing per capita demand and wasteful state use are combining to exacerbate basic supply and demand problems. Corollary resources to water and arable land (particularly food and forest resources) present policymakers similar challenges. Furthermore, structural shortages—a condition where corruption leads to disproportionate resource allocation among elites at the expense of the larger population—are increasingly common in the region. An exhaustive treatment of resource scarcity in Central Asia would therefore include much more than water and arable land. Such an endeavor is beyond the scope of this book; however, water and arable land factors are more than adequate to demonstrate how resource scarcity can contribute to the warlord's rise.

Water Woes

Central Asia faces a water crisis. This most basic resource needed by all living creatures is not plentiful in most of Central Asia; clean, potable water is in even shorter supply. Sources of water are overexploited and dying. The Aral Sea is drying up and may be gone completely by 2012. Only one third of the Aral's surface area remains, while the sea has lost nearly 75 percent of its volume.[14] The two major rivers feeding the Aral, the Amu Darya and Syr Darya, long ago ceased reaching the sea, which is now actually two smaller "lakes." The drying of the Aral Sea has increased the salinity of water in all of western Central Asia, and the extensive amount of residual salt is often whipped up by the winds, coating everything in its path. A severe drought, which some meteorologists contend will be a permanent feature due to loss of the Aral, has gripped the region since 1999. Loss of primary water sources is further complicated by exceptionally poor water infrastructures that lose at least as much water as is transported—evidenced by the hundreds of miles of lush weeds that grow along all major canals and irrigation systems. Other water aggravations include lavish, wasteful uses of water for politically pretentious purposes. For example, Ashgabat boasts both the largest water fountain in the world and has incredible displays of various "water architectures" throughout the city. President Saparmurat Niyazov also declared his intention to create the "Turkmenbashi Sea" just north of Ashgabat—in the middle of the vast Kizilkum Desert—by diverting more water from the already hyper-exploited Amu Darya via the Karakum Canal. In the meantime, a worsening water crisis is augmenting VNSA incubation; indeed, resource scarcities in general could weaken the fabric of both state and society in Central Asia, creating conditions more amenable to VNSA development.

Historically, as with so many resources during Soviet times, water was commonly controlled by the state. As exclusive state property, it was also a free commodity.[15] Water use and allocation were based on the "Fundamentals of Water Legislation of the USSR and the Union Republics" of 1970. This central, nation-wide guidance also crafted the water codes for the individual Soviet Republics.[16] This background is important in two distinct ways. First, as all water utilization and allocation was decided by Moscow, there is no tradition at all in Central Asia for regional water-sharing agreements among the five governments. Second, as with any free resource, water was wasted. In the early days of the Soviet Union, with a low industrial rate and a small population, water utilization could be less than optimal with minimal impact. With populations that are at least doubled since the 1960s and water resources becoming increasingly scarce in much of Central Asia, squandering is no longer a viable option. This well-documented sub-regional scarcity is juxtaposed by the nearly universal Central Asian practice of emptying bowls of water on one's driveway or sidewalk in the morning and in the evening, the many ostentatious fountains in major cities, and the hundreds of miles of leaky, weed-choked canals bringing water to the desert.

Another important factor when discussing water resource scarcity in Central Asia is to note the vast water disparities in the region. While Kazakhstan, Uzbekistan, and Turkmenistan are largely steppe or desert, mountainous Kyrgyzstan and Tajikistan have ample water supply. Indeed, the headwaters of the two most important water sources in the region, the Amu Darya and the Syr Darya, originate in Tajikistan and Kyrgyzstan respectively. The Amu Darya then flows through Uzbekistan and Turkmenistan where it simply dries up before reaching the Aral Sea. The Syr Darya, on the other hand, flows through all the Central Asia republics except Tajikistan, crossing political borders several times, and at least in the case of Uzbekistan, enters, leaves, and re-enters further to the west.

Two things are important regarding this complex hydro-geography. First, Kyrgyzstan and Tajikistan control the headwaters of these rivers and therefore technically control the flow of the waters. Thus, either country is at least theoretically capable of building enough dams or reservoirs to significantly reduce (or for short periods of time, actually stop) the flow of the rivers to the downstream riparian zones. These downstream zones are militarily and economically (with the possible exception of Turkmenistan) more powerful than the upstream riparians zones. Most analysts who study international river basins agree with this arrangement—a stronger downstream riparian zone dependent on water from a weaker upstream riparian zone—is the most unstable and conflict-prone type of basin.

Second, multiple border crossings by both these rivers complicates regional water sharing agreements. In issues of both quantity of water taken and quality of water leaving the country, each country always demands more and higher quality water from its upstream neighbor. Another very significant issue is water utilization. Tajikistan and Kyrgyzstan typically use their water for hydroelectric power production. Thus, they tend to fill their reservoirs during the summer and release water during the winter when more power is needed. Uzbekistan, Turkmenistan and Kazakhstan, on the other hand, need that water released during the summer for irrigation purposes. Thus, the timing of water release from the upstream riparian zones creates a considerable amount of tension as well.

The potential for this to create an interstate resource scarcity conflict is substantial. Tension between states regarding water is already palpable. Some residents in Ferghana, for example, keep their bathtubs full of water for emergency use after 7:00 p.m., when their water is cut off. They politely instruct visitors to try to avoid using the facilities after that time. What is the reason for these emergency stores of water? A tit-for-tat resource conflict had developed between Kyrgyzstan and Uzbekistan. Kyrgyzstan had cut the water flow of the Syr Darya to eastern Uzbekistan. The Uzbek government, in response, stopped electricity flows from power plants in the Ferghana Valley.[17] Additionally, Kyrgyzstan filled the Toktogul Reservoir with waters from the Naryn River, which is fed from snowmelt in the far-off Central Tian Shan Range. This reservoir, lying in the western-most quarter of Kyrgyzstan, is very vulnerable to either an Uzbek or a Kazakh military intrusion; several guides, officials, and individuals expressed fear that if the water situation got worse, Uzbekistan could most likely be the next owner of Toktogul. Several other scenarios exist, for example, the depletion of Lake Balkash waters in Kazakhstan will be accelerated by China's recent decision to divert two rivers that feed into the lake in order to expand irrigation in the Xinjiang province.[18] Certainly this decision will complicate Kazakh-Sino relations in the future.

While water woes do exacerbate tensions between states, they can also increase tensions with non-state actors. As Stefan Klotzli, a noted researcher on Central Asian conflicts, stated in 1994, "Ethnic minorities could use ecological problems as a vehicle for imposing their interests against the titular nation, as has happened in the disintegration of the Soviet Union in many different regions."[19] Based on persistent resource scarcities, the most likely form of non-state conflict in the near term is "deprivation conflict," where sub-state actors will fight one another for water due to low supply and/or unequal or unfair distribution of water. As one possible case, a survey of the entire Aral Sea basin in 1994 identified a total of thirty-two major irrigation systems—twenty-three on the Amu Darya and nine on the Syr Darya. The most ethnically contentious irrigation systems were found in Tajikistan, Kyrgyzstan and Uzbekistan.[20] Some of these irrigation systems lie in ethnically diverse (and torn) areas such as the irrigation systems in the Ferghana Valley. Other irrigation systems straddle political borders—like the system used by the Uzbek minority in Dashoguz, Turkmenistan and the semi-autonomous Karakalpaks in western Uzbekistan. Others go through areas previously torn by civil strife; the Vakhsh/Pyandsh irrigation system is split between Gorno-Badakhshan and Kurgan Tyube, two bitter regional rivals in Tajikistan's civil war.

It is also important to understand that water (and to a lesser extent land) is already established as a flashpoint. For example, the UN reported that in 1989, tensions over access to water resulted in a violent conflict where several people were killed and injured in the village of Samarkandik, a Tajik enclave within western Kyrgyzstan. The following year, the Ferghana Valley city of Osh, Kyrgyzstan, witnessed a much larger conflict over allocation of scarce land resources. The warring parties fell along ethnic lines—Uzbeks fighting Kyrgyz, where at least three hundred people (possibly up to one thousand) were killed, and more than one thousand wounded. Additionally, more than five thousand crimes were reported, including the destruction of homes, robbery, and rapes.

Three different catalysts could cause water shortages to further mobilize various groups to turn violent to advance their goals. First is a continued supply crunch. Central Asia is already consuming far more water than is being naturally replenished. As a result, per capita water availability in 2000 (the last year reliable figures are available) is estimated at 700m³, with some localities having only 300m³,[21] significantly down from the estimated 7500m³ in 1950 and 2000m³ in 1980.[22] By comparison, U.S. citizens enjoy approximately 4000m³ of available water per capita; 1000m³ of water per capita is considered necessary to maintain an adequate standard of living in a moderately developed country. As the per capita water availability continues to shrink (data are not available since 2000, but each successive year will surely be less than 300–700m³ due to the severe drought and expanding demand in the region), localities will be the first to resort to violence for two reasons. First, certain localities are already in critical water shortages, and any further reduction in water supply may push such localities over the edge. One such region is Karakalpakstan (examined more closely in chapter 5), which is located in western Uzbekistan near the Aral Sea. Second, while states may negotiate prior to resorting to force to secure adequate water for their populations, individuals and small groups will mobilize and resort to violence much sooner. Groups that are already formed along some other identity cleavage will be especially prone to violence. An excellent example of this phenomenon is the Kurds in southeastern Turkey and Northern Iraq, who were severely affected by Turkey's Grand Anatolia Project. The Kurds, dependent on the water, claimed the project was "ethnocide" against them and an attempt to destroy their identity.[23] Thus, denial of water was used by that VNSA as both a rallying point for recruiting militants to fight against Turkey and as a raison d'être for their violent ways.

A second possible catalyst for environmental conflict is the further erosion, or possible collapse, of the agricultural sector, especially in Uzbekistan and Turkmenistan. Even with yields already 30 percent below peak production during the Soviet days (largely due to drought and a precipitous drop in water and soil quality) and still generally falling, resulting in increasingly fewer rural jobs, the monoculture of cotton still consumes an enormous amount of the scarce water resources throughout the region. Throughout Uzbekistan and Turkmenistan, thousands of acres of salt-encrusted earth exist where cotton fields used to be. The farmers of the region have had to resort to "washing" their fields prior to planting cotton—actually flooding the fields, then bringing huge vacuums to suck away the then salty water—in order to make the soil marginally useful. Should this already teetering sector of the economy cease delivering what economic security it now provides, rural farmers (who have already demonstrated a penchant for violence while under duress) could choose conflict to express their frustrations.

A third environmental catalyst that could lead to conflict is a massive flight from rural to urban areas due to continued drought, which we explore further under the next section, Demographic Pressures. Already, access to the capital cities in all Central Asia republics is tightly controlled, and the ruling elite would no doubt unfavorably view any massive refugee movement to urban areas. Indeed, many young, unemployed people moving to urban areas report having to pay police in order to simply *be* in the cities—let alone the bribes which would be necessary in order to find employment.[24] Some level of ecologically induced population movement is already evident. As shown in table 2.1, some reports suggest that as many as 270,000 migrants resulted from ecological disaster.[25] In other words, the mass population movement necessary

TABLE 2.1
Central Asian Ecological Migrants (Since 1988)

Aral Sea to Kazakhstan	30,000
Aral Sea to CIS at large	13,000
Aral Sea to Uzbekistan	50,000+
Semipalatinsk w/in Kazakhstan	45,000
Semipalatinsk to CIS at large	116,000
Kyrgyzstan w/in Kyrgyzstan	17,000

for resource-based conflict as described by Homer-Dixon's model is already underway.

To illustrate how these pressures coupled with perceived organized crime and corruption can lead to a nascent VNSA one needs to look no further than the crackdown on cotton smuggling in Uzbekistan during the 2003 harvest. The Uzbek cotton market has not changed much since Soviet times; farmers still must sell their crop to the Uzbek government, typically for a fraction of what they can get in neighboring Kazakhstan or Kyrgzystan. Further, farmers often do not get paid immediately for the cotton they provide to government purchasers, and belief that the system is corrupt is widespread. Due to higher worldwide cotton prices and an even smaller cotton crop than usual in 2003, many cotton farmers decided to smuggle their cotton abroad, thereby collecting higher prices. The Uzbek government, which receives more than one quarter of its entire revenue from cotton sales on the world market, cracked down hard, sending as many as eighteen thousand police and soldiers to the border areas. Some confrontations resulted in the death of several smugglers.[26] Poverty, resource constraints, perceived corruption, and a technology-enabled ability to smuggle large quantities of cotton across state lines led a group of individuals to stop acting in the way they were required to by the state, opting for more self-serving interests. Whether the deaths of the smugglers in the 2003 harvest breaks the smuggling ring or causes it to better organize itself or resort to violence itself remains to be seen.

Demographic Pressures

The forced displacement of central Ashgabat residents described in the opening vignette is one instance among many in Central Asia of how demographic pressure can condition violence. Although there is little evidence to support demographic pressures as a singular cause of armed conflict, there is a growing appreciation for its contributory role. Demographic stresses can accentuate underdevelopment, crime, and resource scarcity. An understanding of demographic pressures provides insight into the future of urban violence, the likely result of dispossessed youth and a weakening state.

Population Ambush

Unlike more traditional and static views of population and national power—determining the number of men or women who can fill the ranks or the number of able-bodied individuals to run the factories—the systems approach treats population as a multi-dimensional input to national and human security.[27] Simply, demographic pressures are a function of a composition that changes over time.[28] Composition refers to the characteristics of a given population, including size, age distribution, and religious/ethnic makeup. The compositional factors most often associated with demographic pressures that contribute to conflict are "youth bulges" (where the population is skewed toward a younger demographic) and urban density. Two of the more salient dynamics are fertility and migration patterns.

Assuming net migration is zero, persistent fertility rates above the replacement value of children per family will obviously cause the population to expand, while the converse—fertility rates below the replacement value—will result in a shrinking population. Such changes in population can be rapid and destabilizing. A rapidly increasing population can place population demands beyond the capacity of the local government, a scenario that is increasingly common in the developing world and specifically in Central Asia. When high fertility rates are combined with rapidly declining death rates, the result is a population explosion that will persist until the demographic transition is completed by a corresponding decline in fertility. This population explosion has been forestalled in Central Asia due primarily to acute underdevelopment in health services and migration, which has kept death rates relatively high. As the data in table 2.2 show, infant mortality rates are high by western standards (6.76 in the United States) and net migration values negative. These two facts have kept Central Asia's population growth manageable.

However, demographic problems do exist, and greater ones wait in the near future. The relatively high fertility rates throughout the region and strong growth rates are creating demographic pressures that will be destabilizing. First, population outflow is slowing; all the ethnic minorities in these countries who could leave have left, and there are fewer of these minorities to leave. Second, as health infrastructures improve, infant mortality will decrease and the average lifespan will increase—both substantially adding to population growth. Even with a high infant mortality, Central Asia's high birth rates created a rapidly expanding and increasing youthful population that is demanding the education, employment, and health care promised at independence.[29] That youth bulge will expand even more when infant mortality is brought under control. Such youth bulges are correlated with greater instability, as the rapid growth in job demand, housing, infrastructure, and environmental stress typically is a shock to government capacity.[30] This is especially challenging for leaders in Dushanbe, Tashkent, Bishkek, Ashgabat, and Astana. They have proven incapable of satisfying expectations they initially raised upon independence. Along the so-called "Broadway" of Tashkent, young men in their late teens and twenties gather in pool halls and on streetcorners. They market cigarettes, cheap wine, and prostitution. Thousands of similar broken young men litter the streets of Central Asia, each a candidate for mobilization into a criminal gang or militant religious movement.

The population growth trends in Central Asia are also certain to reduce the per capita availability of resources, exacerbating water and land depletion.[31]

TABLE 2.2
Central Asian Demographic Data

	Population	Population Growth	Fertility (births per woman)	Infant Mortality (per 1000)	Net Migration (per 1000)	Population Below 30 years of age
Uzbekistan	26,410,416	1.65%	2.97	71.3	−1.72	65.3%
Turkmenistan	4,863,169	1.81%	3.45	73.13	−0.86	66%
Tajikistan	7,011,556	2.14%	4.11	112.13	−2.86	69.4%
Kazakhstan	15,143,704	0.26%	1.9	30.54	−3.35	51.4%
Kyrgyzstan	5,081,429	1.25%	2.71	36.81	−2.45	63%

Source: CIA World Factbook 2004

As argued in our analysis of resource scarcity, dramatic demographic shifts are resulting from ecological decay. According to conservative estimates, over 250,000 people moved out of ecological disaster areas within five years of independence.[32] For example, drought in eastern Uzbekistan stemming from the depletion of water has already driven thousands to urban centers, particularly Tashkent, adding to a significant pool of unemployed youth. These shifts not only transfer stresses from rural to urban areas but also serve as catalysts for group-identity conflicts.[33]

Migration Strains

In addition to ecological decay, substantial demographic shifts can also result from acute underdevelopment, political change and conflict. Migratory pressures include refugees and migrants. Refugees tend to move because they are pushed out, often as a function of government policy or the effects of war.[34] Migrants tend to move as a result of both push and pull factors. In Central Asia, the push of resource scarcity in one region is often accompanied by the false hope for economic opportunity in another. Whether being pushed or pulled, the numbers for Central Asia are staggering. More than 4.2 million people have moved within, from, or to the region since the collapse of the Soviet Union to 1996, when the last data were made available.[35]

The remarkable negative migration rates for each country reflects the out-migration of Russians, Germans and others that are suffering from the collapse of the Soviet system. In Kyrgyzstan alone, more than 450,000 people left the country between 1990–2001, including 62 percent of all Russians.[36] More than 560,000 Germans out of 1.1 million have the left the region for Germany since 1992, which represents a significant loss of professional talent.[37] For the thousands of doctors, teachers and engineers who have not been able to emigrate, life in the newly independent states is a struggle to learn new skills as drivers and janitors. The Russians in particular are new to the minority role, and their dissatisfaction with the new system of preferences and patronages is palatable.

Migration both creates and is created by conflict. Fighting in the Ferghana Valley between Uzbeks and Meskhetian Turks (Turkish minority group) during 1989 left 100 dead and forced the Soviet army to evacuate nearly 74,000 Meskhetians. Two to five hundred people died just a year later as a result of inter-ethnic fighting between Kyrgyz and Uzbeks in Osh and nearby Uzgen. The numbers displaced are not known; however, persistent violence in the Ferghana Valley continues to push individuals out and to the capital cities. In 1994 alone, over 116,000 Kyrgyz moved from the southern rural areas around Osh to the more industrialized north, especially Bishkek.[38] Further north, Kazakhstan hosted an estimated 10,000 Chechen refugees from the war in Chechnya. The most dramatic migratory shifts resulted from the devastating civil war in Tajikistan, which witnessed the displacement of more than 700,000 people, including 60,000 who fled to the war-torn Afghanistan.[39] While many returned home by the mid-1990s, thousands still remain in surrounding countries. According to the UNHCR's Mid-Year Report 2000, which remains the most recently available data, approximately 10,500 remain in Kyrgyzstan, 14,000 Tajik refugees of Turkmen ethnic origin remain in Turkmenistan, 6,000 are in Kazakhstan, and as many as 30,000 may be in Uzbekistan.[40]

The migratory pressures outlined here pose four broad security threats: (1) opposition to the home regime; (2) political risk to the host country; (3) perceived threat to cultural identity; and (4) social or economic burden.[41] Each of these is at play in Central Asia to varying degrees. For example, Afghan refugees were a source of external support for the Northern Alliance. Russians are now perceived as threats to cultural identity, particularly in Turkmenistan and Kazakhstan. Tajik refugees add to the already Tajik character of Samarkand and Bukhara, undermining government efforts to establish these ancient Silk Route cities as loci for Uzbek nationalism. Most important, all migrants and refugees are posing very real social and economic burdens. Although the hard data are not available, there are anecdotal reports suggesting the need for further inquiry into the contribution of migrants and refugees to criminality, dependency, and delinquency.[42] The economic burden is more direct. Migrants and refugees compete for scare jobs, inadequate health care, and insufficient housing.

Compelling Demographics

The demographic pressures in Central Asia are gaining momentum. The out-migration of the 1990s that kept a lid on rapid population growth has nearly stopped. The impact of high fertility rates is just being realized as an expanding "youth bulge" seeks jobs and services that are actually declining. The stresses of population growth are compounded by the perceived and real threats from migrants and refugees. Even if many refugees can be returned to their home countries, they are likely to be greeted by equally distressing socioeconomic deprivation. As weakened regimes thrash about to provide basic services, more and more young men and women are looking to non-state groups to provide access to food and housing. To the teenager of Ashgabat's peripheral slums and the man loitering in a Tashkent pool hall, the consistent monthly salary of a criminal network is increasingly appealing.

Organized Crime and Corruption

A train of donkeys loaded with heroin is intercepted along the Turkmenistan-Afghanistan border. A struggling schoolteacher in Karakol, Kyrgyzstan, accepts a bribe from impoverished parents for a passing grade. Several hundred automatic rifles are smuggled by Uighar separatists across the border from Kazakhstan to Xinjiang province, China. Traditionally considered a domestic rule of law problem, endemic organized crime and corruption have emerged as transnational roots of violence in the developing world. According to former director of central intelligence James R. Woolsey,

> Drug trafficking, links between drug traffickers and terrorists, smuggling of illegal aliens, massive financial and bank fraud, arms smuggling, potential involvement in the theft and sale of nuclear material, political intimidation, and corruption all constitute a poisonous brew—a mixture potentially as deadly as what we faced during the cold war.[43]

The problem is endemic in Central Asia, permeating from the governmental elite to the rural peasant. The roots are fed by the rapid expansion of illicit transnational economic activity, particularly in the global commodities of drugs, small arms, and persons. Underdevelopment, demographic pressures, and resource scarcity foster and result from this destructive duo.

Organized Crime

Crime shifts from a domestic law-and-order problem to a legitimate security threat when it becomes organized and transnational. These groups—especially if they have an ethnic base—are the ones most likely to resort to violence to achieve their goals.[44] As defined by Interpol, organized crime involves "any group having a corporate structure whose primary objective is to obtain money through illegal activities, often surviving on fear and corruption."[45] This definition rightfully embraces the core profit motive, the role of violence, and the key link to corruption. Along the Silk Route, organized crime prospers both outside state authority and in cooperation with it.

In addition to the massive drug trade discussed below, Central Asia experiences robust transnational crime in oil, caviar, metals, humans, and weapons.[46] The most blatant form of crime is the black market in oil. Illegal vendors ply their trade along the roadsides of the now paved Silk Routes, offering used plastic water bottles full of dusty petrol. According to Kyrgyzstan's Interior Ministry, more than 155 tons of oil products were smuggled into the country during 1997 and 1998 alone.[47]

Possibly the most insidious organized criminal activity is the vigorous sex trade.[48] Essentially a form of modern slavery, human trafficking trends indicate at least 700,000 and possibly 2 million women and children are illegally smuggled across international borders every year.[49] Figures for Central Asia are shaky; however, the International Organization for Migration in collaboration with the Organization for Security and Cooperation in Europe (OSCE) report more than 4,000 Kyrgyz women and children were involved in the sex trade during 1999. Other estimates suggest as many as 50,000 to 70,000 in the last few years alone.[50] Additional press reporting suggests that the level of international organization involved in kidnapping and smuggling these women to various parts of the globe has substantially increased as well, possibly accounting for the greater number of such victims.[51]

Like much of the developing world, Central Asia is also home to a robust illegal arms trade. According to Jane's Intelligence Group, an estimated 30 million firearms are circulating throughout the Commonwealth of Independent States.[52] In 1998, an Iranian "humanitarian" aid train bound for the Northern Alliance in Afghanistan was intercepted in Osh. Its seventeen cars held 700 tons of weapons, including anti-tank mines, grenades, machine gun ammunition, 122mm artillery shells, and rocket launchers.[53] In 1999, Kazakhstan "illegally" attempted to smuggle forty MiG-21 fighter aircraft through the Czech Republic to North Korea. Officially unresolved, it is quite likely that well-placed officials were instrumental in the sale, particularly given the mysterious murder of the head of state arms exports shortly thereafter. Non-proliferation efforts are high on the agendas of the U.S. State Department, the OSCE, and other intergovernmental organizations. Russian troops of the 201st Motorized Infantry Division patrol the Tajik-Afghan border in a vain effort to stem the flow between the two weapons-saturated countries.

The transfer of conventional arms is destabilizing enough; however, of greater concern is the potential for the proliferation of weapons of mass destruction (WMD). Fortunately, the threat of nuclear proliferation from the test site in Semey (Semipalatinsk), Kazakhstan, is receding. However, the threat of biological proliferation from the once remote island in the center of the Aral Sea, Ostrov Vozrozhdeniya, was until very recently all too real. The island is increasingly accessible by land as the Aral Sea shrinks. This modest island shared by Uzbekistan and Kazakhstan was until 1992 home to a sophisticated Soviet biological weapons program, with laboratories for creating persistent, weaponized variants of anthrax, plague, Q-fever, and others deadly toxins. Giant steel canisters of anthrax spores and other unknown agents were placed underground during the Cold War, but their status—in regard to both safety and security—was unclear until there was a significant joint effort between Russia and the United States to clean and secure the island.[54] However, Vozrozhdeniya island is not the only WMD concern; for example, in December 2003, officials learned that at least 38 primitive rockets carrying warheads packed with radiological material had disappeared in a break-away region of Moldova known for extensive black market arms sales.[55] Dozens of other WMD stockpiles exist in the region, are poorly protected, and are of high interest to VNSA.

Corruption Corrupts

Corruption shares the profit motive with crime but is more narrowly focused on abuse of entrusted power for private gain.[56] Corruption is not limited to public offices but includes abuse in the private sector. Bribery serves as the main tool; however, corruption also entails theft, fraud, embezzlement, patronage, and nepotism.[57] In traditional state-level analysis, focus is on political corruption, such as election manipulation and the effects on regime legitimacy. Equally important is administrative corruption, which has both an individual and a systemic impact. Administrative corruption involves illegal private gain for doing what is "ordinarily required by law" (according-to-rule) or what is prohibited by law (against-the-rule).[58]

Political and administrative corruption is ubiquitous in Central Asia. Extensive anti-corruption laws and strong official rhetoric are at odds with the realities of daily life. The Transparency International 2003 Corruption Perceptions Index, for example, assesses "the degree of corruption as seen by business people, academics and risk analysts, and ranges between ten (highly clean) and zero (highly corrupt)."[59] Of 133 countries surveyed, Uzbekistan and Kazakhstan tie with four other countries at 100, with a rating of 2.4—down from their 2001 tie at 71st with a rating of 2.7.[60] Kyrgyzstan places 118th with a 2.1 rating, with Tajikistan finishing 124th with a ranking of 1.8.[61] The World Bank estimates one-third of small business annual profits in Uzbekistan go to protection money and bribes.[62] Turkmenistan would likely bottom out with a score near zero if polling were allowed. Anecdotal evidence of embezzlement is pervasive, and graft is an aspect of customary transactions—even prisoners must pay bribes to receive basic necessities.[63] Kyrgyzstan is reflective of the region in that meager earnings—civil servants earn approximately $10–$40 per month—encourage supplementing one's income through bribes. Visitors throughout Central Asia often experience shakedowns from various shady types, ranging from creative plain-clothed men posing as undercover police officers to tough plain-clothed men who simply rob. As reported to us by numerous Peace Corps volunteers, the educational system is being subverted through routine bribery of teachers.[64]

Poppy Problems

In addition to the synergistic effect of the other roots of violence, there are several key environmental factors at work. Organized crime and the associated corruption represent the dark dynamic of globalization. According to prominent organized crime scholar Phil Williams, increased economic interdependence of nation-states, "permeability of national boundaries and the globalization of international financial networks have facilitated the

emergence of what is, in effect, a single global market for both licit and illicit commodities."[65]

Central Asian borders are notoriously porous. The popularity of the so-
called "Northern Route" from the poppy fields of Afghanistan is the direct result of Soviet disintegration and the closing of the Iranian border. Rugged terrain, insufficient border guards, and official corruption contribute to the
region's newly acquired reputation as the primary route for caravans of drugs,
guns, and girls to China, Russia, and on to Europe. The growth of global financial networks has made it increasingly easy to launder money. A globalized
informal economy has emerged beyond the control of the state. On the streets
of Urgench in western Uzbekistan and Ashgabat, the wide divergence in official and black-market exchange rates for dollars provides direct insight to the
advantages for crime and corruption of commercial liberalization. The problem is compounded in Central Asia where weak state institutions and an underdeveloped civil society persists.[66]

The interplay between crime and corruption and the importance of environmental factors is most evident in the burgeoning Central Asian drug trade.
Narcotics are quite likely the only true global commodities, generating an estimated $500 billion a year in revenues for its criminal sponsors.[67] Although
some examples exist of drug cartels using their ill-gotten gains for social good,
this is the rare exception.[68] Among other insidious purposes, they make possible the proliferation of weapons used by VNSA. Silk Route opium, heroin,
and cannabis trafficking are at the center of a global drug addiction.

According to the United Nations, 80 percent of all heroin consumed in
Western Europe originates in Pakistan and Afghanistan, and 50 percent of
these drugs (120 tons of heroin per year) arrive via Central Asia.[69] These estimates are supported by the most recent data on drug seizures as shown in
table 2.3, which represents only the portion of the drug flow that is intercepted. Unfortunately, as the figures for Central Asia are increasingly unflat-
tering, accurate data on this is growing sparse. Afghan and Tajik dealers move
narcotics through Dushanbe and northward through the increasingly popular
Batken route across the mountains between the Batken oblast of Tajikistan
and the Osh oblast of Kyrgyzstan.[70] Although Osh has developed a reputation
as the Bogotá of Asia, new routes are increasingly opening, including seven
known routes from Tajikistan into Uzbekistan and at least two more from
Turkmenistan.[71]

South Asia production is supplemented by rapidly expanding cultivation in
Central Asia. The official cultivation of opium on the high slopes around Lake
Issy-Kul in Kyrgyzstan ended in 1974; however, drug production continues
with the addition of cannabis. Kyrgyz officials indicate one-third of the population is in the business.[72] Fifty grams of marijuana can be bought in any
lakeside village for a mere three to four U.S. dollars. Poppy cultivation also oc-

TABLE 2.3
Central Asian Drug Seizures

Drug Seizures (all drugs in kg)	1995	1996	1997	1998	1999	2000	2001	2002	2003 (Jan.–June)
Kazakhstan	10,400	12,975	31,521	13,368	23,000	20,062	n/a	n/a	n/a
Kyrgyzstan	1,255	2,118	2,428	1,774	3,555	5,370	n/a	n/a	n/a
Tajikistan	1,750	3,565	4,533	2,951	2,000	7,128	1,484	1,482	3,461
Turkmenistan	n/a	14,109	41,216	24,157	39,555	2,200	n/a	n/a	n/a
Uzbekistan	3,017	7,822	3,308	3,206	2,500	n/a	n/a	n/a	n/a

Source: Combined data from UN Office for Drug Control and Crime Prevention

curs near Samarkand and Surkhandaria in Uzbekistan, in the Penjikent Valley of Tajikistan and the Mary and Lebap regions of Turkmenistan. Kazakh officials estimate that over 15,000 acres of land are covered by wild-growing poppy, marijuana, and other narcotic-related plants.[73] State authorities are aggressive in their interdiction and eradication efforts in large part due to the connection between drug trafficking, organized crime, and militant religious movements.

Taking a Toll

Organized crime and corruption take a toll. The World Bank points to losses in government revenue, reductions in foreign direct investment, barriers to small entrepreneurs, and environmental degradation.[74] Moreover, the cancer spreads throughout government, undermining public trust. Systemic crime and corruption can lead common citizens to cynically conclude that it is futile to work through official channels. It alienates the government from the governed, making them all the more vulnerable for VNSA recruitment; when ordinary citizens turn to illegal activity for basic needs, or even for survival, they quickly become easy recruits for predatory gangs offering a return on illicit activities that dwarfs the average regional salary of $10–$15 a month. The fact that a non-state organization can provide such goods when the state can not or will not makes that non-state actor all the more legitimate and accepted in society. Invariably, the emerging transnational criminal organizations (TCOs) rival the state's power, contributing to its weakness and failing legitimacy.

Socio-Economic Deprivation

A young girl, maybe eight or nine, in a tattered yellow dress pushes single cigarettes by briskly circling the plastic tables of an outdoor café in Almaty. An elderly man in the traditional black and white Uzbek skull cap offers a gaze at the moon through his antiquated telescope for a mere five cents. A mother, worn beyond her years, squats behind a cardboard box table, waiting with a seasoned patience for an equally destitute resident of Turkmenabat to buy a handful of sunflower seeds. Standards of living vary across Central Asia, from rural to urban and from one state to another; however, a common thread of daily struggle exists for all but the small percentage of government and criminal elite. The disparity between Kyrgyz families living in yurts, or huts, in high Tian Shan alpine valleys and Kazakh officials residing in the thick woods above Almaty is striking. The widening gap between rich and poor draws our attention to the socio-economic roots of violence. Building on the intellectual tradition of economic sources for internal rebellion, our analysis incorporates a broader understanding of degenerative human development as a contributor to the emergence of VNSA.

Rethinking Developmental Conflict

This current wave of internal violence bears similarity to the spate of civil conflict in the developing world during the period of decolonization. During the Cold War, our understanding of this trend was rooted in the development process itself. Essentially, the shedding of the colonial yoke leads to rising expectations that ill-equipped governments are not able to satisfy. In his seminal work *Why Men Rebel*, Ted Gurr refers to this as relative deprivation: "the perceived discrepancy between value expectations and value capabilities."[75] The resulting frustration turns to aggression as individuals realize they are being denied the basic necessities they deserve. The evidence of the period also seemed to suggest that instability is most likely during periods of rapid development.[76]

This earlier thinking warrants reconsideration since many contemporary conflicts are occurring where such developmental processes are not present. Individuals are aware of their deprivation and turning to collective violence earlier. Donald M. Snow, author of *Uncivil Wars: International Security and the New Internal Conflicts*,[77] suggests two contributory factors that are consistent with our assertions regarding the impact of globalization. First, developmental activity in which resources are unfairly allocated is not only a trigger for rebellion for closely clustered groups of people, but also for any group of people who feel they are unfairly disadvantaged when compared to any other group of people anywhere in the world.[78] As the global media has brought disparity to the doorstep of even the most rural of peasants, individuals are able to compare themselves to essentially any group in the world, not just groups of people in close proximity. Prior to information globalization, resource disparities created interactions between heterogeneous but geographically close groups; now, geographic proximity is no longer required for rebellion to occur. Second, the ideological justification for traditional insurgencies waned.[79] Very few Marxist and Maoist VNSA exist, and those that do, such as the Revolutionary Armed Forces of Colombia (FARC), are loosed from their ideological moorings. Only in Nepal is an active insurgency still both viable and loosely Maoist. Current motivations are not always focused on shaping or controlling the developmental process and therefore can emerge in societies that are moribund or degenerating.

The concept of development has also transformed beyond a strict consideration of hard economic indicators. Perceived relative deprivation is not just a function of gross national product (GNP), but of a broader range of individual values to include expectations for education, health care, sanitation, food, shelter, and even dignity. In order to measure a state's ability to provide these basic human needs, the United Nations Development Program (UNDP) established the Human Development Index (HDI).[80] The HDI seeks to capture as many aspects of human development as possible in one index. The index rates countries from 0 (the lowest possible score) to 1 (the highest possible score), with .5 or lower considered to be low development. In 2003, the United Nations provided HDI rankings for 157 other countries, with data unavailable for 29 countries. Despite a universal decline in HDI score and relative ranking from 2001, Central Asian states were, in 2002, ranked in the medium development range: Kazakhstan .75 / 79, Kyrgyzstan .712 / 102, Tajikistan .667 / 112, Turkmenistan .741 / 87, and Uzbekistan .727 / 95.[81] As there is only one prior year of HDI scores on four of the five countries, it is difficult to tell if the fact that all five countries fell both in HDI and in rank from 2001 is a trend or just a statistical blip. For this, we must go behind the aggregate numbers.

Derelict Development

Central Asia is experiencing postponed decolonization. Independence in 1991 was supposed to bring freedom and prosperity. Although holdover communist bosses knew the loss of Soviet funding would be devastating, they nonetheless generated high expectations in an effort to remain in power. They are failing. Across the region, the general population is experiencing persistent socio-economic deprivation. A wide range of indicators is commonly available to get a sense of the situation. These measures of human well-being tend to focus in three broad areas: poverty, education, and health. Central Asia is problematic due to the distinct absence of key indicators as revealed by a survey of statistical resources, including the UNDP, World Bank, and Central Intelligence Agency (CIA). Table 2.4 captures relevant and available indicators as a first step toward understanding the situation. Perspective is provided by comparison with U.S. indicators. Combining this limited data set with expert observations strengthens our contention that the governments of Central Asia are failing to adequately meet the basic needs of citizens.

As articulated by the World Bank Group, "poverty is hunger, homelessness, sickness, illiteracy and powerlessness . . . it is living day to day with no hope for the future."[82] A person is considered poor if his or her consumption or income level falls below some minimum level necessary to meet basic needs. This minimum level, known as the "poverty line," varies, as each country establishes this line using values appropriate to its level of development and social norms.[83] To make meaningful comparisons between countries, a construct known as the Purchasing Power Parity (PPP) is used to account for the relative purchasing power of currencies across countries. These constructs paint a bleak picture in Central Asia. Despite poverty lines set at artificially

TABLE 2.4
Central Asian Human Development Data

	Poverty			Education		Health	
	% Below Provety Line (2003, CIA)	% Unemployment (2003, CIA)	GDP Per Capita - PPP US$ (2003, CIA)	Gross Enrollment (1999, UNDP)	Adult Literacy (1999, UNDP)	Physicians per 1,000 (1999, World Bank)	Infant Mortality per 1,000 (2003, CIA)
Uzbekistan	NA	10.00%	$2,500	76.00%	88.50%	2.8	71.51
Turkmenistan	34.40%	NA	$5,500	81.00%	98.00%	3.6 (1990)	73.17
Tajikistan	40.00%	40.00%	$1,250	67.00%	99.10%	2	113.43
Kazakhstan	26.00%	8.80%	$6,300	77.00%	99.00%	4.3	58.73
Kyrgyzstan	55.00%	7.20%	$2,800	68.00%	97.00%	3	75.34
United States	12.70%	6.00%	$37,600	95.00%	100.00%	2.7	6.75

Sources: CIA, World Bank, UNDP

low levels, a high percentage of the Central Asian population still lives below those lines. Although Uzbekistan is not available, unemployment and PPP indicators suggest around 50 percent of the population live in poverty. PPP values indicate that average citizens survive on $3.20 a day in Tajikistan to $13.70 a day in Kazakhstan. Given that most professionals earn less than $50 a month, these PPP values are artificially skewed, most likely due to the extravagant incomes of high level governmental and business elites. In the Uzbek Ferghana Valley, for example, monthly incomes average $10 as compared to $15 in the rest of the country.[84] On the Tajik side of the border, incomes average under $8 per month.

Just as PPP values are brought into question by street-level inquiry, so too are unemployment rates. Official employment rates in the region do not reflect under-employment, which probably exceeds 40 percent across the region. The grandmother selling sunflower seeds for two cents a cup on the streets of Khiva is technically employed even though she may make $1 in a week, if lucky. Unemployment rates are also considerably higher in rural areas. According to Dr. Fiona Hill of the Brookings Institution, as many as 95 percent of male high school graduates are unable to find jobs.[85] The potential for unemployment to contribute to social tension is compounded by disproportionately high rates for those under thirty, the failure of the state to provide promised unemployment payments, and uneven distribution of jobs across ethnic groups.[86]

Poverty is difficult to overcome when the education system is also impoverished. Gross enrollment and literacy indicators do not do justice to the deficiencies in regional educational systems. State funding has been on a precipitous decline since the early 1980s. As one example, the Ferghana Valley Working Group, a scholarly investigative team sponsored by the Council on Foreign Relations, reports that the non-wage element of the education budget has fallen by an estimated 70 percent in real terms, "resulting in shortages of textbooks and teaching materials and inadequate maintenance of school buildings.[87] Teachers are forced to take bribes to supplement meager earnings, which are often in arrears, and classes take place in rooms with crumbling walls, dirt floors, and no plumbing. Teachers in Tajikistan earn $12 per month with bribes increasing for higher grades or more prestigious programs like the Medical University in Dushanbe.[88] In Turkmenistan, budget cuts led to the elimination of an entire grade, ostensibly to be replaced by a year learning vocational skills as an apprentice. This is a fiction, as there are no apprenticeships in Turkmenistan, unless one counts the drug and sex trade. With funds so limited, the state is precluded from delivering educational programs in multiple languages, which has developed as an additional source of tension among nationalities. Any optimism for near-term improvement in the region springs from the growing role of foreign investment, international governmental organizations (IGOs) and non-governmental organizations (NGOs).

Closing

Central Asia provides grim examples of the relationship between environmental conditions and VNSA formation. The optimism of 1991 is waning. A complex combination of corruption and incompetence as well as the structural legacies of a defunct communist system undermine most prospects for progress. The situation, however, has yet to descend to such a desperate level that socio-economic deprivation can generate violence on its own. Moreover, grass roots organizations, such as the *makhallas* in Uzbekistan, have taken the place of the state in trying to ensure that families have sufficient food and water; currently, these non-violent non-state actors are working mightily to address the conditions of violence. However, they can only do so much. Unless current regimes weed out corruption and embrace difficult reforms, such as the privatization of collective farms, the region is unlikely to turn the corner. In the meantime, the ranks of the exploited and unemployed will grow along with disillusionment and even anger. Will the young girl in the tattered yellow dress still be selling cigarettes in five years, or will she have moved on to a more lucrative heroin trade?

Violence grows where desperation lingers. At the individual level, where people struggle to survive, an ideological nudge here and a suggestion of blame there can move them from passive citizens to individuals who display growing dissatisfaction with their existing leadership. Some groups will be easy to motivate to engage in activities inimical to the state, especially in regions where citizenship is a foreign notion but a long tradition of violence exists. On the other hand, some may be more difficult to motivate to violence due to countervailing environmental factors. For example, more than seventy years of Soviet domination and ten years of indigenous authoritarianism have engendered a political and social passivity that restrains collective violence in Central Asia. In comparison to the paranoia of the Soviet era, even the authoritarian rule of Turkmenbashi can be sold as "freedom." Moreover, the economic retardation caused by Soviet planning still serves as a source of blame to deflect criticism from present failings. Despite these environmental constraints in the region, individual attitudes are slowly sliding toward a resentment that cannot be pacified through state coercion or pleas for patience. With the states in the region failing, non-state identity groups are gaining prominence as a socioeconomic provider. Legitimate non-state actors like Counter-Part Consortium, funded in part by the U.S. Agency for International Development, bypass state bureaucracies to work directly with these non-state actors in an effort to provide basic health and educational services. Identity cleavages are deepened as identity groups vie for scare resources, jobs and services. For the most part, these non-state actors supplanting the state has been peaceful; however, incidents of non-state violence have precedent and are likely to grow in frequency as the roots of violence become more acute. Standing next to the Turkmen father, who watched solemnly as another Ashgabat apartment building crumbled, one sensed not only resignation but a quietly simmering rage.

Notes

1. Refer to *Uncivil Wars: International Security and the New Internal Conflicts* by Donald Snow, (Boulder, CO: Lynne Rienner Publishers, 1996); or Mary Kaldor, *New and Old Wars: Organized Violence in a Global System* (Stanford, CA: Stanford University Press, 1999).

2. The state's characteristic of "impermeability" and the impact of advanced weapons is discussed in John Herz, "Rise and Demise of the Territorial State, *World Politics* 9, no. 4 (July 1957): 473–793.

3. Barry Buzan, *People, States and Fear: An Agenda for International Security Studies in the Post-Cold War Era* (Boulder, CO: Lynne Rienner Publishers, 1991), introduction.

4. Several of the leading "stresses" on human security are discussed by Michael T. Klare, "Redefining Security: The New Global Schisms," *Current History* (November 1996): 353.

5. For a more complete discussion of affordances, see "Affordance, Convention and Design," *Interactions* (May 1999): 38–43. Also available at: www.jnd.org/dn.mss/affordances-interactions .html as of January 10, 2004.

6. Martha Crenshaw, "Theories of Terrorism: Instrumental and Organizational Approaches," in *Inside Terrorist Organizations*, ed. David Rapoport (Portland, OR: Frank Cass Publishers, January 2001), 21–23.

7. Kim Cragin and Peter Chalk, *Terrorism and Development: Using Social and Economic Development to Inhibit a Resurgence of Terrorism* (Santa Monica, CA: RAND Corporation, 2003), ix–xiv.

8. Importantly, the pre-existing identity cleavages are correlates in the sense that an identity entrepreneur can exploit them. The authors strongly reject the notion of primordialism, which posits that people fight one another simply because they are different.

9. Discussed by Donald M. Snow and Eugene Brown in *International Relations: The Changing Contours of Power* (New York: Longman, 2000), 46.

10. Thomas F. Homer-Dixon, "Environmental Scarcity and Violent Conflict," *Scientific American*, February 1993, 38–45.

11. Lester R. Brown, "Redefining National Security," *Worldwatch Paper* 14 (October 1977): 37.

12. Refer to paper "The State Failure Project: Early Warning Research for U.S. Foreign Policy Planning" by Daniel C. Esty, Jack Goldstone, Ted Robert Gurr, Barbara Harff, Pamela T. Surko, Alan N. Unger, and Robert Chen, presented at "Failed States and International Security: Causes, Prospects, and Consequences," conference at Purdue University, February 25–27, 1998. Available on line at www.ippu.purdue.edu/failed_states/1998/papers/gurr.html. Additional updates on this on-going project can be found on line at www.cidcm.umd.edu/inscr/stfail/. Both accessed on January 10, 2004. From the Correlates of War databases, see, for example, Bremer, Stuart, J. David Singer, and Urs Luterbacher. "The Population Density and War Proneness of European Nations, 1816–1965," *Comparative Political Studies* 6 (1973): 329–48; reprinted in J. David Singer

and Associates, *Explaining War* (Beverly Hills, CA: Sage, 1979), 189–207; and Michael, Altfeld and Alan Sabrosky, "Indicators of Power: National Versus Battlefield Capabilities in the Post-1945 Era" in Charles Gochman and Alan Sabrosky, eds., *Prisoners of War: Nation-States in the Modern Era* (Lexington, MA: Lexington Books, May 1990), 257–70.

13. Homer-Dixon, "Environmental," 38–45.

14. Abdukhalil Razzakov, "Water Shortage in Central Asia and Re-Routing of Siberian Rivers to Central Asia," *The Times of Central Asia* (June 14, 2001, vol. 3, no. 24), 1.

15. G. E. Hollis, "The Falling Levels of the Caspian and Aral Seas," *The Geographical Journal* 144 (1978): 77.

16. Dante A. Caponera, *Principles of Water Law and Administration: National and International*, (Rotterdam, The Netherlands: Brookfield Press, May 1992), 85.

17. Gregory Gleason, "Mixing Oil and Water: Central Asia's Emerging Energy Market," 27 August 2001. Available at www.eurasianet.org/departments/business/articles/eav082701.shtml. Accessed on January 10, 2004.

18. British Broadcasting Company, as reported by the *Central Asia/Caucuses Analyst*. Available at 209.58.150.225/cacianalyst/August_2/newsbitesaug2.htm. Accessed on September 8, 2001.

19. Stefan Klotzli, "The Water and Soil Crisis in Central Asia—A Source for Future Conflicts?" *ENCOP Occasional Paper No. 11*, Center for Security Policy and Conflict Research/Swiss Peace Foundation, Zurich/Berne, May 1994.

20. P. Raskin, E. Hansen, Z. Zhu, M. Iwra, "Simulation of Water Supply and Demand in the Aral Sea Region," *Water International* 17 (1992): 56.

21. Arthur C. McIntosh. "Asian Water Supplies: Reaching the Urban Poor" (IWA Publishing, London, August 2003), 25. Sponsored by the Asian Development Bank and International Water Association. Available at www.adb.org/Documents/Books/Asian_Water_Supplies/asian_water_supplies.pdf. as of January 10, 2004.

22. Peter Gleick, ed., *Water in Crisis. A Guide to the World Fresh Water Resources* (New York: Oxford, 1993), 127.

23. Kristina Koivunen, "The Invisible War in North Kurdistan," (Ph.D., University of Helsinki, 2002). Available at ethesis.helsinki.fi/julkaisut/val/sospo/vk/koivunen/theinvis.pdf. Accessed on January 10, 2004.

24. International Crisis Group, "Incubators of Conflict: Central Asia's Localised Poverty and Social Unrest," Available at www.crisisweb.org/home/index.cfm. Accessed on January 10, 2004.

25. United Nations High Commission for Refugees, "The State of the World's Refugees: A Humanitarian Agenda," 1997. Available at www.unhcr.ch/cgi-bin/texis/vtx/home?page=PUBLandid=3eef1d896andID=3eef1d896andPUBLISHER=TWO. Accessed on January 10, 2004.

26. Several news sources carried varied accounts of the cotton smuggling efforts. One of the better accounts is by Esmer Islamov, "Anti-Smuggling Efforts Imperil Uzbekistan's Cotton Farmers," 23 October 2003. Available on Eurasia-Net at www.eurasianet.org/departments/business/articles/eav102303.shtml. Accessed on January 10, 2004.

27. This evolving view of demography and national security is explained by Brian Nichiporuk, *The Security Dynamics of Demographic Factors* (Santa Monica, CA: RAND, 2000), 5–7.

28. The available data is defined in terms of the nation-state. Given our focus on non-state actors, many of which are transnational, this data provides only partial insight to the dynamics working at the sub-national level. Ibid., 3.

29. From the International Population Database of the U.S. Census Bureau available at www.census.gov./. Accessed on January 10, 2004.

30. For a thorough discussion of this concept, see Anne Hendrickson's, *The "Youth Bulge": Defining the Next Generation of Young Men as a Threat to the Future,* Population and Development

Program, Hampshire College 19 (Winter 2003). Available at clpp.hampshire.edu/PDF/ DifferenTakes percent2019.pdf as of January 10, 2004.

31. The relationship between population growth and resource availability is examined in our section on resource scarcity (p. 26) and is based on research by Thomas-Homer Dixon. Among other articles, consider "Environmental Scarcities and Violent Conflict," from *International Security* 19, no. 1 (Summer 1994): 5–40.

32. United Nations High Commission on Refugees (UNHCR), "Displacement in the Commonwealth of Independent States," 1996. Available at www.unhcr.ch./pubs/ as of January 10, 2004.

33. Ibid., 19.

34. Internally displaced persons are included in our concept of refugees.

35. UNHCR, "Displacement," 1.

36. Field Report, "New Splash of Migration of the Kyrgyz Population," *Analyst* (Central Asia–Caucasus Institute, Johns Hopkins University, July 4, 2001). Available at www.cacianalyst.org/ as of January 10, 2004.

37. UNHCR, "Displacement," 1.

38. Ibid.

39. Ibid.

40. UNHCR, "Mid Year Report 2000." Available at www.unhcr.ch/ as of January 10, 2004.

41. Myron Weiner outlines these threats to include a fifth, refugees as potential hostages, in "Security, Stability and International Migration," *International Security* 17, no. 3 (Winter 1992/1992): 106–20.

42. Ibid., 15.

43. Statement appears on the website of the Global Organized Crime Project for Center for Strategic and International Studies, available at www.csis.org/goc/ as of January 10, 2004.

44. United Nations Office on Drugs and Crime, *Results of a Pilot Study of Forty Selected Criminal Groups in Sixteen Countries*, September 2002. Available at www.unodc.org/pdf/crime/ publications/Pilot_survey.pdf as of January 10, 2004.

45. Fenton Bresler, *Interpol* (London, UK: Penguin, 1992). Referenced in Tara Kartha, "Organised Crime and the Illegal Market in Weapons in Southern Asia," *Strategic Analysis: A Monthly Journal of the IDSA* 24, no. 2 (May 2000).

46. With the exception of the drug trade, reliable statistics for transnational criminal activities are not available. The United Nations is pursuing the development of such a database through its crime prevention program at www.unodc.org/unodc/en/crime_cicp_commission .html.

47. Tamara Makarenko, "Patterns of Crime in the Caspian Basin," *Jane's Intelligence Review* 13, no. 4 (April 1, 2001). Obtained through LEXIS-NEXIS.

48. The Victims of Trafficking and Violence Protection Act of 2000 defines sex trafficking as the inducement of a commercial sex act by "force, fraud, or coercion, or in which the person induced to perform such act has not attained 18 years of age." U.S. Department of State, *Trafficking in Persons Report*, 2001, 2.

49. Amy O'Neill Richard, "International Trafficking in Women to the United States: A Contemporary Manifestation of Slavery and Organized Crime," *DCI Exceptional Intelligence Program: An Intelligence Monograph* (Washington, DC: Center for the Study of Intelligence, April 2000), 3.

50. Field Report by Faniya Mussayeva, South Kazakhstan State University, for *The Analyst*, (Central Asia–Caucasus Institute, Johns Hopkins University, Washington, DC, July 18, 2001).

51. "Kyrgyzstan: Focus on Poverty as a Stimulus to the Sex Trade in the South," Integrated Regional Information Network, United Nation Office for Coordination of Humanitarian Affairs. Available at www.irinnews.org/report.asp?ReportID=37821andSelectRegion=Central_Asiaand SelectCountry=KYRGYZSTAN as of January 10, 2004.

52. Chris Smith, "Light Weapons Proliferation: A Global Survey," *Jane's Intelligence Review* 11, no. 7 (July 1, 1999). Obtained through LEXIS-NEXIS.

53. Martha Brill Olcott and Natalia Udalova, "Drug Trafficking on the Great Silk Road: The Security Environment in Central Asia" (Working Paper for the Russian and Eurasian Program, Carnegie Endowment for International Peace, no. 11 Washington, DC, March 2000), 23.

54. For excellent audio report on the biological threat originating from Ostrov Vozrozhdeniya, listen to the National Public Radio report by Aileen Garres, *All Things Considered,* September 27, 2001, at www.npr.org/ramfiles/atc/20010927.atc.05.ram accessed on January 10, 2004.

55. Joby Warrick, "Missing Rockets Heighten Fear of 'Dirty Bomb' Terrorist Attack," *Washington Post,* as reported in the *Charleston Post and Carrier,* December 9, 2003. Available at www.charleston.net/stories/120903/ter_09dirty.shtml as of January 10, 2004.

56. As put forth by the World Bank's General Counsel, Ibrahim Shihata, "in all cases, a position of trust is being exploited to realize private gains beyond what the position holder is entitled to." The World Bank Group, "Helping Countries Combat Corruption: The Role of the World Bank," Poverty Reduction and Economic Management Program, the World Bank, September 1997, 20. Available at www1.worldbank.org/publicsector/anticorrupt/corruptn/corrptn.pdf as of January 10, 2004.

57. Ibid.

58. From "Chapter 1: The Challenge of Renovation," in the *TI Source Book 2000,* Transparency International. Available at www.transparency.org/sourcebook/01.html as of January 10, 2004.

59. 2003 Corruption Perceptions Index, Transparency International. Available at www.transparency.org/cpi/2003/cpi2003.en.html as of January 10, 2004. Additionally, Alena Ledeneva thoroughly discusses corruption issues in the Commonwealth of Independent States in her 2003 report for Transparency International, available at www.globalcorruptionreport.org/download/gcr2003/16_CIS_(Ledeneva).pdf as of January 10, 2004.

60. 2003 Corruption Perceptions Index, Transparency International. Available at www.transparency.org/cpi/2003/cpi2003.en.html.

61. Restrictions prohibited polling in Turkmenistan.

62. Freedom House, "Uzbekistan," *Nations in Transit 2001.* Available at www.freedomhouse.org/research/nattransit.htm as of January 10, 2004.

63. Freedom House, "Turkmenistan," ibid.

64. Author interviews with Peace Corps volunteers in Bishkek and Karakol, Kyrgyzstan, June 19–20, 2001.

65. Phil Williams, "Transnational Criminal Organizations and International Security," *Survival* 36, no. 1, (Spring 1994.). Appears in *In Athena's Camp: Preparing for Conflict in the Information Age* (Santa Monica, CA: RAND, 1997), 316.

66. This view is not only intuitive, but also supported by research of the U.S. Agency for International Development in the *USAID Handbook for Fighting Corruption,* 1998, 7. Available at www.usaid.gov/democracy/anticorruption/resources.html as of January 10, 2004.

67. Williams, "Transnational," 320.

68. Several press reports indicate Pablo Escobar, the late head of the notorious Medellin cartel in Colombia, used his lavish riches for several social causes. See, for example, Mark Bowden's *Killing Pablo: The Hunt for the World's Greatest Outlaw* (New York: Penguin, 2001)

69. Data is from the United National International Drug Control Program and is provided in Olcott and Udalova, "Drug Trafficking," 4.

70. Ibid., 12.

71. Ibid.

72. Ibid., 10.

73. Ibid.

74. The World Bank Group, "Helping Countries Combat Corruption: The Role of the World Bank," Available at www.worldbank.org/html/extdr/corruptn/cor02.htm as of January 10, 2004.

75. Tedd Robert Gurr, *Why Men Rebel* (Princeton, NJ: Princeton University Press, 1970), 36.

76. Charles Tilly effectively outlines and critiques the dominant theories during the Cold War in *From Mobilization to Revolution* (New York: Random House, 1978), 12–51.

77. Snow, *Uncivil Wars.*

78. Ibid., 55.

79. Ibid.

80. United Nations Development Program, *Human Development Report: 2002.* Available at hdr.undp.org/reports/global/2002/en/ as of January 10, 2004.

81. Ibid.

82. World Bank Group, "Understanding Poverty." Available at www.worldbank.org/poverty/mission/up1.htm as of January 10, 2004.

83. World Bank Group, "Measuring Poverty." Available at www.worldbank.org/poverty/mission/up1.htm as of January 10, 2004.

84. All PPP figures are taken from Nancy Lubin, Keith Martin, and Barnett Rubin, *Calming the Ferghana Valley: Development and Dialogue in the Heart of Central Asia* (New York: Council for Foreign Relations—Ferghana Valley Working Group, 1999), 62.

85. Remarks by Dr. Fiona Hill during an open forum by the Open Society Institute on June 11, 2001. Recap of forum available at www.eurasianet.org/departments/recaps/articles/eav061201.shtml as of January 10, 2004.

86. Council on Foreign Relations, *Calming the Ferghana Valley,* 66.

87. Ibid., 73.

88. Konstantin Parshin, "The Cost of Education in Tajikistan," *Analyst* (Central Asia–Caucasus Institute, Johns Hopkins University, 14 February 2001). Available at www.google.com/url?sa=Uandstart=1andq=http://www.sais-jhu.edu/cacianalyst/Feb_14_2001/cost_of_Education_in_Tajikistan.htmande=7370 as of January 10, 2004.

3

Violent Transformations

The frustrated young man was just told he needed to get a boat permit in order to run tours along the Madre de Dios River near the Bolivian border. Tourism in this part of Peru was increasing, and he wanted to set up his own business instead of scraping by one odd job to the next. But to get an appointment to even see the local bureaucrat who could issue the permit, he would have to give the bureaucrat's secretary a bribe of about 100 pesos—nearly 20 dollars, an enormous sum. Worse, an appointment didn't guarantee a permit—another bribe would be needed to get the permit itself, perhaps as much as 500 pesos. A business opportunity was knocking, but the free market wasn't so free—extortion, excessive bureaucracy, and bribery were all barriers to his success. As the young indigenous man walked back to his crumbling yet crowded house in Puerto Maldonado, he passed a mural celebrating Abimael Guzman, the former head of the Sendero Luminoso, Che Guevera, Victor Raul Haya de La Torre, the founder of the Peruvian Communist Party, and some Incan Indian he'd heard about in school but didn't recognize. Things were better when the Incan rulers were in charge, he'd been told in school. He was also told things were better when Guzman was helping the peasants. He wondered how things would change if that Shining Path rural movement got started again. He also thought about his cousin who moved up north, near Iquitos, where he had a job paying up to 25 pesos a day working in coca fields. Perhaps his cousin could get him a job. Anything was better than the situation he was in.

ORGANIZED AND SUSTAINED COLLECTIVE violence is not an event resulting from the natural order of things, nor is it a spontaneous outgrowth of the conditions of violence discussed in the last chapter. Rather, the roots of violence are the substrata upon which organized collective violence builds; they create the conditions necessary and shape individuals to be ripe for mobilization. They are a necessary, but not sufficient, condition for VNSA to emerge. Incubation requires something more, transformational processes that take the unstructured, yet simmering potential of a primed population and push it toward group membership and, ultimately, collective violence. This chapter explores these transformational processes.

Our open systems framework in figure 3.1 provides visual insight to the key relational dynamics between a sufficiently "prepared" population and the transformational processes that spawn VNSA—failures in governance, identity cleavages, and identity mobilization. First, the state fails its citizens as a result of illegitimacy, impotence, or oppression. Second, existing identity-based divisions exist that compete with citizenship for attention and loyalty. Finally, mobilization transforms passivity into active participation in a non-state group. Despite being presented as an orderly evolution, the transformation from a population primed for collective violence to a functioning VNSA is not linear. A population can languish under intolerable conditions for many years, but without a competing identity, a VNSA is unlikely to emerge. North Korea, the most ethnically homogenous and completely stifling country in the world, is a prime example.

On the other hand, a population can exist in relative calm for some time, and as soon as the roots of violence reach a tipping point, alternative identi-

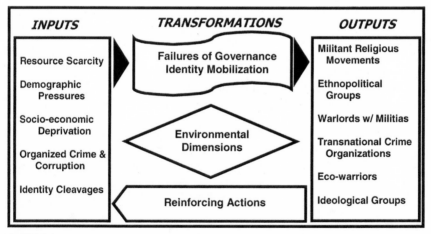

FIGURE 3.1
Open Systems Framework

ties are exploited along ethnic, political, or religious lines. The Balkans is a harrowing illustration of this dynamic.

Failures of Governance

The state is the arbiter of conflict within its borders—it sets up and administers the rules by which everyone plays. A fully sovereign state controls all matters of governance, administrative control, and most importantly, holds ultimate and monopolistic command and control of the means of coercion.[1] With power come responsibilities, and more importantly, expectations by citizens. Citizens desire safety and security, a relatively equal application of justice, and a legitimate distribution of goods and resources. When government fails to deliver, the affected sectors of the population will seek alternative means to obtain resources and provide services.

Three types of state failure exist: (1) *illegitimacy*, whereby the citizens of a state do not see the leadership of the state as the rightful wielders of power; (2) *incapacity* or impotence, whereby the wielders of power do not have the means to address the problems facing their citizens, and (3) *excessive force*, whereby the use of coercive power is an oppressive response to problems. This last form of state failure is special in that an excessively harsh response by the state can contribute to the other two forms of state failure.

As an analogy, the black market can be understood as a consequence of open market failure. When the open market either cannot (reflecting the market's incapacity) or will not produce certain goods that are demanded (possibly leading to the market losing legitimacy), a black market for those goods will develop. In other words, the black market can be viewed as a failure of the "legitimate market" to provide goods and services demanded by the population. Likewise, identity entrepreneurs create black markets and encourage individuals to participate; black markets are created and sustained in response to an environmental stimulus, namely an under-supply of goods and services. For example, in centrally controlled economies, such as the former Soviet Union, consumer demand was muted as an influence on what the central government decided to produce. Consequently, many products demanded by Soviet citizens were under-provided in the Soviet market. The result was an impressive black market, where the Soviet market's impotency resulted in its loss of legitimacy. With the right connections and the right amount of cash, the black market eventually produced just about anything demanded. Note that the Soviet economy had not completely collapsed before a significant black market emerged—it merely was inadequate in certain areas for "non-state market actors" to begin filling in the voids.

Just as black markets emerge from economic failures, non-state actors form, or existing ones spread to, areas where goods and services normally provided by the state are under-produced by either intent or inability. Whether that non-state actor will be a legitimate non-violent organization, such as the Red Cross or Doctors without Borders, or an illegitimate group like Hamas may depend on who gets there first and what type of organization best meets the demand. Not all non-state actors responding to state failure will be illegitimate, and not all illegitimate organizations will be violent—but some will be.

A complete state collapse is not necessary for non-state actors to begin filling small political vacuums as they become apparent—a form of niche construction. Once created, these power vacuums are typically short-lived. Other states or international organizations, such as the United Nations, attempt to fill the voids. Indeed, states that cannot provide all the services necessary ask for governance assistance. On the other hand, illegitimate— and sometimes violent—non-state actors may fill the voids before legitimate ones can or are allowed to step in. Colombia provides an illustrative example of how all types of political actors can move to fill a power vacuum. Bogota, attempting to exert its command over various parts of the hinterlands, receives aid from the United States. Additionally, the country is getting plenty of aid from more than one hundred NGOs around the world (themselves a type of legitimate non-state actors). Nonetheless, it remains mired in civil war with a very different type of non-state actor, the drug-running, psuedo-communist FARC and, to a lesser extent, the National Liberation Army (ELN). Complicating matters further are the right-wing paramilitaries such as United Self-Defense Forces of Colombia (AUC) fighting the leftist cocaine-based groups—ostensibly fighting on behalf of the state but certainly operating outside of it. Caught in the middle of all these cross-currents is the average Colombian who faces violence, kidnapping, extortion, and chaos on a daily basis—themselves continually shaped by this violence-prone environment, with some reaching that tipping point where they too feel that it is time to abandon loyalty to the state.

While political vacuums can be filled by any sort of outside influence, it is the violent non-state organizations that pose the thorniest security problems. Illegitimacy, impotence, or excessive coercion do not necessarily occur chronologically but can act on the population in a simultaneous and reinforcing manner. First, states suffer a loss of legitimacy due to incompatibility in governance ideology. Next, states illustrate incompetence or incapacity through a loss, abdication or rejection of legitimate state power, or excessive corruption and/or failed markets. Finally, states that rely on excessive coercion or oppression typically are not supported by their populace, with some members, if given the opportunity, willing to resort to violence to harm or over-throw that government.

Illegitimacy

Ideological incompatibility broadly refers to a group within a country that is opposed to the ideology the state uses to rule. It is more than a matter of credibility; it has to do with acceptance of the government as legitimate based on a belief system or worldview. No state's ideology is perfectly compatible with all its population; however, many states have mechanisms through which the citizens can satisfactorily express that incompatibility. Democracies, for example, have voting procedures where citizens are allowed to choose between political parties that pursue ideologically different agendas. There is agreement about the rules. Even the fractured country of Afghanistan for centuries used the *loya jirga* ("grand council" in Pashto, one of the local dialects), where influential elders and chiefs of various tribes gathered to select their king, adopt constitutions, and settle disputes. Afghans, by and large, accepted the results of the *loya jirga* outcomes, until the Cold War introduced outside powers that began influencing the process.[2] As the in-fighting in Afghanistan suggests after the communist revolution there in 1978, problems arise within a state when such mechanisms to express discontent do not exist or citizens refuse to accept those mechanisms as legitimate. As long as the accommodative capacity of the state to register ideological discontent is sufficient, the state has less to fear regarding VNSA mobilization.

When coupled with other roots of violence, the first case—where "ideological expression mechanisms" or political "safety valves" do not exist—presents fertile ground for VNSA incubation.[3] Disgruntled citizens who do not believe in the ruling ideology and have no legitimate means to express their own ideology or challenge the existing one may turn to illegitimate means. This condition can help explain the rise of al Qaida. Upset that the House of Saud was not observing certain elements of the *sharia* and had allowed non-Muslim forces to be stationed in the "land of the two Holy Places" (Saudi Arabia),[4] bin Laden protested to King Fah'd. When he was rebuffed and had no other legal course of action to protest this perceived ideological failure, he turned to illegal activities within Saudi Arabia, to include protesting against the House of Saud, calling its rulers false Muslims (*jahiliyya*) and apostates and generally fomenting discontent within the kingdom. At that point, he was stripped of his Saudi citizenship and expelled from the country.[5] As the kingdom rarely registers discontent from its citizens, one cannot accurately say that mechanisms to express discontent or exercise influences existed. When bin Laden's early non-violent efforts failed, he turned to violent means, and a significantly different chapter of history was written because of it.

The second condition—where the mechanisms by which citizens can express their ideological differences exist but lose legitimacy—also provides some fertile ground for VNSA incubation, but it is a more complex situation. Institutional legitimacy may be lost for a variety of reasons, to include corruption, failure of that institution to do what it is designed to do, etc. As mentioned earlier, Afghans generally stopped trusting the *loya jirga* process after they perceived it as corrupted by outside influences, even though the communists still wanted the process to be used and accepted. On the other hand, some organizations or individuals may be interested in actually creating the perception of corruption so that certain populations will actively oppose it. For example, during the Cold War, the Soviet Union, Cuba, and other communist nations funded and fomented ideologically-based insurgencies around the world. In some cases, especially in Latin America where the existing government institutions were doing a particularly poor job of providing basic services to their citizens, the task of convincing citizens that their current government was illegitimate was not difficult. Anti-government movements using violence, such as in Cuba, El Salvador, and other states were the result. In other cases, such as in Portugal where the roots of violence were not quite so deep, rejection of the democratic state system was avoided. And in other cases, such as in the United States, most of Europe, and Japan, where the roots of violence were quite shallow, the only thing the communists could do was to form small terrorist groups such as the Red Brigades, the Baader-Meinhoff Gang (also known as the Red Army Faction), and the November 17th Movement. In these cases, the contest was essentially between capitalism and communism; an ideologically-driven entity attempted to convince elements of a population that the institutions by which they expressed their various political beliefs were illegitimate. In populations where the roots of violence were strong, this message resonated, and large VNSA resulted. In populations where such conditions did not exist, small VNSA resulted, and once the outside sponsor of communism was gone, so were the VNSA.

Ideological incompatibilities today find their roots less in political ideology than in religious beliefs. The origins of large terrorist groups can be traced back to populations steeped in the roots of violence, living under an ideologically incompatible government. For example, al Jihad (which recently merged with al Qaida) sprang from the Muslim Brotherhood, an organization founded in 1928 by Hasan al-Banna, a twenty-two-year-old elementary school teacher. The movement began as an Islamic revivalist movement following the collapse of the Ottoman Empire and the subsequent ban of the caliphate system of government that had united the Muslims for hundreds of years. As Banna saw Islam as not only a religion but also a comprehensive way of life, he was dismayed at the increasingly secular Egyptian government. Coupled with the grinding poverty, corruption, and other conditions of violence in Egypt at the time and no formal institutions to pursue their Islamic goals, the Brotherhood turned to violence, and the Egyptian state cracked down.[6] Over seventy-five years later, the Muslim Brotherhood morphed to al Jihad, which subsequently joined the al Qaida terror network.

As al Qaida expanded around the world, those states that were vulnerable to the call to *jihad* were largely those states with populations shaped by the environmental conditions outlined in chapter 2. Indonesia, the southern Philippines, western China, Pakistan, and Algeria all have receptive populations sufficiently conditioned by environmental factors. In the Philippines, the Bangsamoro, an Islamic tribe living in the southern Philippines, is a microcosm of this phenomenon. While the history of the Moro people is far richer than can be expressed here, the history of fighting against the Philippine government in the late 1960s and early 1970s is illustrative. While fighting for the independence of the Moro people, the Moro National Liberation Front (MNLF) declared itself in existence in the early 1970s. After the 1976 Tripoli Agreement between the Marcos government and the MNLF, the Moro Islamic Liberation Front (MILF), one that espoused the Islamic religion rather than the Moro culture—emerged as a splinter group. By 1991, the Abu Sayyaf, ("bearer of the sword" in Arabic), was the second Islamic-based VNSA split off from the MNLF.[7] To highlight the increasing influence of religion on VNSA in the country, the MNLF felt compelled to merge with the MILF in October 2001; thus, the two major VNSA in the Philippines are now both based on religion rather than on ethnicity, despite the Philippines being one of the most ethnically diverse countries in the world.

Interestingly, not all states fell under al Qaida's siren song. States that did not have deep roots of violence appeared to be able to prevent VNSA from taking root. Singapore, for example, with 500,000 Muslims in its 3 million population did not prove to be a fertile spot for operations or sympathy, as more than one al Qaida operative found upon their arrest. It is no coincidence that Singapore has both a higher standard of living than the Asian countries where al Qaida did resonate. Further, the Singaporean government stresses a single Singaporean identity, despite its ethnically diverse population. Indeed, "Forging the Singaporean Identity" is a key goal of the Singaporean Ministry of Education.[8] The lack of environmental conditions conducive to violence and an active governmental effort to ensure no identity cleavages existed prevented a strong VNSA from penetrating.

Incapacity

Theoretically, the state has control of the means of coercion. If the state lacks this capacity, alternative authority mechanisms emerge to fill the void. The origin of the Sicilian mafias—which dates back to the latter half of the nineteenth

century, right after the unification of Italy—provides an interesting illustration
of VNSA development under this phenomenon. Having a long tradition of resistance to outside domination coupled with the new Italian state unwillingness (perhaps because it realized it was unable) to extend its authority into the
island, the Sicilians tended to "use new systems of private protection for secur-
ing their land and property"; these "new systems" were simply local families
who were well-known and well-trusted by the majority of the local populace.[9]
Thus, the mafia began simply as a trusted power structure that existed outside
the state, but was capable of arbitrating disputes, enforcing contracts, and providing protection in the absence of the "legitimate" state's ability.[10] These
rather innocuous roots have led to a powerful VNSA today. As Roberto
Scarpinato, a full-time mafia prosecutor stated, "the Mafia's determination to
establish itself as a state within a state is what makes it unique."[11]

While the Sicilian mafia can trace its origins to political activities a century
and a half ago, this is not unlike how and why many modern-day VNSA come
to be. Some states, such as Somalia, were completely incapable of performing
basic governance functions. Present-day Afghanistan, even after the routing of
the Taliban, also has a weak ability to project its power much beyond the city
limits of Kabul. In these cases, alternative power structures exist that have the
ability to arbitrate disputes and enforce contracts; Somalia has its Colonel
Bihis and Afghanistan has its Hekmatyars and Khans. These black holes of
state power are occupied by powerful figures that build VNSA.

Across the security landscape, the problem of ungoverned space is growing.
A recent World Bank study of governance in 196 countries cautiously asserted
"evidence is suggestive of deterioration, at the very least in key dimensions
such as control of corruption, rule of law, political stability and government effectiveness."[12] Further analysis out of the Institute for National Security Studies indicates approximately 50 percent of the 196 countries evaluated by the
World Bank qualified as weak, very weak, or failed.[13] Not surprisingly, these
states are concentrated in the strategic ghettos of Africa, the Middle East, and
Asia. Of the remaining states, one quarter rated as fair, leaving only about 20
percent of the surveyed countries in the categories of excellent and good.[14] Out
of ninety-plus failing states, "terrorist groups, as well as insurgent and criminal
organizations, are located in the remote parts of more than 20 countries."[15]
Over the last twenty years, U.S. military deployments have been to "very weak"
or "failed" states with few exceptions.[16] It is an unremitting trend.

Excessive corruption

A sign of governmental incapacity or incompetence is excessive corruption.
The World Bank, in an extensive examination of the effects of corruption on
state power, made this observation regarding corruption:

Yet all forms of state [corruption] directed towards extracting rents (or advantages) from the state for a narrow range of individuals, firms or sectors through distorting the basic legal and regulatory framework, with potentially enormous losses for the society at large. (sic) They thrive where economic power is highly concentrated, countervailing social interests are weak, and the formal channels of political influence and interest intermediation are underdeveloped.[17]

The World Bank followed that statement with the observation that the expansion of corruption in various regions in the world coincided with a sharp, initial decline in economic output and significantly higher levels of poverty and inequality. While admitting that the causal connection was not absolutely certain, one certainty is that the poor bear the heaviest effects of corruption. "Corruption weakens public service delivery, misdirects public resources, and holds back the growth that is necessary to pull people out of poverty," and "some countries risk becoming trapped in a vicious circle in which pervasive corruption reduces public revenues, undermines public trust, and weakens the credibility of the state, unless decisive leadership can push through the necessary reforms."[18] Corruption itself is a root of violence and further reinforces and deepens other roots of violence.

Corruption is also an active process eroding the trust between the populace and the state. Governments that extort, require bribes, arbitrarily enforce laws, seize private goods, or behave in otherwise kleptocratic manners not only increase economic inefficiencies, stunt growth, and reinforce the roots of violence, but they prove they are an ineffective enforcer of contracts and law and that such extralegal methods of exchange are acceptable. In other words, such a government not only alienates its citizenry, but it simultaneously shows its citizenry that illegality is an acceptable modus operandi.

These lessons can have many effects, two of which that are particularly important here. First, the alienated citizenry is far more easily recruited into non-state actors. Feeling no special loyalty (indeed, resentment or hostility may be a more common reaction) to a state that unfairly attempts to extract as much from them as possible, their loyalty is easily won by any number of competing organizations. Second, their norms and expectations of behavior are similarly reduced. Consequently, when less than noble organizations—especially those organizations which resort to or rely on violence—approach the citizenry, they are less likely to reject these organizations based on having high ethical, moral, or social norms.

Excessive corruption is correlated to organized crime, transnational criminal organizations, and, to a more limited extent, insurgency.[19] Various regions in the world that rank high in all forms and types of corruption—to include former Soviet states and Eastern Europe—also rank high in local and regional mafia activity as well, with black markets providing many of the goods and services for the population. The Chinese Triads managed to flourish under the corrupt Chinese political and economic system, with a cycle of reinforcing in-centives making both problems worse. Corruption allowed the Triads to be-come so powerful in the first place, and the Triads are increasing the corrup-tion in the Chinese government. In 2001, for example, over 2,600 influential officials in China were implicated in corruption, with the Triads increasingly involved in these cases.[20]

Excessive Coercion

While not universally true, weak states resort to excessive coercion or op-pression more so than strong states. Strong states boast healthy economies, solid infrastructure, and conditions that generally satisfy their populations. Weak states, on the other hand, have difficulty providing the basic goods and services to their populations; their citizens have reason to question or in some cases rebel against state authority. Therefore, it is typically the weak states that must resort to greater coercive measures to control their populations; they face a greater likelihood of challenge. Harvard University researcher Robert Rot-berg summed this condition well:

> In most cases, driven by ethnic or other intercommunal hostility or by regime insecurity, failed states prey on their own citizens. As in Mobutu Sese Seko's Zaire or the Taliban's Afghanistan, ruling cadres increasingly oppress, extort, and ha-rass the majority of their own compatriots while favoring a narrowly based elite. As in Zaire, Angola, Siaka Stevens's Sierra Leone, or Hassan al-Turabi's pre-2001 Sudan, patrimonial rule depends on a patronage-based system of extraction from ordinary citizens. The typical weak-state plunges toward failure when this kind of ruler-led oppression provokes a countervailing reaction on the part of resentful groups or newly emerged rebels.[21]

As such, excessive coercion can be seen as much as an indicator of a weak state as it can be viewed as a failure of governance in its own right. Typically other prob-lems beset a state that relies on oppression to stay in power; the decision to resort to oppression reflects state failure *prima facia*. Therefore, this type of state failure feeds directly into the two previously discussed state failures—illegitimacy and incapacity. Continuing to rely on oppression or excessive coercion will continue to erode the legitimacy of that government, as harsh treatment is not a sustain-able ruling ideology. Further, a state that appears to be skilled only at arrests, truncheons, and imprisonment cannot be viewed as competent. Often, such a state must put significant quantities of resources and energy into its internal se-curity apparatus in order to continue pursuing its repressive reign. When the only tool in which the state invests is internal security, other mechanisms that could be used to address security challenges are vestigial and undeveloped. The capacity of the state to have a multi-dimensional response to the various prob-lems and challenges it faces is thus reduced. As such, the state can no longer count on the fabric of shared values or consensus to hold the state together; the basis of state authority in such situations then shifts to the unstable solution of state coercion.[22]

Failures of governance begin when populations (either in whole or in substantial parts) perceive that their state no longer thinks or acts properly. Perceived illegitimacy, incapacity, or excessive coercion can all lead individuals to view the state not as an avenue for protecting or enhancing their lives but as an entity that is undermining them or blocking their efforts at improving their existence. Where identity cleavages exist or can be created, the potential for mobilization is high.

Identity Cleavages

Pre-existing identity cleavages were mentioned as a root of violence in chapter 2. Unlike poverty or demographic pressures, divisions within a society based on alternative identities are a special condition for violence. People do not fight each other simply because they are different from one another. Rather, alternative identities provide an avenue for an identity entrepreneur—an individual who has a vested interest in created conflict along such lines—to exploit. Exploiting identity and mobilizing the individual along similar lines, either by creating competing identities where none previously existed or exacerbating existing identity differences, is an important aspect of the individual's conversion from citizen to VNSA member.

With failures in governance resulting in a loss of regime legitimacy and undermining the notion of "citizenry," identity cleavages further serve to alienate the individual from the state and lure them toward non-state actors. These identity cleavages are the nucleus around which VNSA recruit members and develop group cohesion. An increasing number of states, the increasing wealth gap between the world's haves and have-nots, the worldwide wave of religious revivals, and the increasing awareness of "us" versus "them" resulting from the greater exposure to other parts of the world courtesy of the information revolution have created "identity-threats" that brings even latent group identities to the forefront.[23] In other words, globalization is raising individual awareness of ethnic, cultural, religious, or other identity. These identity-threats, coupled with the roots of violence and perceived state failures, advance the cause of the VNSA at the expense of the state. In this section, we examine several types of identity cleavages that are a basis for mobilization.

Ethno-Political Identity Cleavages

An "ethnic group" designates a people that is predominantly biologically self-propagating, that holds a common set of fundamental values, that constitutes a field of interaction and communication, and that has a membership that identifies itself and is identified by others as constituting a category that can be distinguished from other categories of the same order.[24] Importantly, the continued existence of these groups is dependent upon the establishment and maintenance of social, cultural, religious, and sometimes geographic boundaries by which they define themselves and are defined as distinct by others.

The Central Asian Republics serve as a somewhat distressing case study of ethnic identity cleavages. Under the autocratic rule of the Soviet system, ethnic groups were suppressed in favor of creating the Soviet Man. While some expressions of nationalism or ethnicity were allowed, they were the rare exception rather than the proverbial rule. Consequently, the desire to propagate one's own ethnic group, thereby creating the necessary boundaries to do so, was rare. This has changed significantly. In the post-Soviet vacuum, ethnic groups are emerging—and thus asserting or reasserting the norms and values that define them.

Citizenship

The first aspect of identity in Central Asia is nation-state citizenship. Efforts are underway to formally codify state boundaries and solidify citizenship. This attempt cuts across the grain of Central Asian culture and history, and the act of "creating" the state and citizenship generates tension of its own.

According to Dr. Igor Torbakov, a Russian historian, the ideas of an ethnic identity, statehood, citizenship, or nationality were largely alien to the peoples of Central Asia. Indeed, as late as 1927, Vasiliy Barthold, Moscow's leading specialist in Oriental affairs, stated "The settled peoples of Central Asia regard themselves first as Muslims and then as inhabitants of any given town or region; ethnic concepts having virtually no significance in their eyes."[25] It was only under the Soviet program of "national delimitation" (*natsional'noe razmezhevaniye*) that occurred in 1924–1925, where swaths of formerly un-demarcated Asia territory were turned into Soviet Socialist Republics and given titular names, did the political creations now known as Uzbekistan, Kazakhstan, Tajikistan, Kyrgyzstan, and Turkmenistan come into being. However, these "creations" did little to create eponymous identities, as Soviet policies were strictly from Moscow and ethnic expressions were largely suppressed.[26]

In the wake of the Soviet collapse, the Communist Party leaders who inherited their respective Soviet Socialist Republic immediately faced the task of nation building. They approached the task in a variety of ways—demarcating boundaries (in Uzbekistan's case, unilaterally), relaying historiographies, establishing national heroes, political elites attempting to be the most important in the region, and competing for once-shared resources. The process of getting individuals to swear their loyalty to them proved difficult. Nation-building efforts have created certain external instabilities as well. Once dormant border disputes are now serious points of contention between governments, and resources are now weapons (as illustrated by the water and electricity tit-for-tat between Kyrgyzstan and Uzbekistan described earlier). To quote Torbakov, "efforts by both countries to forge distinct identities in the post-Soviet era are a source of considerable friction between peoples who have co-existed relatively peacefully in the same region for centuries."[27]

Nation

A second but closely related identity cleavage is the "nation" half of nation-state. As opposed to the period before Russian colonization and Soviet annexation, awareness of national identity is now an established social practice in the Central Asian region. As is often the legacy in recently de-colonized areas, the newly independent populace embraces ethnicity as a significant and legitimate category of assessment—a phenomenon the Hutu–Tutsi rivalry in Rwanda and Burundi illustrates horrifyingly well. Discrimination, especially in the militaries, is rampant; individuals who do not speak the ethnic language of their country are often singled out for harassment and punishment.[28] The codification of the nation-state mix is illustrated by examining an Uzbek passport—clearly, the holder of an Uzbek passport is an Uzbek citizen, but "nationality" is an additional required identifier on the passport. For a group of peoples where Muslim identity traditionally masked ethnic differences, such an awareness of ethnicity coupled with identity mobilization can be dangerous.

Perhaps more ominous is the increasing trend of "nationalizing," or the attempt to make the nation and state coterminous. Kazakhstan provides an excellent example of "nationalizing" policies, which aim to promote the Kazakhs, while assimilating, marginalizing, or expelling non-dominant ethnic groups. For example, although nearly everyone in Kazakhstan speaks Russian, the "official language," the "state language" is Kazakh. While the difference between these two terms is vague and uncertain, other laws have more concrete effects—stipulating phasing-in of exclusive use of Kazakh for state employees, for example. Linguists and sociologists alike point out that even 25 percent of ethnic Kazakhs speak Russian as their first language; only those communities that resisted Russification during Soviet times are still using Kazakh as their first language.[29] Using such preferences has the effect of staffing the government bureaucracy almost entirely with ethnically-aware Kazakhs. While many other such laws and programs exist which structurally favor Kazakhs over non-Kazakhs (especially Russians), this example makes the point—laws are creating new winners and losers in Kazakhstan, and individuals are placed in each category based on their ethnicity.

A clear indicator of early mobilization among Russians is their massive out-migration, with estimates showing that from 1989 to 1999, more than 1.5 million Russians, or 25 percent of the Russian population of Kazakhstan, left the country permanently. Many of the remaining Russians moved to the highly Russified areas of Kazakhstan—in the north and east, close to the Russian border. A second visible effect is the emergence of largely Russian groups and political movements in northern Kazakhstan that actually have secessionist goals. While these groups are small (so far), their influence may be limited more by state actions (such as media restrictions, constraints on their ability to meet, and organization) and a lack of support from Russia than as a reflection of low resonance among that population.[30] Of particular interest is Kazakhstan's November 1999 arrest of twenty-two men—twelve of whom were Russian citizens—in Ust-Kamennogorsk, the administrative capital of East Kazakhstan Oblast. They were charged with planning to overthrow the oblast's leadership and proclaim the region a "Russian Altai Republic."[31] Despite steady Slav out-migration since Kazakhstan became independent, only 12 percent of the population of Ust-Kamennogorsk are Kazakh, suggesting that separatist tendencies will not subside soon. While measures such as media restrictions and arrests may be effective in keeping Russian irredentism capped in the short term, they may only reinforce the Russian-Kazakh identity cleavage and exacerbate mobilization effects over the long term.

Such nationalizing actions are observable from each of the five Central Asian republics. Saparmurat Niyazov, the peculiar president of Turkmenistan, proclaimed himself leader of all Turkmen and declared the twenty-first century to be the Golden Age of the Turkmen. Other slogans, splashed over everything (to include buildings, airliners, and mountainsides) proclaim "Halk! Watan! Turkmenbashi!" loosely translated as "The people! The Land! The Leader of all Turkmen!" Such popular pronouncements definitely promote Turkmen nationalism; however, one could not fault non-Turkmen citizens for feeling uneasy going into the new Golden Age. Even the Tajiks, with perhaps the most difficult job of creating a state, are attempting to build their nation around the old Saminid dynasty.

These two aspects of identity cleavages become all the more difficult given Josef Stalin's population-mixing programs of the 1920s. Stalin removed all Koreans on the Russo-Korean border and relocated them in the Ferghana Valley and central Uzbekistan. Moreover, Stalin gerrymandered the political boundaries of the Ferghana Valley so it would be divided among Tajikistan, Uzbekistan, and Kyrgyzstan—all in an effort to divide the Muslim population there. Large numbers of Russians, and to a lesser degree Ukrainians and Belorussians were sent to the new Soviet Socialist Republics to help the natives conform to the requirements of socialism. Later in Soviet history, many of the German and Japanese soldiers captured in World War II were relocated to

Central Asia, and their descendents still live there. In the Ferghana Valley city of Osh, Kyrgyzstan, there are at least eighty-three nationalities.[32]

As these Central Asian examples suggest, creating a national identity can cause a backlash from those who exist outside that identity. Further, even the majority of those who would fall inside the created identity may not agree with it. For example, Mohammad Reza Shah Pahlavi, the Shah of Iran, attempting to counteract the rise of Islamic fundamentalism in his country in the 1970s; he presented the pre-Islamic Persepolis greatness of Iran to his people on many occasions even going so far as to hold ceremonies to celebrate Persian (rather than Islamic) holidays. Such activities were criticized by conservative clerics, since celebrations were rooted in Iran's pre-Islamic Zoroastrian culture. The Shah's attempt to steer the national identity away from the very elements that led to a violent overthrow of his government may have actually exacerbated the conditions feeding the populace's discontent.

Tribe and clan

A third significant ethno-political identity cleavage is the clan or tribal identity. Within Turkmenistan, for example, there are five tribes, but three dominant ones: the Tekke in the center, the Ersary on the eastern Afghan border, and the Yomud in the west.[33] While President Niyazov has gone to great lengths to erase tribal identity, it still exists—Turkmen will only marry within their own tribe, and will also typically hire within their own tribe.[34] Only three generations ago, these tribes were distinct separate social, political, and economic entities often in conflict with one another; only since becoming a Soviet Socialist Republic were these tribes tied together by the uncomfortable cord of a state boundary. Kazakhstan provides another excellent example of the sub-national identity; these once nomadic people categorize themselves by *zhuz* or *ordas* (tribal confederations), and then through *ru* and *taipa* (clans and tribes). These identities continued through the Soviet era, and retain some level of importance after independence.[35]

Meta-identities

The fourth dimension of ethno-political identity is the meta-identity. This is an affinity of those that have broad, general similar histories, share a religion, and/or come from a similar linguistic family. Central Asia is divided (by population, and increasingly geographically, as the various groups settle into more homogenous "sub-communities" and diasporas) into those who come from a Muslim cultural heritage and those who do not, and those who are Turkic and those who are not. A Muslim cultural heritage, for example, would group Uzbeks and Tajiks together but separate Russian, Ukrainian, and German individuals. A Turkic meta-identity, for example, would focus on shared linguistic roots, grouping Uzbeks and Turkmen but marginalizing Kazakhs, Koreans, Ukrainians, and Russians.[36]

Civilizations

A fifth cleavage is Samuel Huntington's classical civilization fault lines introduced in his work *Clash of Civilizations and the Remaking of World Order.*[37] If our system of conflict is truly open, actors who are not physically in Central Asia but have influence there must be considered. Central Asia is the intersection of several civilization fault lines—one between the Muslim and Sinic civilizations, along the Muslim and Slavic/Orthodox civilizations, and one along the European/Muslim civilizations. The proximity of the Muslim/Buddhist fault line must also be mentioned. China and Russia both have political, economic, and security interests in the area. India has an additional indirect interest in the area due to its conflict with Islamic militants over Jammu and Kashmir, besides its continuing struggle with Pakistan. To again reject the primordialist explanation of conflict, these civilizations will not fight one another simply because they are different—an actual cause for fighting must exist; the various "fault lines" simply provide pre-drawn identities to further divide the competing sides.

Economic Identity Cleavages

Political dynamics often mirror economic dynamics. The collapse of communism as a competing ideology to capitalism opened many markets around the world to a new way of "doing business." The sudden arrival of notionally free markets in large swaths of the world allowed individuals to capture large elements of productive economies. The former Soviet Union provides the best example, as privatization there ended up concentrating wealth in the hands of a very few individuals. While corruption and the Communist Party system in the former Soviet Union obviously thwarted the Marxist notion of equality, the disparity between rich and poor witnessed in the region is orders of magnitude greater than anything seen in the USSR—and the difference continues to grow. Now, these ultra-rich individuals in the Russian state—the billionaires such as former Yukos Oil chief executive Mikhail Khodorkovsky—are targets of other identities, such as the former powerhouses in the Soviet state, leaders of the KGB. In the background, crime has increased in Russia, as various organized criminal elements, gangs, and petty thieves are all trying to get their share of the economic pie.

This is not an unusual turn of events. Nearly every region struggling in its immediate post-colonial days witnessed acquisition of wealth by a few. The identity of the new economic elite and their relationship with their kindred poor are of great importance. As noted Central Asian scholar Martha Brill Olcott asserts,

> The prospects of social and political instability are also more pronounced. Decolonization has always provided enormous economic opportunities for the new political winners, but the totality of the economic transformation is something quite new, and . . . the losers—be they the masses or among the political elite—have little or no economic assets to fall back on, because private property was virtually non-existent.[38]

While Olcott was referring specifically to the post-Soviet states, her analysis is easily applied elsewhere. The emergence and solidification of such economic strata in a weak state can certainly make populations more vulnerable to exploitation. As economically developing societies such as Vietnam, China, Indonesia, and others develop the institutions and norms related to handling an increasing number of economic transactions, friction or competition may develop other existing traditions and norms. Certain elements of the population may sacrifice "social capital" for economic capital, creating fissures in society.[39] As Drs. Fiona Hill and John Shoeberlein recently testified at the Open Society Institute in New York, poverty is a—perhaps *the*—critical ingredient in the increasing violent tension in Central Asia.[40] According to the Central Asia Project, stratification of economic elites can create instability as well. In the post-independence chaos, wealth accumulated in a very select group of hands.[41] The emergence of such a small group of prosperous elite left the majority of Central Asians below the poverty line. While this level of poverty grinds the population down, certain elites continue to gain wealth—a recipe for at least widespread resentment, and possibly widespread violence. The International Crisis Group concludes:

> there is a sharply growing disparity between the narrow elite, which benefits appreciably from privatization and other market reforms, and the larger part of the population, which is being driven towards economic desperation. Even more worrying, there are significant sub-regions and localities in [Uzbekistan, Tajikistan and Kyrgyzstan] where the situation is so [economically] dire for the vast majority of the population that patience is beginning to evaporate and unrest to grow sharply. While most Central Asians have been steadfastly passive in the face of post-Soviet upheaval, indications are increasing in some localities that a breaking point is near. If it is reached, spontaneous uprising or organized underground political activity, increasing militancy, and a readiness to seek the overthrow of current regimes can all be anticipated. The most dangerous social force is a desperate population that has little to lose.[42]

Another potential avenue for violence springs from economic identities in the form of the loss of the middle class. Examples from other states suggest that a small middle class in countries with such skewed wealth distributions is small and typically does not survive—a trend that unfortunately is being confirmed throughout Central Asia. The erosion of the middle class makes that particular caste prey for radical groups. As Alisher Ilkhamov, a 2000 IREX fellow at Harvard University, stated, "the IMU [Islamic Movement of Uzbekistan] not only [appealed] to the impoverished peasants of the Ferghana Valley, but also to a significant number of Uzbekistan's' shrinking middle class."[43]

Religious Identity Cleavages

The concept of identity threats and violence is nowhere as important as they are when dealing with religious identities. In the age of globalization, when more and more individuals of a given faith are exposed to the practices and beliefs of those of different faiths, the potential for creating more and threatening "them-groups" is high. The likelihood of these religious identity groups to resort to violence is similarly high for at least two reasons, although given the complexity of this issue, others are certain to warrant some consideration.

First, every major religion has a vision of divinely legitimized violence—under certain circumstances.[44] The Jewish faith has its Just Wars, Christianity has the Holy War, Islam has *jihad*, Hindus have a cycle of violence and peacefulness, and even Buddhist myths speak of the Seven Days of the Sword. Outside the theological ideas, these religions all have observable histories of violence. Christians have the Crusades and the modern-day Christian patriots. Buddhists have stained much of Sri Lanka with blood. Jews and Muslims, especially in the past two generations, are entangled in extraordinary violence. Hindus and Muslims within and between India and Pakistan also have far too rich a history of brutality. In all these cases, it is a requirement of the truly faithful. Note that most of this violence was not directed by the state—the Muslim and Hindu communities slaughtered each other in Hyderabad in 1990; extremist Jews and Muslims kill both one another and members of their own religious identity for perceived failures in keeping the faith. People kill abortion doctors and clinics in the name of Christianity. None of this violence exploits a state-based identity—rather, it is violence shaped by those who are exploiting non-state identities.

Second, religious identity generally brings greater emotional intensity and a deeper motivation than any other kind of identity can hope to arouse. Outside the western world where a tradition of separation of church and state is ostensibly the norm, religious identity is a comprehensive construct. Even in the western world, however, church and state is co-joined in the minds of various groups, making religious identity a paramount statement.

A perceived threat to the community aspect of religious identity gives birth to greater identity commitment, communalism, intolerance of the threatening entity, and a greater acceptance of social violence. Indeed, when the religious identity is perceived as threatened, individuals have the tendency to forego all other identities and develop a greater sense of connection with their co-religionists.[45] Religious identity in the Islamic world is so important, for example, that no revolutionary has ever been able or willing to renounce that Muslim religious heritage.

Again, Central Asia provides an excellent canvas for painting a picture of religious identity cleavages and their relationship to VNSA formation. The Muslim community, or *umma*, of Central Asia emerged after seventy-four years of totalitarian administration to find itself part of nationalist struggles for independence. With the Islamic awakening came regional and Western anxieties over the possibility of a fundamentalist revolution based on an Iranian model. The *umma* also became a target and an object of concern for varied foreign powers seeking to establish influence. Although the revolution did not materialize, external efforts to shape the *umma* persist. Despite renewed international interest in Central Asia, current examinations have failed to sufficiently delineate the cleavages of the Muslim community.

Islam has been integral in defining the culture, political behavior, and economic interaction of Central Asians since the Arab invasion in the seventh century. Hence, its resurgence is neither surprising nor unintelligible. The current revival has its roots in *glasnost, perestroika,* and the collapse of the Soviet empire and takes place in a community of over 50 million Muslims. Sunni Muslims of the Hanafi school, or *madrassah,* are an overwhelming majority (70 percent), although approximately 1.5 million Sunnis follow the Shafi'i *madrassah.* Other religious groupings include Sufis, Twelvers (Ja'farite), Shi'ites, Ismailis and Bahais. Despite diversity, the *umma* has remained relatively homogenous. Although Sunni and Shi'a Muslims are historically ambivalent, this traditional enmity was dampened in the region due to shared resistance to Russian and before it, Soviet rule. Indeed, both Sunni and Shi'a delegations to the 1905 Third Congress of Muslims in Russia declared Ja'farite Shi'ism as a fifth legal school, equivalent to the Hanafi, Maliki, Hanbali, and Shafi'i *madrassahs.*[46] *Madrassahs* enable a network of persons, who share not only a common religious identity but also a common language, to form. The Qu'ran is memorized in Arabic, and most religious instruction takes place in that language. So, the faithful of any city (even if it is full of, say, ethnic Turkmen who speak only Turkish) will also have some ability to speak Arabic. For example, while traveling in the foothills town of Sheki in Azerbaijan, the authors were able to speak little Azeri, but when they stumbled upon a mosque and *madrassah* in the center of the city, they were suddenly able to converse in Arabic.

Parallel Islam

Although cleavages in Islam are often examined as a function of the dominant sect, branch, or school, the *umma*'s fissures in Central Asia can be better understood on four levels. The first is at the grassroots level, which can be examined in degrees of "religiosity"; a term corresponding to the observance of Islamic traditions.[47] Covertly organized communities and Sufi brotherhoods also functioned at this sub-national level. The Islamic establishments of the ex-Soviet regime and current authoritarian regimes operate on another level. Political-religious movements can be considered on a fourth level and are the focus of more detailed analysis in our chapter on VNSA.

Despite bans on unofficial religious activity, Islam received widespread allegiance at the grassroots level during the Soviet period. This so-called "Parallel" Islam remains active today. Expressed in terms of religiosity, this unorganized activity can be readily observed as a function of life-cycle rituals. Various studies have revealed the extensive observance of religious rites to include circumcision, religious burials, marriage, and the payment of the bride price, or *kalym*. Other commonly practiced rituals include observing *Ramadan* (the month of fasting), *Bairam* (the feast of sacrifice), and *mawlud* (communal prayers celebrating the date of Mohammad's birth).[48] Moreover, many take to wearing religious symbols, painting Quranic verses on their automobiles, and giving their children distinctly Islamic names. One of the most extensive and overt practices is the pilgrimage to various holy places, of which there are many. Bukhara and Samarkand in particular were centers for Islamic learning over a several-century period.

Parallel Islam revolves around loosely organized communities, which follow an unofficial mullah or highly structured Sufi brotherhoods called *tariqas* (the path leading to God). Sufi brotherhoods date back to the eleventh century and exert substantial influence over public opinion. Two *tariqas* are the most prevalent; the Naqshbandi, originating in Bukhara, and the Qadiri, originally founded in Baghdad. They advocated both the spiritual advancement of individual Muslims and the establishment of Allah's rule on earth through the *umma*. One might consider, however, that the mystical and personal nature of Sufism is less conducive to political activity than other sects such as Shi'ism.

Only Sunni and Shi'a Islam were officially recognized by the Soviet Union and only to the extent that they submitted to state control. This trend has continued under current regimes. The state appoints the overall spiritual head, the Mufti of Tashkent for example, as well as imams and mullah at prominent mosques and *madrassahs*. Official Islam is tasked with regulating religious activity, operating official mosques, supervising religious publications, and directing the educational institutions in a manner consistent with governmental policies. To many, these co-opted religious leaders are illegitimate because their loyalty is to the state. A more recent phenomenon has been the emergence of political-religious movements. Although many consider these new "revolutionaries" to be the inheritors of the Basmachi opposition in the 1920s, they represent a unique reaction to contemporary conditions. The politicization of Islam also reflects a symbiosis between nationalism and religion. These movements form the nucleus of Islam's role in the current situation.[49] The dynamic composition of the Central Asian *umma* contributes to its tenacity. Official Islam, which allowed for limited expression, is supplemented by other modes of activity. Parallel Islam provides the basis for popular action in the event the current regime and official Islam prove insufficient in meeting the *umma*'s religious demands.

Political Islam

Islam is directly involved in the unfolding political process in Central Asia. At independence, Islam quickly became inextricably linked with the nationalist movements. Prominent regional scholar, Ahmed Rashid, makes the point that Islam has become a convenient symbol "which allows local nationalists to distance themselves from Slavic culture and aspirations."[50] Unfortunately, it is also intertwined with inter-ethnic conflict. Many of the communist leaders in power prior to the breakup of the Soviet Union, with the lone exception of Kyrgyzstan, retain prominent government positions. According to some experts, Islam may be the only force strong enough to overcome the continued monopolization of power by these ex-Soviets.

External powers also seek to influence the relationship between the *umma* and the state. Turkey, capitalizing on shared linguistic traits with all Central Asians except Tajiks, offers a secular model with a market economy. Its impressive efforts since independence, to include business investments, school construction and other financial involvement, are directed at the current leaders, the new middle class and the indigenous intelligentsia. Iran's influence is primarily directed at Azerbaijan, Turkmenistan, and Tajikistan. Iranian influence is more prominent in Tajikistan since both speak a version of Persian, or Farsi, and because there are approximately 100,000 Ismailis living in the Badakhshan region.[51] Like Iran, Saudi Arabian influence is directed at grass-roots activity and a growing Wahhabi movement (examined in chapter 4). The Wahhabi, or Salafist, movement is currently the most potent in the region, and the source of a highly conservative theology embraced by religious VNSA. There were also strong linkages between this movement, centered in the Ferghana Valley, and the Taliban in Afghanistan.

The political-religious movements can be classified according to their objectives. The first, often termed "fundamentalist," seeks the establishment of an Islamic republic based on Islamic law, or *shari'a*. Generally speaking, the previously non-registered mullahs and the Islamic Renaissance Party (IRP) lead these movements. The second, coined "secularists," advocate the establishment of a secular state, but with Islam playing some major but non-political role. The remnants of official Islam tend to prefer this option, as do numerous unregistered clerics and some moderate ex-communist leaders. A third political grouping seeks to prevent any official role for Islam in government and in society. Its advocates are primarily the reactionary ex-communists and remaining European and Russian settlers. There has also been widespread speculation over pan-Islam and pan-Turkic ideologies. Given the widespread ethnic diversity and conflict, accentuated by state-specific nationalism, any pan-movement is destined for failure. This typology suggests that the political process can be seen as a struggle for power among the fundamentalists, secularists, and the current regime.

Fractured Identities

If one could draw a multi-dimensional map that juxtaposed political, ethnic, national, religious, sub-national, and civilization demarcations—as well as the contentious political borders—simultaneously, the resulting jumble would illustrate how fractured this part of the world truly is. Indeed, thorough examinations of all the competing identity cleavages in Central Asia makes the political borders seem insignificant. While some effort is underway to formally demarcate them, the borders in Central Asia are best described by Alexi Maleshenko as "[they are] virtual in the sense that they are less a matter of physical demarcation and more a function of what people in the region think them to be."[52] The multiple "other" borders rarely coincide with administrative borders; governments typically will focus much of their energy defending such administrative borders, while non-state actors often see such borders as mere inconveniences.

For example, the eastern parts of Kyrgyzstan and Kazakhstan, and the Xinjiang province of China (political entities) are populated by the Uighars (a Turkic nationality), which straddles the fault line between the Sinic and Muslim civilizations, and is itself a subset of the meta-state Muslim/Turkic identity. Intermingled in this largely Uighar-populated area are Russians, Tajiks, Uzbeks, Ukrainians, Germans, Tartars, and Belorussians, in addition to the Kyrgyz and Kazakhs. For China, Kyrgyzstan, and Kazakhstan to be able to convince all those different identities at all levels to stay faithful subjects of the state is quite the difficult task. This is but one of the many dozen identity Rubik's Cubes in the region.

Identity Mobilization

In order to understand how and why individuals eventually become VNSA members, we need to better grasp both how individual identity is formed and how individual identities interact with groups and cultures to shape a sense of collective identity. While this section makes no claim to be an exhaustive examination, it sets the stage for better understanding the organizational functions VNSA develops to better recruit from vulnerable populations and to reinforce role behaviors. Applying the following ideas generally to VNSA is straightforward. Groups of individuals feeling they share a common fate, a common identity, a common threat, common needs, or common alternative identity (especially a religious one) are abundant. When such groups are present in violent environments reinforced by failures of governance they are especially prone to even greater identity mobilization, with the individual increasingly identifying with the competing identity group rather than with the political state.

Constructing Identity

From childhood through adulthood, individuals learn and grow; the beliefs, values, and attitudes acquired and elaborated during such learning are critical for self-identity. We become the selves we are as learning anneals into identity over time and as this complex of beliefs, values, and attitudes becomes (more or less) stable. David Sears and Sheri Levy provide an excellent summary of the socio-political development of identity in their essay "Childhood and Adult Political Development."[53] They break this research down into several areas, including moral and cognitive development, development of racial and ethnic identity, and development of prejudice.

Moral and cognitive development is critical for self-identity. Who I am is determined in part by what I am willing to do: Am I willing to kill innocent people to achieve a political objective? Two major paradigms that discuss moral development are stage models and social-cognitive domain models. Stage models are based on the pioneering work of Jean Piaget, but reached their apex in Lawrence Kohlberg's formulation of a six-stage scheme of moral development. Stage models characterize children's moral learning as proceeding through basically invariant stages, with each succeeding stage being superior to its predecessor. In Kohlberg's model, the highest stage consists in principled moral reasoning unaffected by mere self interest (which characterizes stages one and two) or standard convention (stages three and four). Whether or not one is willing to intentionally kill an innocent person to achieve a group's objectives will be determined in large part by where one falls in these stages (when the principles implicit in each stage are applied to the facts at hand . . . for instance, if I am a stage-three group-oriented reasoner, whether or not I am willing to use terrorist tactics will depend on whether or not the group with which I identify has sanctioned their use). More recent work has focused on the domain-specificity of moral reasoning and hence has tended to reflect the findings of the second paradigm: moral reasoning is distinct from, "but coordinated with, social-conventional reasoning and personal reasoning."[54] One highly influential approach maintains that children develop three subsystems that influence judgment and decision making. One is keyed to *social conventions* such as tradition and custom; another is cued by *moral* issues (fairness, equality, rights, etc.); the third is influenced by *psychological factors* (autonomy, personal goals, relationship to authority, and the like).[55] Moral development issues constitute an important part of the identity picture.

In a globalizing world, issues of race and ethnicity are an important component of identity. Whether or not I am successfully mobilized by VNSA that has goals of racial or ethnic hegemony will depend on whether or not I consider myself to be a part of the group whose interests will be served by the VNSA. Jean Phinney and William Cross have developed similar models that posit three stages of ethnic identity (although as discussed in the last section, there are other identities besides ethnic ones). These stages are presented here to complement those introduced in chapter 5 as part of our discussion of ethno-political groups.[56] In the first stage, "unexamined ethnic identity" or "pre-encounter," there is little to no self-awareness about ethnicity; children have not explored their own conceptions of self vis-à-vis skin color or lineage. In the second stage, children seek out information about the group they are a member of; this is called "encounter and immersion" or "ethnic identity search." This stage is a turning point in development and can precipitate an identity crisis. In stage three, "internalization" or "achieved ethnic identity," adolescents have in place positive self-concepts as group members; on some stories, this can lead to prejudice with regards to other groups, although contemporary research indicates that a secure ethnic or racial identity can actually prevent prejudice.[57]

Social context is critically important for racial and ethnic acculturation. This is no surprise, as there is an entire theory (called "social learning theory") dedicated to the role that social and group interaction plays in the development of attitudes and skills.[58] Social learning did not require that there be rewards and punishments for learned behavior to occur (as in the neo-behaviorist paradigm); rather, all that was required were the "minimal components of attention to a behavioral sequence, retention of its form, and the ability to reproduce the behavioral sequence."[59] The core components of personal *cum* group identity are learned, on this picture, and such behavior as prejudice or discrimination (or even a willingness to resort to violence to solve problems) is transmitted through various social groups because children hear and see such attitudes in action in their peers, parents, and authority figures. It is easy to see how the development of prejudice, which may be a necessary (though not sufficient) condition for organized violence to be committed against out-groups, is contingent upon cultural and social factors.

If we are to understand VNSA, we must understand how individual identity/group identity interactions occur, and how these interactions can reinforce group-oriented functional roles.

According to Leonie Huddy, "group identification involves a subjective sense of membership and can be divided into two kinds of attachments— social identity and a sense of realistic interdependence or common fate."[60] Social identity requires that a person realize that she shares a common characteristic with a group and hence can come to identify with that group; in addition, she needs to attach emotional significance to that act of identification.

Of note, as Shelley Taylor suggests, "not all forms of group attachment are necessarily predicated on identity. A sense of subjective interdependence or shared common fate with other group members simply depends on the recognition that group members share similar interests or face a similar threat"[61] Taylor points out that the four major theoretical approaches regarding the construction of group identity (which consist of the cognitive approach, realistic interest approaches, social identity theory, and social constructivist theory) all make somewhat different predictions regarding sources of commonality and critical issues around which members may mobilize. A thumbnail sketch of these approaches will help us understand her conclusion. The *cognitive approach* to formation of group identity emphasizes the importance of self-perception in the development of cohesive groups: individuals become group members because they identify with the group and wish to emulate typical group members. *Realistic interest approaches* stress the common interests that groups share and advance; common fate is thus especially critical . . . if all of Islam is threatened, and we are Muslims, then it is more likely that we will become cohesive so as to achieve the common objective of protecting the shared interests of our group.[62] *Social identity theorists* emphasize the importance of symbolic interactions between groups and potential members; group members endorse group memberships because of a need to achieve a positive sense of social identity that will differentiate their own group from others.[63] *Social constructivism* takes social identity one step further: concepts derive their meaning from social practices; this theory stresses how social identities form even among strangers so long as enough shared interactions can occur to generate the construction of the group as a group.

Taylor rightly notes that

> the cognitive approach predicts cohesion among the members of any salient group; realistic interest theory confines cohesion to groups whose members share a common fate; social identity theory points to unity among widely stigmatized groups, such as low-status ethnic or racial groups, religious sects (etc.), whose members cannot easily pass as belonging to a higher status group; and a social constructivist perspective predicts cohesion among members who share a common understanding of group membership.[64]

Resolving the tensions among these various approaches to group identification is beyond the scope of our book; suffice it to say that our VNSA species
break-out and discussion of identity cleavages includes organizational forms
that leverage all four conversions of group identity to varying degrees, some
more so than others. A pragmatic approach would dictate that until the "psychological dust" settles, we pick from among the successful research programs
so as to produce a workable understanding of a maximal number of potentially violent groups.

Before pressing on to briefly discuss "need frustration" and how it may be
related to group mobilization, it is worth noting that external non-group
threats can both increase in-group unity and inflame out-group hostility.[65] In
other words, one way to reinforce group identity and boost the chances that
the in-group will be more likely to adopt a hostile attitude toward other groups,
is by *threatening* the group.[66]

The relationship among group identity, aggressive action, and basic human
needs is difficult to quantify. However, it probably plays a role in helping us understand why the variables discussed earlier (resource scarcity, demographic
pressures, socio-economic deprivation, etc.) are such good forecasters of the
potential for violent non-state group action. In some way or another, these
variables all influence a population's ability to satisfy basic psychological needs
(such as those discussed by Abraham Maslow); in like vein, Ervin Staub suggests that some basic needs include security, control, positive identity, positive
connection, comprehension of reality, independence, self-transcendence, and
long-term satisfaction.[67] He explains that social upheavals (of the kind generated, for example, by resource scarcity or severe demographic pressure)
threaten and frustrate individual's abilities to fulfill these basic needs. Need satisfaction, in turn, generates group identification, group elevation, scapegoat-
ing, and the embracing of totalizing ideologies. These reactions are then the
starting point for group versus group persecution and violence.[68]

These thoughts explain some recent developments in the literature on terrorism (a form of collective violence often selected by violent non-state actors) which link the rise in terrorist organizations to a frustration with the
modern worldview and with the existential malaise generated by it.[69] Eric
Hoffer's classic study of those inclined to terrorism or to other movements
(particularly fundamentalist terrorism) is instructive: all mass movements
"draw their early adherents from the same types of humanity," frustrated people, "who, for one reason or another, feel that their lives are spoiled or
wasted."[70] The frustration of some basic psychological needs may very well explain why resource scarcity and demographic pressures can cause people, especially those with pre-existing fault lines upon which identity entrepreneurs
can focus so as to spur mobilization, to organize groups that may adopt in-
discriminant violence as a means to their various ends.

Identity entrepreneurs

Another concept to be introduced into this already volatile mixture—conditions of violence combined with competing alternative identities—is that of the identity entrepreneur.[71] An identity entrepreneur is an individual or group of individuals who find it desirable, profitable, or otherwise utilitarian to create or reinforce group identities. They will specifically seek to exploit such volatile situations and will do so by reinforcing perceived identity cleavages or create new ones. The identity entrepreneur is typically a charismatic voice that appeals more to the emotional (rather than rational) side of the individual. This can be done by highlighting, or in many instances embellishing or even creating, injustices to the identity group, myth-creation about the significance of the group in other times or places, and bringing the borders between the "us" (those in the identity group) and "them" (those outside the identity group, most typically the "enemy") into sharper focus. Creating such consciousness—real or false—and then exploiting that to move a group toward collective action is the goal of the identity entrepreneur.

Unlike Slobodan Milosevic of Serbia, not all identity entrepreneurs are associated with a state; many are associated with a non-state organization. Abdullah Ocalan, the captured chief of the Kurdish Worker's Party, a Kurdish identity group violently fighting the Turkish state, is an excellent example. Other variations of the identity entrepreneur exist: Vladimir Zhirinovksy is a Russian identity entrepreneur who attempted to use the Russian state to assume power, but failed; Osama bin Laden is an identity entrepreneur for radical Islam, with the enemy being the West.

This "creation" aspect of identity mobilization stands in stark contrast to the primordialist approach to identity conflict. While fighting often does fall along identity fissures, such competitive demarcations are coincidental to other, deeper reasons for conflict as well as falling victim to identity entrepreneurs' exploitation of ethnic differences for their own selfish reasons. In other words, the transformation of identity groups to VNSA requires much more than the simple fact that identity groups exist; mythical historiographies, exaggerated claims or embellished injustices appealing to emotion are all tasks the identity entrepreneur must successfully complete before an identity group will move to action. The identity entrepreneur simply exploits the fact that easily observed differences to generate violence that is actually a result of these other factors.

Reinforcing Actions

Among the aspects of our open systems framework, reinforcing actions are probably the most difficult to understand without direct access to VNSA leaders. Essentially, we are proposing that the VNSA behave in a manner that sustains, and even expands, the cycle of collective violence. Warlords recognize that they can only exist in the context of a weak state. Drug lords understand they can only increase their profits if the government fails to intervene or is a corrupt element in the system. Leaders of militant religious movements recognize the value of a corrupt, incapacitated state to the furtherance of their efforts to bring down a regime. Identity entrepreneurs of armed ethno-political groups are aware that they will be less successful in mobilizing based on socio-economic disparities if the state can successfully reconcile differences. Each group has a vested interest in expanding their recruiting pool and undermining state efforts to govern effectively. Because VNSA are typically not focused on the public good or the betterment of all society, they do not necessarily work to pull up the roots of violence. Since their foot soldiers come from the ranks of the impoverished and dispossessed, they do not have a stake in seeing this pool immediately shrink.

That nation-states also take actions to reinforce the growth of VNSA is obvious enough. A failure to redress the root causes of recruitment, for example, or even taking actions that exacerbate those roots, can construct a fertile environment that will encourage rather than hamper violent non-state actor ontogeny.

Niche Construction

Returning to our inter-disciplinary assertion that VNSA resemble organisms, there is increasing recognition that all organisms modify their environments, and that such environments in turn share feedback relationships with the organisms that modify them. The more radical insight, however, has been to note that organisms can affect more than just their local ecology; their attempts to change their environment influence the very forces of natural selection that shape their future evolution as a species. This process is called *niche construction*.[72] For instance, beavers engineer dams, and the existence of those dams increases both the likelihood that individual beavers will thrive and that future beavers will share the traits necessary to thrive in a dam-laden environment (broad, flat tails; waterproof fur; etc.). Birds construct nests. The existence of nests then drives the evolutionary pathway that birds of the next generation must follow to be fecund. These creatures change their environments, and in both the short and long run these changes in environments lead to novel adaptations in the creatures.

Ecological niches constructed by living organisms force us to think of evolutionary processes not in linear terms but rather in cyclical terms; niche construction should be recognized as a significant cause of evolution, "on a par with natural selection. . . . By accepting that organisms shape environments as surely as environments shape organisms, evolution is transformed from a linear to a cyclic process."[73] It is cyclical because organisms shape environments that in turn shape organisms that shape their environment, and so on. A proper understanding of evolutionary change requires us to consider, therefore, not only the genetic inheritance of an organism but also its environmental inheritance. As noted by K. N. Laland and F. J. Odling-Smee,

> the net result is a dual inheritance system, involving the inheritance both of genetically encoded information and of environmental resources. Active organisms inherit an 'information package' from their 'genetic ancestors' in the form of whatever information is encoded by their naturally selected genes. However, they also inherit a 'resource package,' namely the resources of living space, energy, and materials, which are provided by their local habitats.[74]

The critical upshot for understanding VNSA is that fit or lack of fit only relative to particular environments. If VNSA are at all like organisms, then reinforcing actions become critically important for driving VNSA development.

States can take actions that create niches that promote survival and development opportunities for VNSA; they can also fail to address the niche construction that a developing VNSA takes to ensure its survival. For example, support (at least passive, and ideally active) of the population in which a terrorist organization lives is, except in unusual cases, a practical necessity for the organization's survival. In the case of the Basque separatist movement, the ETA (Euskadi ta Askatasuna, or "the Basque Fatherland and Liberty" group) operates primarily in Spain for the purpose of establishing an independent Basque nation in the northern portion of that country. ETA was established in 1959 as a nationalist movement to resist the political oppression of the Basque people that came into fashion after the Spanish Civil War ended in 1939. One tactic the Spanish government has used to address ETA is to disperse captured militia members to separate prison facilities when they are captured. Understandably, the Spanish government did not want ETA members to be able to collaborate secretly when they were imprisoned; indeed, the policy was enacted beginning in 1998 by Minister of the Interior Enrique Mugica, an ethnic Basque and a member of the Socialist Party.[75] While the policy may have prevented some collaboration, it had the adverse effect of breeding sympathy for convicted terrorists among the general population, as families had to travel many miles to visit imprisoned friends and relatives. "The families, therefore, develop a sense of resentment against the central authorities. That resentment had bred sympathy for the basic demands of the terrorist group."[76] This counterterrorist policy constitutes a reinforcing action on the part of Spain, constructing a niche in the environment in which ETA can flourish.

Another example of a reinforcing action that fuels niche construction deals with how the corrupt police of Ayacucho dealt with Sendero Luminoso activity in their district. Rather than confront the Marxist insurgency, Ayacucho police fed Alberto Guzman's recruitment activity by spending most of their time in discotheques and brothels. The poverty of Ayacucho forced the young women in the area to consort with the police in order to meet their basic economic needs; this enraged citizens of what was a relatively conservative and law-abiding city. As Gustavo Gorriti notes, "the sight of police officers strutting their plumage in the company of more or less shamefaced young girls, watched with disapproval by older Ayacuchans and fury by Ayacucho's young men, were common."[77] This fueled sympathy for Sendero Luminoso's cause, and while it is difficult to say with certainty whether it fueled recruitment into the organization, it is certainly reasonable to assume that it did.

For an example of a reinforcing action where the state fails to address active VNSA niche construction, consider India's experience with terrorist organizations in the contested regions of Jammu and Kashmir, where Pakistan has laid claim to parcels of land controlled by India. In that case, Indian officials initially treated Pakistani-sponsored terrorism as a mere law and order problem: There were a few gun smugglers and black market con artists, but nothing that required redressing root causes or that couldn't be dealt with by local police forces. The initial half-hearted Indian response allowed terrorist organizations like Al Faran to niche construct by consolidating sympathy in the local Muslim population, and to solidify supply line connections to Pakistani backers. India has also dealt with Sikh separatists in the Punjab region using a "law and order" model rather than a counterterrorism model, allowing groups like Akali Dal to consolidate support and logistics.[78]

On the offensive side, states can actively destroy the niches that VNSA attempt to create for themselves; or VNSA can, owing to their short-sightedness, take actions that destroy the very niches they have created. The "flip side" of niche construction is *niche destruction*; in the long run, organisms can "niche destruct" just as they can "niche construct," or they can have the niches they have been building destroyed by outside forces such as those of the state. An example of a self-inflicted niche-destruction relationship, where a VNSA acted short-sightedly in such a way that their environment eventually hampered their growth, is Sendero Luminoso's attack upon Allpachaka, an experimental peasant training farm administered by the University of Huamanga, but under the control of Sendero. When the Sendero had to retreat in the face of a government offensive, they destroyed much of the farm, killing a great deal of livestock, and otherwise laying waste to what had been a model experiment on the university's part. Soon after Sendero departed, professors and university students traveled to Allpachaka in two buses to begin reconstruction, but they were stopped by Senderistos who claimed responsibility for the destruction and called the Allpachaka program "a center of imperialist penetration and re-formist illusions," prohibiting any attempt to rebuild.[79] This fed public percep-tion that the Sendero had become a Pol Pot–style insurgency, as much of a menace to the people as to the state.[80]

For an example of a state action that constituted niche destruction, we need look no further than Turkey's attempts to "drain the swamp" in the remote vil-lages and hamlets of southeast Turkey; towns were evacuated and residents re-located to safer zones, depriving the Kurdistan Workers' Party (PKK—*Pariya Karkaren Kurdistan*) of safe havens that in some cases they had taken great pains to cultivate. The Turkish government conducted targeted evacuations of about 300,000 people (the entire population of the emergency region was ap-proximately 6 million people).[81]

The ability of a state to engage in niche destruction of the niches that en-courage undesirable VNSA, or in niche construction that encourages the growth of non-violent alternatives, is very much contingent upon the culture of the state: does the state have the appropriate intelligence capacities to de-tect niche construction, and the wherewithal to coordinate effective policy responses? Conversely, the ability of a VNSA to construct its own niches, and rebuild niches that the state is seeking to destroy, is culturally contingent. As Laland and Odling-Smee note, "culture greatly enhances the human capac-ity for niche construction."[82] Of note, an organization's *internal* ecology will be greatly influenced by its ability to control and influence its culture (niche construction takes place internally as well as externally). One of the primary functions of the maintenance sub-system is the socialization of members to an organizational culture via the propagation of rewards and punishments to members for satisfying the demands of role-required behaviors. One note of caution: certain mutations in microorganisms that are neutral under nor-mal growing conditions can become advantageous under stress.[83] Similarly, when confronting VNSA, states should ensure that they are not playing to VNSA capacities that are designed to function best under conditions of ad-versity.

VNSA may not establish specific objectives with regard to sustaining the sys-tem; however, the nature of their activities does deepen the roots of violence, whether they intend it or not. VNSA almost always raise funds through illegal means. Both derail productive engagement in civil society and engender greater violence. Collective violence has its own reinforcing effects. It now only creates a climate of fear, but it often forces the state, particularly authoritarian regimes, to divert limited resources to law enforcement and counter-insurgency/terrorism. In our analysis of VNSA types in chapter 5, we present evidence of these behaviors, which are at odds with the legitimate, non-violent efforts of NGOs to improve human development in Central Asia and in other areas of the world.

A particularly telling comparative analysis of two different VNSA—the IRA and the Islamic insurgency in the Philippines—and the policy responses to them serve as a fitting closing that illustrates this chapter's concepts.[84] Without delving into the fascinating history behind both of these situations, many parallels between the two situations exist. First, both the government of the United Kingdom and the Philippines are entangled in the crosscurrent of multiple identities. In Northern Ireland, the conflict pitted Catholics against Protestants, those of Irish descent against those of English descent, the poor against the rich. In the Philippines, the identity cleavages were similar: Catholic versus Muslim, the Moro people against other Filipinos, and an underdeveloped, poor region against the (only relatively) more developed northern Philippines. Both states responded to the VNSA presence through a variety of programs—military action, police work, peace accords, and socioeconomic development efforts. London pursued the Belfast Agreement, the Good Friday Accords, and the Supplementary Framework, all of which included substantial socio-economic development plans for Northern Ireland. Mindanao pursued similar programs that also included various socio-economic development programs, sponsored largely through the Davao Consensus. This framework created the Autonomous Region of Muslim Mindanao, the Special Zone for Peace and Development, and the Southern Philippine Council for Peace and Development. Funds to pursue these goals came from the UN, the United States, and the Philippine government. These socio-economic development efforts in both countries were designed to alleviate poverty and create jobs as part of a multi-pronged effort at ending the violence in the troubled regions.

Yet, the outcomes were different. In the United Kingdom, the socio-economic development programs were specifically designed to go primarily to small communities, with considerable local input as to how the funds were to be dispersed and used. Further, the funding process was completely transparent. As a result, most of those funds went to education, housing, and encouraging foreign direct investment, with the majority of the Irish seeing the funding process and results as legitimate efforts to improve their situation. Consequently, the needs and effectiveness evaluations reported commissioned in 2002 by the Northern Ireland First Prime Minister showed that there is now virtually no difference between Catholics and Protestants in terms of education, health, and housing. Given the disparities that existed in the 1960s (for example, Irish Catholic communities faced 20 percent unemployment, whereas only 8 percent of Protestants were unemployed[85]), this is substantial progress. Interpreted differently, the efforts in the United Kingdom successfully eased the roots of violence in Northern Ireland while simultaneously erasing the reinforcing alternative economic and political identity cleavages existing there—all within a single generation. The vestigial remnants of the warring parties—the Real IRA and the Loyalist Volunteer Force—are small, and made up of hard-core members that pursue organizational self-preservation (which unfortunately includes some violence) rather than any real political change.

The result in the Philippines is not nearly as successful. Much of the funds for development in the region did not go to local communities nor was local input used in how the funds were dispersed. For example, much of the funds went to high-profile projects, such as hotels, airports, and "circumferential" roads (roads built around an island, such as the 87-mile road around Sulu). These projects were geared primarily to encourage tourism, not to develop a more broad-based local economy. Ironically, most of these projects could only be pursued in areas that had some minimal level of infrastructure already—which was primarily the Christian portions of the Southern Philippines rather than the completely underdeveloped Muslim portions. Thus, both the process and results of these development efforts only exacerbated the underlying causes of the conflict. The Muslim populations felt that the development funds given to the Philippine government were co-opted by corrupt officials and steered towards their cronies, further entrenching the notion that Mindanao was illegitimate and an enemy. Additionally, the fact that relatively richer Christian portions of the region—rather than the Muslim communities—benefited from the development funds only worsened the underlying roots of the conflict and reinforced the economic identity cleavage between the Muslims and the Catholics. The continued violence in the region testifies to the importance of understanding roots of violence and identity cleavages when crafting government policy.

Closing

The conditions of violence outlined in chapter two represent potential. This chapter examines how and why elements of such an exploitable population undergo the conversion from a suffering but passive population to an active VNSA. These critical mechanisms are the "point of entry" for the VNSA; presence of these mechanisms is a good indicator that a VNSA may soon emerge and is likely to prosper.

Failures in governance—be they represented by an unwillingness to act, an incapacity to act, or through the use of excessive coercion when acting—are key to the conversion process. Each of these undermines the legitimacy of the government. Once a properly primed population no longer sees the government as a rightful or effective wielder of political power, what few barriers that existed between that population and the persuasive message of an identity entrepreneur are swept away. Large or widespread demonstrations, increasingly negative media reporting, and a variety of other visible indications are relatively clear messages that important elements of a country question or reject their government's legitimacy. Should that government cling to power or crack down on the populace, underground and potentially violence groups are likely to form.

The likelihood of these shadowy groups to form—representing the gestation of VNSA—is compounded when pre-existing identity cleavages are present in a given population. An ethnically diverse population is perhaps one of the most easily categorized. Indeed, the ethnically diverse Balkan region of Europe is the basis for the neologism "Balkanization," representing the fracturing of a society or organization. However, many other phenomena besides ethnicity can categorize a population—rich versus poor, religious beliefs, political power and freedoms, etc. An especially dangerous combination is when multiple categorizations reinforce each other. A given ethnicity in a country that is also poor, politically disenfranchised, and has a unique religion is far more likely to be the basis or source for a VNSA than a pre-existing identity cleavage that is not reinforced by other identities.

Of special interest are the identity entrepreneurs who understand these dynamics. An effective identity entrepreneur can create identity where none exists, can magnify identity in such a manner as to create nostalgia for a greatness or stature that may have never existed, or can manipulate or distort identity to the point of convincing his audience that their identity is synonymous with victimhood, injustice, and discrimination. Just as reinforcing identity cleavages increases the potential of VNSA formation, presence of an agitating force like an identity entrepreneur increases the likelihood of VNSA formation.

Once a VNSA gestates, it benefits from modifying its environment. This modification includes possible exacerbating of the conditions which provide it, the VNSA, legitimacy in the eyes of the populace, exploring new avenues of generating legitimacy, beginning to build stores of negative entropy, or otherwise pursuing niche construction to increase the probability it will survive.

Once the ontogeny of a VNSA reaches the point of being able to modify its environment in order to increase its ability to survive, it is presenting the first signs of growth, sub-system development, and functional differentiation. The VNSA life cycle has begun.

Notes

1. Thomas S. Szayna, ed., *Identifying Potential Ethnic Conflict: Application of a Process Model* (Santa Monica, CA: RAND Corporation, 2000), 33.

2. *History of Afghanistan: The Loya Jirga.* Available at www.afghanland.com/history/loyajirga .html as of January 10, 2004.

3. Simply observing this can provide the analyst or policy maker with their first option—to create such safety valves, thereby shaping the environment in such a way that provides the individual with more choices, thus denying VNSA agitation and recruiting opportunities. These and other options will be further discussed in chapter 7.

4. Rohan Gunaratna, *Inside Al Qaeda: Global Network of Terror* (New York: Columbia University Press, 2002), 28–29.

5. Michael Donovan, "Islam and Instability in Saudi Arabia," *CDI Terrorism Project* 13 (November, 2001). Available at www.cdi.org/terrorism/saudi-pr.cfm as of January 10, 2004.

6. Refer to Abd Al-Fattah M El-Awaisi, "Education and the Society of the Egyptian Muslim Brothers: 1928–49," *Journal of Beliefs and Values* 21 (2000): 213–25.

7. Council on Foreign Relations, *Encyclopedia of Terrorism*. Available at www.cfr.org/reg_issues.php?id=131 as of January 10, 2004. See also the MNLF homepage, available at mnlf.net/index.htm. Accessed on January 10, 2004.

8. Government of Singapore, "Contact," Ministry of Education Newsletter (volume 11, August 1999). Available at: www1.moe.edu.sg/contact/vol11/pers.htm as of January 10, 2004.

9. Annelise Anderson, "Organized Crime, Mafia and Governments." In Gianluca Fiorentini and Sam Peltzman, ed., *The Economics of Organized Crime* (Cambridge, UK: Cambridge University Press, 1995), 34–35.

10. See Raimondo Catanzaro, *Men of Respect: A Social History of the Sicilian Mafia* (New York: The Free Press, July 1992). See also Diego Gambetta's, *The Sicilian Mafia: The Business of Private Protection* (Boston, MA: Harvard University Press, 1996).

11. "A State Within the State," *The Economist*, 24 April 1993, 21–22.

12. Daniel Kaufmann, Aart Kraay, Massimo Mastruzzi, "Governance Matters III: Governance Indicators for 1996–2002" (Washington, DC: World Bank, June 20, 2003), 32. The trend was reconfirmed by Kaufmann in "Corruption, Governance and Security: Challenges for the Rich Countries and the World," *Global Competitiveness Report 2004/2005* (Washington, DC: World Bank, September 2004), 84; "Revisiting the long-term trend evidence . . . we find that, overall, this stagnating trend does not appear to have been reversed over the past year." In addition to these four dimensions of governance, states were also evaluated in the areas of "voice and accountability" and "regularity quality."

13. Richard H. Shultz, Douglas Farah, and Itamara V. Lochard, *Armed Groups: A Tier-One Security Priority*, Occasional Paper 57 (USAF Academy, CO: Institute for National Security Studies, September 2004), 55.

14. Shultz, 55.

15. Shultz, 8.

16. Shultz, 58.

17. World Bank, "Anticorruption in Transition: A Contribution to Policy Debate," 2000, xv–xvi. Available at www.worldbank.org/wbi/governance/pdf/contribution.pdf as of January 10, 2004.

18. Ibid., xiii–xiv.

19. Extensive empirical studies testing these correlations are an area that admittedly needs further study. However, some empirical work does exist. See Leslie Janzen and Alpa Patel's excellent study, *The Economic Impact of Non-State Actors on State Failure* (Annapolis, MD: U.S. Naval Academy, 2001). Available at www.ippu.purdue.edu/failed_states/2001/papers/Janzen_Patel.pdf as of January 10, 2004.

20. CNN On Line, "China Corruption Linked to Triads," March 10, 2002. Available at edition.cnn.com/2002/WORLD/asiapcf/east/03/10/china.npclaw/ as of November 13, 2003.

21. Robert Rotberg, "The New Nature of Nation-State Failure," *The Washington Quarterly*, Summer 2002.

22. Donald Snow, *Uncivil Wars: International Security and the New Internal Conflicts* (Boulder, CO: Lynne Rienner Publishers, Inc., 1996), 35.

23. Sudhir Kakar, *The Colors of Violence: Cultural Identities, Religion, and Conflict* (Chicago, IL: University of Chicago Press, 1996), 186–89.

24. Frederick Barth, *Ethnic Groups and Boundaries: The Social Organization of Culture Difference* (Boston, MA: Little, Brown, 1969), 10–11, 14.

25. As quoted by Igor Torbakov, "Tajik-Uzbek Relations: Divergent National Historiographies Threaten To Aggravate Tensions," *Eurasianet.org*, June 12, 2001. Available at www.eurasianet.org/departments/culture/articles/eav061201.shtml as of January 10, 2004.

26. Ibid.

27. Ibid.

28. Jennifer Balfour, "Many Families Fear for Sons' Safety in Uzbek Military," June 15, 2001. Available at www.eurasianet.org/departments/insight/articles/eav061501.shtml as of January 10, 2004.

29. William Fierman, "Language and Identity in Kazakhstan: Formulations in Policy Documents 1987–1997," *Communist and Post-Communist Studies* 31:2 (1998): 171–86.

30. Olga Oliker, Thomas Szayna, and Sergej Mahnovski, *Potential Sources of Conflict in the Caspian Region* (Santa Monica, CA: RAND Corporation, March 2001), 65.

31. Liz Fuller, "Trial of 'Separatists' Highlights Plight of Kazakhstan's Russians," *Kazakhstan Daily Digest*, as posted by *Eurasianet.org* at www.eurasianet.org/resource/kazakhstan/hypermail/200005/0013.html as of January 10, 2004.

32. United Nations High Commission for Refugees (UNHCR), "Displacement within the Commonwealth of Independent States," May 1996. Available at www.unhcr.ch/pubs/cis96/cis9603.htm as of January 10, 2004.

33. *The Dorling Kindersley World Reference Atlas* (London, UK: Dorling Kindersley, 1994), 550.

34. Personal interview with our translator, Otajon, June 2001, Bukhara, Uzbekistan.

35. Edward Schatz, "The Politics of Multiple Identities: Lineage and Ethnicity in Kazakhstan," *Europe-Asia Studies* 52:3 (2000): 489–506.

36. Oliker, "Potential Sources of Conflict in Central Asia," 56.

37. Samuel Huntington, *Clash of Civilizations and the Remaking of World Order* (New York: Simon and Schuster, 1996.)

38. Martha Brill Olcott, "Central Asia's Security Issues," *Carnegie Endowment for International Peace* (April 10, 2001) 3. Paper presented for the Spring 2001 meetings of the Schlesinger Working Group on Strategic Surprises, an initiative of the Institute for the Study of Diplomacy of Georgetown University.

39. See, for example, Gerd Mutz and Antje Schmidt, *Economic Identities: About the Value of Underlying Value Systems*, available at www.socialscience.de/VortragPetersburg2.pdf as of January 10, 2004. See also MIT professor Michael Piore's paper, *From Economic Identities and Collective Bargaining to Social Identities and Employment Rights: Notes on Shifting Regimes in Labor Market Regulation and Changing Axes of Political Mobilization*. Forthcoming from MIT Press, Cambridge, MA, in 2004.

40. Erin Finnerty, "Poverty a Crucial Element Leading to Tension and Violence in Central Asia—Experts," June 12, 2001. Available at www.eurasianet.org/departments/recaps/articles/eav061201.shtml as of January 10, 2004.

41. Alec Applebaum, "Post-Soviet Experience Shows There Are No Easy Economic Solutions for Caucusus, Central Asia," *Eurasianet.org*, August 20, 2001. Available at www.eurasianet.org/departments/business/articles/eav082001.shtml as of January 10, 2004.

42. Ibid.

43. Quoted in Applebaum, "Post-Soviet Experience."

44. John W. Bowker, "The Burning Fuse: The Unacceptable Face of Religion," Zygon Center for the Study of Religion and Science 21, no. 4 (1986): 501–18.

45. Kakar, *The Colors*, 191.

46. Alexandre Bennigsen and S. Enders Wimbush, *Muslims of the Soviet Empire* (Bloomington, IN: Indiana University Press, 1986), 14.

47. Alexandre Bennigsen, "Islam in Retrospect," *Central Asian Survey* 8 (1989): 89–91.

48. William Fierman, *Soviet Central Asia: The Failed Transformation* (Boulder, CO: Westview Press, 1991), 193.

49. Troy Thomas provides a thorough examination of the Central Asia *umma* at the time of independence in "The Central Asian *Umma*: Composition and Prospect," May 4, 1992. Available from the author at troysthomas@hotmail.com.

50. Ahmed Rashid, "Clout of the Clergy," *Far Eastern Economic Review*, January 9, 1992, 18.

51. Anthony Hyman, "Suddenly, Everyone's Interested," *The Middle East*, February 1992, 14.

52. Alexi Mashenko and Martha Brill Olcott, eds., *Multidimensional Borders of Asia* (New York: Carnegie Endowment for International Peace, April 2000). Available at pubs.carnegie.ru/english/books/default.asp?n=ethnicity as of January 10, 2004.

53. David Sears, et al., ed., *Oxford Handbook of Political Psychology* (New York: Oxford University Press, 2003), 60–109.

54. Ibid., 64.

55. Developed by Elliot Turiel and colleagues; see Sears for a succinct summary.

56. Completion of this 3-staged process completes the first step in an ethno-political group turning to violence to achieve its goals

57. Ibid., 68.

58. Social learning theory was most comprehensively articulated by Albert Bandura in the 1960s and 1970s. Bandura placed special emphasis on how new behavior is acquired through observational learning via cognitive processes.

59. Shelley Taylor, "The Social Being in Social Psychology," in Daniel T. Gilbert et al., *The Handbook of Social Psychology, Fourth Edition: Volume One* (Boston, MA: McGraw-Hill, 1998), 66.

60. "Group Identity and Political Cohesion," from the *Oxford Handbook of Political Psychology*

61. Ibid., 514.

62. Osama bin Laden has been especially skillful in employing this technique in motivating individuals and groups to support his efforts. For example, in an interview with *Nida 'Ul Islam* in 1996, bin Laden states "What bears no doubt in this fierce Judeo-Christian campaign against the Muslim world, the likes of which has never been seen before, is that the Muslims must prepare all the possible might to repel the enemy on the military, economic, missionary, and all other areas." A transcript of the interview is available at www.osama-bin-laden.tmfweb.nl/interviews.htm as of January 10, 2004.

63. "Group Identity," 519.

64. Ibid., 521. "Etc." inserted by authors and should be read as a ". . . ."

65. Ibid., 541.

66. See also the essays in Russell Spears, et al., ed. *The Social Psychology of Stereotyping and Group Life* (Cambridge, UK: Blackwell Publishers, 1997).

67. Ervin Staub, *The Psychology of Good and Evil: Why Children, Adults, and Groups Help and Harm Others* (New York: Cambridge University Press, 2003), 55–61.

68. Ibid., 54.

69. See, e.g., Michael J. Mazarr's paper "Existentialism, Fundamentalism, Terrorism," available from the author at the Center for Strategic and International Studies (MazarrM@NDU.edu).

70. Eric Hoffer, *The True Believer; Thoughts on the Nature of Mass Movements* (New York: Harper and Row, 1951), 169. Our thanks to Michael Mazarr for pointing out these quotations.

71. Barbara Ballis Lal, "Identity Entrepreneurs: Do We Want Them? Do We Need Them?" Unpublished manuscript. As used by Szayna, *Identifying*, 45.

72. See K. N. Laland, F. J. Smee, and M. W. Feldman, "Evolutionary Consequences of Niche Construction and Their Implications for Ecology," *Proceedings of the National Academy of Sciences* 96 (August 1999): 10242–10247.

73. K. Laland and F. J. Smee, "Life's Little Builders," *New Scientist* 180, no. 2421 (15 November 2003): 43.

74. F. J. Odling-Smee, "Niche Construction, Evolution and Culture," in Tim Ingold ed. *The Companion Encyclopedia of Anthropology*, (New York, NY: Routledge, 1994), 178.

75. See Antonio Remiro Brotons and Carlos Esposito's essay "Spain," in Yonah Alexander ed., *Combating Terrorism: Strategies of Ten Countries*, (Ann Arbor, MI: University of Michigan Press, 2002).

76. Ibid., 173.

77. Gustavo Gorriti, *The Shining Path: A History of the Millenarian War in Peru* (Chapel Hill, NC: The University of North Carolina Press, 1999), 258.

78. Ibid., citing Ved Marwah's "India" essay, 301–14.

79. Gorritti, *The Shining Path*, 225.

80. Ibid., 225. The Pol Pot comparison is Gorritti's.

81. See "Turkey," by Gunduz S. Aktan and Ali M. Koknar, as printed in Alexander, *Combating Terrorism*, 277.

82. Kevin Laland and John Odling-Smee, "Niche Construction, Biological Evolution and Cultural Change," *Behavioral and Brain Sciences* 23:1 (2000): 131–75. This article contains the "niche destruct" locution. For an excellent online resource for more literature on the theory of niche construction, see www.st-andrews.ac.uk/~seal/niche/publications.html. Available as of January 10, 2004.

83. See, e.g., the discussion in Mary Jane West-Eberhard, *Developmental Plasticity and Evolution* (New York: Oxford, 2003), 508.

84. The ensuing summary is largely taken from Kim Cragin and Peter Chalk, *Terrorism and Development: Using Social and Economic Development to Inhibit a Resurgence of Terrorism* (Santa Monica, CA: RAND Corporation, 2002).

85. Paul Mitchell and Rick Wilford, ed., *Politics in Northern Ireland* (Boulder, CO: Westview Press, 1999), 30.

4

Violent Systems

Hidden down a narrow alley in the old quarter, or Parte Vieja of San Se-
bastian in the Basque province of Spain is one of many small bars. It is
crammed with young people wearing t-shirts championing Basque nationalism and chain smoking under a large poster of Che Guevara. The bar is
loosely associated with the recently banned Herri Batasuna (Popular
Unity) political party, which was linked in its 1979 origins with the terrorist organization ETA (Basque Homeland [Euskadi] and Freedom). Among
these youth, several if not many, will spend the early hours before daybreak
spray painting "ETA" and other nationalist slogans across the old city—a
ritual being simultaneously conducted in the province's other major urban
centers of Vitoria and Bilbao. From among these rebellious youth, several
will one day be approached by ETA recruiters, and if selected, their participation in vandalism will cease while their indoctrination and training in
terrorism will begin. Given the arrests of key ETA leaders over the decades,
and several in the last two years, the rebellious youth of the back alley bar
may even rise to the rank of senior military leader within a few years.[1]

A CCORDING TO OFFICIALS of the Basque Nationalist Party, recruitment is becoming more difficult for ETA. Improved economic conditions as well as
the increased societal rejection of violence have reduced the pool of potential
recruits, forcing ETA to consider less than optimal new members or face
dwindling numbers. How ETA responds to a declining recruiting pool and
waves of leadership purges will offer insight into its ability to adapt to an environment that has become increasingly turbulent in the post–September 11
and March 11 era. A contextual understanding of VNSA such as ETA is im-
perative; however, it only goes part of the way toward a useful diagnosis of the

organization. In the previous chapters we sought to delineate the central dynamics of this environment and relate them to VNSA development. Analysis of the super-system provides insight to the conditions most likely to foster and shape identity mobilization, and it orients analysis to environmental constraints and opportunities. For our analysis to be complete, we must go inside the social organization to expose its organs and determine how internal functions interact to forge organizational-level or system characteristics. Thus, our diagnosis of the VNSA system continues in this chapter at the system and subsystems levels.

The open systems framework as developed and applied in this analysis is guided by modern organization theory. As a way of thinking about organizations of all types, organizational theory has evolved beyond the rigid emphasis on scientific management and bureaucratic structures, which characterize mechanistic organizations, to a contingency-based view based on natural and biological systems.[2] Organization theory as intended for businesses, nonprofits, and legitimate political organizations enables the diagnosis of organizations for the purpose of understanding and solving organizational problems to improve performance. We turn this on its head. Our approach applies open systems-based organizational theory to a different but related purpose: solving threat assessment problems in order to decrease and deny VNSA performance. Our approach provides a framework for analysis at three levels, or, as suggested before, the scaffolding on which the unique signature of a VNSA can be understood and confronted.

We begin by examining the VNSA as a whole, building on and clarifying our baseline definition of VNSA as organizations that exist and operate outside the classical state system, resorting to collective violence to achieve goals. In so doing, we draw out the value of the open systems approach as contrasted against the structural (also termed instrumental) lens of classical organization theory. As with other organizations, such as corporations or bureaucracies, the structural emphasis does not capture the dynamic reality of the VNSA. That is, structural theory does not reveal the inner workings of the organizations to include the complex formal and informal interactions that constitute the "real" organization. Our analysis must go beyond formal structural theory to appreciate these complexities as an aspect of the dynamic, even organic character of the VNSA.

At the system level, all social organizations are "sets of interacting elements" that acquire inputs from the environment, convert the inputs, and discharge outputs back to the external super-system.[3] At this most basic level of analysis, our attention is drawn to the organization's relationship to the environment and the importance of interactions among system functions. The input-conversion-output dynamics are the most obvious, but not the only, or even the most important system-level characteristics. In the course of this chapter, our analysis also explores three often overlooked but critically important or-

1.)   2.)   3.)

ganizational properties—negative entropy, congruence, and life cycles. *Negative entropy* is essential for survival. Organizations must overcome "the universal law of nature in which all forms of organization move toward disorganization or death."[4] Social organizations, because they are open systems, can import more energy from the environment than is immediately required and store it for use during periods of crisis, such as a concentrated counter-insurgency campaign. Smart VNSA will recognize their impressive ability to continuously arrest the entropic process and build their reserves to ensure a comfortable margin of operation.[5] Until the negative entropy pond is drained, the VNSA will survive. *In a distinct form, tho?*

Inducing positive entropy at the environmental and organizational levels can undermine the congruence of VNSA. *Congruence*, sometimes referred to as fit or alignment, is a systems term used to describe "relations among internal system components and between organizations and their environments."[6] A VNSA has good congruence when its internal elements, or sub-systems, are functioning in a reinforcing manner and optimizing coordination and information exchanges so as to reduce inefficiency and uncertainty.[7] Good matches between environmental opportunities/constraints and system functions also evidence good congruence. Al Qaida demonstrates good environment-system congruence by shifting to soft targets in Africa when the hardening of targets in the United States and Europe make operational success less likely. Misfit, or bad congruence, can contribute to organizational failure. ETA shows poor congruence when it recruits undisciplined youth to carry out highly complex attacks that demand strict adherence to operational secrecy. VNSA that cannot adapt their organizations to the external environment or achieve some degree of harmony among internal functions are likely to struggle beyond gestation.

Our inter-disciplinary approach to VNSA, which draws heavily on the social and physical sciences, demands an appreciation for the evolutionary or at least changing nature of organizations. Our attention to the organizational *life cycle* is predicated on the need to grasp the importance of a VNSA's developmental history, in part to forecast the future, but more important, to diagnose the strengths and weaknesses of the VNSA depending on its location in the evolutionary process. This implies a linear process, which is somewhat misleading. Although most organizational life cycles do flow definitively through a series of phases—gestation, growth, maturity, and transformation—other options exist. Some VNSA never emerge from gestation, while others oscillate between "periods of convergence around distinctive strategies."[8] The Irish Republican Army (IRA), for example, might shift between armed insurrection and political dialogue. In other cases, such as Mao's popular war, returning to a previous phase—shifting from mobile operations to guerrilla operations—is necessitated by changing conditions as well as battlefield losses; Mao is actually arguing for congruence, or a good fit between the organization and the environment's demands. Regardless of the flow, a VNSA's position in the life

Self-awareness

cycle has real implications for how it operates, how it adapts, and where its development is likely to lead.

In addition to addressing these system characteristics, this chapter also probes inside the organization to look at the four key sub-systems that make up all social organizations—support, maintenance, cognitive, and conversion. The labels are less important than the concept of sub-systems as grouped functions. Functions are made up of highly specified patterns of activities involving people, places, and objects over time. The support sub-system, for example, manages boundary relations, while maintenance works on people, cognitive decides strategy, and conversion delivers violence. As we examine the key functions of each sub-system, we are careful to highlight its contribution to negative entropy and congruence. While we do not address every function performed by VNSA, the eleven we diagnose are the most relevant to the performance of all VNSA. Moreover, we evaluate functions and sub-systems in relationship to the life cycle, which provides insight to critical requirements, vulnerabilities, and, in military parlance, centers of gravity. This assessment of life cycle vulnerabilities serves as a guidepost for developing strategy against all VNSA but must be complemented by a tailored analysis of the unique patterns of activity that constitute the functions of a specific VNSA. It is unlikely for any analytical frame to fully capture the high degree of complexity and dynamism inherent in social organizations. That said, the systems approach to diagnosing organizations has proven to be a highly valuable framework over the decades, and it provides the only comprehensive framework for addressing one of today's most pressing security challenges.

System Level

Like the modern nation-state, VNSA are too often treated as "rationally ordered instruments for the achievement of stated goals."[9] Rationality is achieved through defined rules and highly institutionalized relationships, which allow the entire structure to become subject to manipulation—an instrument of rational action.[10] To achieve this high degree of control and coordination, the formal organization is also treated as a closed system. It is seen as a self-contained unit, functioning independent of changes in its environment.

The formal, structural approach fails to deliver an accurate picture of the VNSA (and most organizations for that matter) for three reasons. First, the formal structure never fully succeeds in "conquering the non-rational dimensions of organizational behavior."[11] An informal structure exists as well, which deviates from the well-defined roles imposed by the rational structure. Or, as put by Philip Selznick in his seminal article "Foundations of the Theory of Organizations," individuals have a "propensity to resist depersonalization, to spill

Closed systems - orgs. act w/in boundaries they've set for themselves
Open Systems - orgs. act in relation to/against the boundaries set by
the status-quo system.

over the boundaries of their segmented roles, to participate as wholes."[12] The formal structure cannot adequately accommodate the deviations from rationality introduced by individual action. People misbehave, react emotionally, or simply fail to adhere to role performance expectations, often due to a lack of skill or will. Thus, it is better to view VNSA as cooperative systems, consisting of "individuals interacting as wholes" in relation to an organization's formal structures and rules.[13]

As cooperative systems, VNSA are also open systems. The rationality of the organizations cannot be simplified by examining them independent of their environment and static in time. The closed system approach is appealing, particularly since it allows us to apply the laws of physics to organizational behavior and control for environmental change. While convenient, the approach denies the reality that organizations are also living, social entities, adapting to a dynamic environment and simultaneously impacting the environment by their actions. Returning to Daniel Katz and Robert Kahn in their important text *The Social Psychology of Organizations*, the open systems approach frees us from the shackles of physics and leads us to the more applicable science of biology.[14]

The VNSA as open systems can be understood in terms of several key characteristics, which directly relate to the system of violence examined earlier.[15] These groups share certain system characteristics: (1) importation of energy; (2) through-put (energy conversion); (3) export of product to the environment; (4) cyclic pattern of activities; (5) negative entropy; and (6) feedback.[16] For example, the Revolutionary Armed Forces of Colombia (FARC) imports recruits as well as guns, training (this includes training from outside VNSA, such as the urban tactic training provided by the Provisional IRA) and drug monies. Second, the FARC converts, or transforms the recruits into trained guerrillas. Third, the reorganized input is exported to the environment; the recruits join a unit and conduct attacks on Colombian armed forces. Fourth, this pattern of activity is cyclic; the attacks generate new inputs—recruits, resources, governmental responses, etc. Fifth, the FARC seeks to avoid inevitable disorganization and death by importing more energy (recruits, guns, funds) than it expends.[17] Indeed, it is this adaptive characteristic that has enabled the FARC to survive periodic increases in counter-insurgency and counter-terrorism efforts. Sixth, the energy inputs are also informative, providing intelligence about the environment. The quality of available recruits provides insight into changes in the socio-economic dimensions of the environment, and changes in the payment schedules by the drug cartels provide intelligence on the current profitability of the drug market. In more obvious feedback cases, the FARC conducts covert surveillance against a police station to determine vulnerabilities, which in turn impacts operational planning. Defeat in combat also provides the negative feedback required to drive a fundamental shift in tactics.

Turning an OODA Loop

The importance of viewing the VNSA as an open system leads to the final reason for rejecting formal organization theory. Organisms have life cycles. They do not spontaneously appear on the international scene as mature beings with well-ordered structures. Rather, they pass through a distinct series of stages in form and function. The organizational life cycle parallels that of an organism, transitioning from gestation through growth to maturity. Decline normally follows maturity; however, the ability of VNSA to acquire negative entropy suggests the need to think in terms of transformation rather than an inevitable death, although it may very well be that a subset of possible transformations includes elimination. Despite chronological sequencing, each stage is highly interrelated. A mature VNSA like ETA continues to experience aspects of gestation, growth, and transformation as it interacts with its environment.

The life cycle begins with gestation, or the initial conception of an idea for collective violent action. At gestation, the idea is no more than an embryo in the minds of one or several identity entrepreneurs who are part of an at-risk identity cleavage. Gestation occurs at the intersection of the conditions of violence, failures in governance, and identity mobilization. At this crossroads, the identity entrepreneurs are engaged in environmental scanning. These future VNSA leaders are evaluating the state's response to the salient roots of violence and drawing conclusions about the need and prospects for violent action as a means to achieve non-specified goals of survival, political power, profit, or even vengeance. The organization has yet to take form or differentiate its functions; there are no recruits, training programs, facilities, or sustainable resources. Although gestation may involve rational decision making by the identity entrepreneurs, there is a distinct lack of organizational rationality.

The Yomud tribe of Turkmenistan, for example, is a strong candidate for an embryonic VNSA. Already a non-state group with identifiable leaders, the deep roots of discontent and continued state failure by the enigmatic regime of Turkmenbashi (dominated by the Tekke tribe) are probably sufficient to lead tribal leaders to conceive of violent action as another option to continued socio-economic decay and political marginalization. Because of its lack of form, the gestating VNSA is the most difficult to identify, but it is also the most susceptible to a deterrence strategy of environmental shaping. At this stage, the VNSA may be articulating a foundational mythology justifying its existence and may be actively creating exemplars that "fall out" of these myths and stories.

The VNSA moves from gestation to growth at the point when goals are specified, an organization takes initial form, and basic functions ensue. Growth occurs at the intersection of state failure and identity mobilization with gestation continuing as long as the conditions for violence persist. The development of specific, prioritized goals by VNSA leadership as part of the cognitive sub-system opens the door to traditional deterrence; however, the adolescent nature of the organization limits the group's ability to differentiate alternatives, assess outcomes, and orchestrate functions that consistently reflect purpose.[18] The VNSA remains heavily focused on recruitment, developing resources, and establishing an organizational model (hierarchal, network, cells, etc.) to eventually conduct a sustained campaign of violent action. While sporadic violent acts can be expected during the growth stage, these are more likely to establish legitimacy, enhance recruiting, collect intelligence, and test tactics.

By way of example, the Uighur militants of Xinjiang Province in China were a growing VNSA prior to September 11, 2001. Enver Can, president of the East Turkestan National Congress, led a political front to a grassroots separatist movement, which is based largely in Kazakhstan and Kyrgystan. Uighur militants received training and resources from the Taliban and al Qaida in Afghanistan and conducted several small-scale bombings and assassinations against Chinese officials and facilities throughout Xinjiang.[19] The movement remained adolescent due to a diffuse and informal organization, limited resources, and pressure from the Chinese government.

It is in maturity that the VNSA achieves its closest approximation to the formal organization of structural theory, thus providing the greatest opportunity for the application of rationality-based coercion strategies. A mature VNSA has completed its development, achieving the form and functions that are optimal, or nearly so, for it to achieve specified, prioritized objectives. The VNSA engages in environmental scanning, reorganizes inputs, and exports a product back to the environment. Patterns of activity, cognitive relationships, and membership are all discernable, and preferred forms of collective violence are actively employed as part of a sustained campaign.

It is important that functions are differentiated in a process known as progressive mechanization; organizations shift toward greater elaboration and multiplication of increasingly specialized roles.[20] Progressive mechanization recognizes that the patterns of regulation in an embryonic organization involve dynamic interaction.[21] As the organization reaches maturity, "fixed arrangements and conditions of constraint are established which render the system and its parts more efficient."[22] Essentially, the mature organization may be more efficient, but it also loses its equifinality, or ability to achieve its optimal performance in relation to its environment.[23] To put it more directly, the regulation of behavior by VNSA members during gestation and early growth is more likely to be dynamic and driven by individual relationships and the norms of group behaviors. As the VNSA grows, the requirement to perform a greater number of increasingly complex functions leads to increased regulations, often formalized in edicts, instructions, or simply rules, to achieve great efficiency and increase the reliability of role behaviors. This movement toward a more rigid, mechanistic organization may improve efficiency and reduce uncertainty, but it also reduces ability to adapt and pursue alternative strategies unless the organization can retain a balance between decentralization and integration. Al Qaida's ability to survive a coalition onslaught in the fall of 2001 indicates that previous efforts to differentiate through training and decentralize operations were partially successful.

Progressive mechanization and the increased rationality it engenders make the VNSA more vulnerable to traditional coercion or even conventional warfighting. As an example, the al Aqsa Martyr's Brigade emerged as a mature organization on October 12, 2000, during a paramilitary parade in Nablus, Palestinian Territories.[24] According to David Eshel, reporting for *Jane's Intelligence Review*, the Brigades were "a loose coalition of irregulars, hurriedly trained in basic individual combat and equipped with privately owned small arms. Operatives wore plainclothes and limited their activities to roadside shootings."[25] This growth phase included efforts to create a formal military organization, establish infrastructure, acquire arms, develop tactical leadership, and attract recruits to their secular version of the Hamas suicide squads. Upon maturity, a cell-based structure emerged under the senior command of Marwan Barghouti. Progressive differentiation was evidenced in the formation of an intelligence division (learning through environmental scanning), a military logistics division, special combat teams, suicide bomber volunteer forces, and chapters in at least six West Bank towns.[26] Additionally, the Brigades clarified their goals: (1) end Israeli occupation and (2) create a sovereign Palestinian state. Although not deterred from the bombing campaign by the Israeli Defence Forces, the mature Brigades were sufficiently developed to make rational choices and direct organizational behavior on this basis.

Ultimately, increased formalization left the Brigades vulnerable to direct military action, as evidenced by the temporary destruction of their infrastructure and capture of senior leaders during Israeli military operations in April 2002. The result is the transformation of the Brigades, which serves as just one example of how a VNSA may transform over time. The VNSA can survive transformation in two key ways. First, it can choose to end hostility due to a fundamental change in state capacity or policy. This outcome is often the purpose of efforts to build nation states through good governance programs while simultaneously negotiating a peaceful resolution to the conflict. Second, the VNSA can suffer a devastating blow, which would normally result in its ultimate death unless it has built sufficient negative entropy. In the case of the Brigades, the decentralized organizational structure, rich supplies of arms, and ready access to external resources meant it had sufficient negative entropy to weather the storm. In fact, Israeli defense and intelligence officials expected the Brigades to successfully rebuild their operational capabilities.[27] Like the Brigades, the longevity of al Qaida, ETA, IMU, FARC, and others will depend on its ability to navigate the transformation stage.

Internal Functions

Thus far, we have introduced tools for assessing the environment in terms of broad inputs, transformations, and outputs. We have also defined whole system properties and championed the value of life cycle analysis to more accurately characterize the organization. By now looking inside the organization to its functions, we complete our dissection of the organism and reveal vulnerable relationships.

All organizations are made of similar sub-systems and functions. VNSA variation is found primarily in the patterns of activity that make up functions and in terms of the specific nature of their interface with the environment. Collectively, functions do not add up to equal the system, since the system is more than, or at least different from, the sum of its parts. Reducing the Abkhazian ethno-political separatist movement in Georgia to its sub-systems builds an incomplete picture—we may be able to discern the skeleton, but we cannot comprehend the organism's holistic properties without first and second levels of systems analysis. We may learn names of leaders and numbers of militants under arms, but we fail to understand the criticality of the movement's relationship with Russian organized crime, or the efficacy of its efforts to build negative entropy through weapons acquisition and cash accumulation.

Organizational theory is replete with sub-system types and labels. Analysis of non-state groups, however, requires the employment of sub-systems that lend themselves to collection, analysis, and effects-based operations. Fortunately, such sub-systems exist, and their value to organizational diagnosis has withstood scrutiny over the decades. Applying sub-systems and their associated functions to the problem of VNSAs results in four core sub-systems: support, maintenance, cognitive, and conversion. As shown in figure 4.1, these

[handwritten margin note: i.e., there can be more, or fewer, functions within the system.]

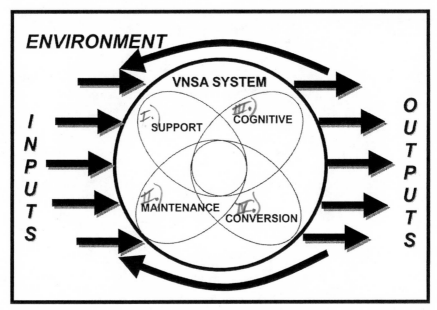

FIGURE 4.1
Violent Non-State Actor System

sub-systems are embedded in the VNSA system, which is exchanging energy and information with its environment.

I. Support Sub-system

Religious students in Islamic schools, or *madrassahs*, are identified and recruited for *jihad*, money is collected and laundered through a front charity, small arms are purchased on the black market, and communiqués are faxed to media outlets around the world. These are just a few of the routine activities that constitute the system dynamics of the support sub-system. In modern organizational theory, support sub-systems "carry out environmental transactions of procuring the input or disposing of the output or aiding in these processes."[28] Essentially, the support sub-system works at the boundary of the VNSA, monitoring and managing relations with the environment. Five types of environmental transactions are most critical to the VNSA: recruitment, resource acquisition, stakeholder associations, learning, and operational employment. The last two are carried out by the cognitive and conversion sub-systems respectively.

A. Recruitment

The recruitment mechanism can take many forms but generally involves linking needs and expectations within a ripe population, or identity cleavage, with the agenda of a gestating VNSA. Identity mobilization is among the first instances of congruence where the leader, or identity entrepreneur, is fitting organizational goals to the likely at-risk population segment. Well after gestation, recruitment continues to attract members from among a sympathetic social cleavage. Once congruence is achieved between the VNSA and its potential members, the group will employ a variety of incentives to close the deal, including, but certainly not limited to, the tangible benefits of a salary, training, or shelter (transactional) and the more persuasive intangible incentives of ideology, sense of belonging, power, greed, and possibly the promise of eternal life (transcendental). The specific patterns of activities, consisting of recruiting agents, incentives, and procedures will vary by VNSA type. Militant religious movements recruit through mosques and *madrassahs* to support a radical theology. Warlords with private militias recruit through family and clan associations to support predatory wealth accumulation. Maoist insurgents recruit students through universities or rural peasants to support an ideological vision. And as evidenced on the streets of Baghdad and Tikrit during 2003–2004, ethno political Sunni groups hired one-shot insurgents using hard cash payments of more than $2500.[29]

An important and often overlooked aspect of recruitment is selection. Selection preserves stability by weeding out risky, low performing recruits or those that might prove difficult to socialize. From the VNSA perspective, a large recruiting pool improves prospects for greater selectivity based on a variety of criteria, which again are tailored to the VNSA type. While most VNSA types are likely to select initially based on a recruit's perceived commitment to the group's agenda, other factors play a role. In small, cell-based, highly secretive organizations like ETA or November 17, dedication to the nationalist cause is not sufficient. Members must also be highly disciplined, capable of sustained covert activity, and capable of learning required skills to include the preparation of improvised explosive devices. As in our ETA example, the specific selection criteria and procedures are likely to be fluid, reflecting the group's adaptation to environmental change. Changes in recruitment and selection over time offer valuable insight into an organization's vulnerabilities and present an opportunity for exploitation if accurately judged.

In the appendix to this book, we introduce an initial effort to model the recruitment function as a first step toward modeling each of the functions using the systems approach. While the process is in its infancy, the appendix offers a first attempt at organizing and relating the key variables involved in the patterns of activity that make up the recruitment function. The Sendero Luminoso serves as our test case due in part to the availability of data.

B. Resource acquisition

The resource acquisition function involves manipulation of the environment in order to obtain requirements for system performance.[30] Or to put it more simply, to acquire what is needed to grow and operate. Like organisms, the resources required to sustain an organization's life become increasingly elaborated during their life cycle and can also change with changes in strategy. This function can be analyzed to determine the importance of specific requirements in three phases. First, the full-range of identified and suspected resource requirements for the target VNSA are inventoried. Requirements are many, but generally include money, weapons, training materials, logistical supplies, false documents, transportation, information technology, communication systems, ideology, etc.[31] For example, the requirements of the FARC during its gestation and early growth phases in the mid 1960s included such basic needs as food, clothing, and supplies.[32] As the FARC reached maturity in the 1980s, expanding its initial force of 350 fighters to the 15,000–20,000 today, its requirements increased and shifted to include training support, advanced weapons systems such as surface-to-air missiles, satellite phones, jamming equipment, and more.[33]

Second, the specific patterns of activity or mechanism for acquiring the resources are identified. Mechanisms vary widely for every requirement. For example, information technology may be acquired through front companies, direct acquisition at trade shows, theft from businesses, or illegal bartering with corrupt government agencies. Weapons can be readily obtained through black markets, theft, raids on police, corruption of security forces, or defeat of an

adversary. Returning to the FARC, resources were acquired during the gestation phase through ambushes on security forces, raids on farms, kidnapping
of hostages for ransom, blackmailing officials, and propaganda appeals to
peasants.[34] In the 1980s, increased resource demands necessitated a shift to expanded alliances with drug cartels as well as exploiting primary commodities
such as cattle, oil, and gold.[35]

Once all resources and the mechanisms for acquisition are identified, we
draw on the well-developed social science theory of *resource dependency* for
determining the extent to which the VNSA is dependent on specific resources
for performance. According to resource dependency theory, the environment
is a powerful constraint on organizations, and therefore resource dependen-
cies must be effectively managed to guarantee the organization's survival and
"to secure, if possible, more independence and freedom from external constraints."[36] Dependency is measured in terms of criticality and scarcity. *Critical* resources are vital to system function. In fact, the system dies when its critical resources are exhausted unless it can find substitutes, which often requires
advance planning and significant organizational transformation. Critical resources for the FARC are the coca crops, and more importantly, the agricultural migrants associated with the drug industry, which are its social base.[37]
Scarce resources are not widely available in the environment, and there is often
competition for them—diamonds and plutonium are scarce, landmines are
not.[38] Resources that are critical and scarce demand the greatest organizational attention while also offering an appropriate focus for a countering
strategy. Critical resources that are widely available, or scarce resource that are
critical, reveal a second level of vulnerability, while non-critical, abundant resources do not provide a profitable countering opportunity. Importantly, critical and/or scarce resources must be acquired in sufficient quantity and with
appropriate timing to ensure that the VNSA can survive temporary interference with its dependent relationship. Such a well-developed and executed resource acquisition strategy is a form of negative entropy.

C. *Stakeholder associations*

The stakeholder association dynamic involves obtaining social support and
legitimacy through societal manipulation and integration.[39] *Stakeholder dependency* is closely related to resource dependency, since many stakeholders
control key resources. The evaluation of stakeholder associations provides direct insight into the relative importance of key relationships that must be sustained to ensure survival as well as relationships that exert influence on the behavior of the VNSA. For example, it is widely held that the Revolutionary
Guard of the Iranian armed forces maintains a stakeholder interest in the
Hezbollah in Lebanon, providing a wide range of support services to include

money, sanctuary, and training. Strings are attached, although their strength remains a matter of dispute. In its February 16, 1985, foundational letter, Hezbollah asserted that

> We, the sons of Hizb Allah's nation, whose vanguard God has given victory in Iran and which has established the nucleus of the world's central Islamic state, abide the orders of a single wise and just command currently embodied in the supreme Ayatollah Ruhollah al-Musavi al-Khomeini, the rightly guided imam who combines all the qualities of the total imam.[40]

With the death of al-Khomeini, the rise of more moderate political forces in Iran, and Hezbollah's growth into a dominant social, political, economic, and military organization in Lebanon, it can be reasonably argued Hezbollah no longer takes orders from Tehran. Therefore, the character of this important stakeholder relationship has changed.

For Hezbollah and other VNSA, the first analytical step in determining the extent and influence of these relationships is to map the network of stakeholder associations. Network analysis provides a complex web of relationships in which the VNSA is embedded.[41] It begins by inventorying all possible stakeholders, including, but not limited to state sponsors, sanctuary or safe haven providers, identity entrepreneurs, non-governmental organizations, weapons suppliers, diasporas, corrupt officials or agencies, sympathetic identity cleavages, financial institutions, and other VNSA. As one example, the Tamil rebels in Sri Lanka, the Liberation Tigers of Tamil Eelam (LTTE), are supported by stakeholders among the Tamil Diaspora, including migrant communities, charitable NGOs, and front companies.[42] When feasible, specific stakeholders must be identified such as in the case of Shun Sunder. Sunder is a medical practitioner in California who has provided an estimated $4 million to LTTE during the 1990s.[43] Notably, not all stakeholder associations are defined in terms of financial support. In many cases, such as celebrity support for an independent Tibet, the association may provide no more than publicity.

With all stakeholders inventoried, the next step is to assess the mechanisms for sustaining relationships. While the association is often in the form of financial transactions through banks, donor bodies, or front companies, support can also be managed through direct mailings, e-mail, telephone hotlines, community libraries, television and radio programs, conferences, and websites.[44] The LTTE relies heavily on the Internet to build support, leading experts to conclude that it has been able to establish a truly global presence, permitting the group to "virtually and instantaneously transmit propaganda, mobilize active supporters and sway potential backers."[45]

Relative importance or the *centrality* of stakeholder associations is difficult to measure. Centrality is a function of both the actual and perceived value of an association to the VNSA. One method to determine centrality is to examine the VNSA's strategy for dealing with stakeholders. *Proaction* involves extensive effort to maintain relations, address stakeholder interests, and anticipate future requirements.[46] Proaction appropriately characterized Hezbollah's relationship with Iran in the 1980s. *Accommodation* is a less active strategy that might entail infrequent interface or only partial efforts to satisfy interests. Accommodation is suggestive of Hezbollah's relationship to Tehran in the 1990s. The *defense* strategy involves doing the minimum required to keep the relationship alive, while *reaction* typically entails ignoring or rejecting the relationship.[47] The LTTE must be proactive in dealing with donor organizations in the Tamil Diaspora, whereas it takes a defensive or even reactive approach to dealing with moderates and scholars in Tamil society who do not share their agenda.[48]

Resource acquisition and stakeholder associations are not the only two functions of the support sub-system, but they are the most critical to developing negative entropy and thus reducing the uncertainty that can derail congruence. Excess critical and scarce resources are needed for the FARC to survive sustained counter-insurgency and counter-narcotic operations. Reliable access to these resources is essential to growth and expansion. In all associations, the ability of the relationship to survive crises is a function of how the strategy is applied over time. That is, a central stakeholder association that has been approached proactively over decades is more likely to survive misunderstanding, deceit, and disloyalty than a new relationship that has been handled defensively or reactively.

Maintenance Sub-system

Jihadist are groomed through *madrassahs*, training camps, and religious media, a Maoist insurgent is executed for collaboration with the state, and an assassin is promoted for successfully killing a justice minister. These activities are among the primary functions of the maintenance sub-system. This sub-system mediates between task demands and human needs to maintain stability and predictability.[49] Its over-aching goal is to protect the VNSA organism and its organs (sub-systems) from uncertainty and positive entropy—survival. Maintenance activities seek to preserve equilibrium, primarily through the socialization of personnel and a scheme of sanctions and rewards to maintain role performance.[50] Where the support sub-system focuses on accessing critical requirements, maintenance dynamics center on the "equipment for getting the work done"; in the case of VNSAs, the "work consists of patterned human behavior and the 'equipment' consists of the human beings."[51] The primary functions of the maintenance sub-system are socialization and rewarding and sanctioning.[52] The interplay of these functions results in a trend to a more mechanistic organization structure due to increased formalization and institutionalization. Disrupting any of the functions has the effect of increasing positive entropy, and if sustained over time, can lead to system failure.

A_0) Socialization *Support* *Maintenance*

Recruitment gathers prospective members, while socialization weds them to a set of organizational norms and values. Norms and values may not be clearly articulated early in the VNSA's life cycle, but they must become explicit during growth and before maturity in order to integrate members toward its goals. Breaking it down, "norms make explicit the forms of behavior appropriate for members of the system."[53] To determine if a norm is a system property, the following criteria must be met: (1) There is evidence of beliefs by individual members that certain behaviors are expected; (2) a majority of group members share the belief; and (3) there is general awareness that the norm is supported by most of the group's members, not just the leadership.[54]

Collectively, values constitute the group's ideology and provide a more "elaborate and generalized justification both for appropriate behavior and for the activities and functions of the system."[55] Values become norms when they are operationalized by the group members in terms of specific behaviors. Despite a broad range of VNSA types, two value systems tend to dominate: transcendental and transactional.[56] *Ch.5* Militant religious groups, ideological organizations, eco-warriors, and others generally embrace a transcendental value system, which places emphasis on morality, sacred duty, the supernatural, and symbolism. Transcendental values are difficult to inculcate, but tend to be more effective in sustaining loyalty. Transnational Criminal Organizations (TCO) and warlords with private militias epitomize the transactional or pragmatic value system with their emphasis on amassing wealth or power. The transactional value system can be rapidly developed, but it is also more susceptible to disruption and defection in the face of a superior threat or more lucrative alternatives for members. The most effective VNSAs foster a dual value system, manipulating symbols and delivering tangible value. Dual value systems have the added advantage of offering reinforcing sources of negative entropy; faith can be often be sustained even when cash runs short.

VNSA culture emerges from the evolution and propagation of norms and values. Diagnosing culture is exceedingly difficult, but when successful, cultural insight provides answers to practical issues, including: Who matters, where are the boundaries, why and how does work get accomplished, what are problems and what is most important to the VNSA?[57] Cultural strength, or the extent to which members share the norms and values, is the system's glue. It is a strong and often overlooked source of congruence in social organizations. A VNSA with a strong culture, such as the IRA or Hezbollah, is more likely to have congruent sub-systems and to enjoy greater member commitment. In this respect, culture may be one of the most powerful forms of negative entropy. An organization with an inflexible or weak culture will have greater difficulty dealing with environmental turbulence.

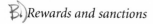

B. *Rewards and sanctions*

Rewarding and sanctioning reinforces culture, generating the negative entropy to survive betrayals and defections by members. This maintenance function works to maintain role performance through an allocation schedule, generally based on proscribed behaviors. In the world of VNSAs, members who display cowardice, reveal operational secrets to the government, or betray the organization in any way are often killed. On the other hand, increased pay, promotion, prestige and even promises of a martyr's paradise are used to reward a job well done. Diagnosis of the "allocation parameters, or who gets what and why," reveals opportunities for undermining role performance. The Real IRA militant who expects to gain promotion and prestige by bombing a police station is less likely to carry out future attacks if the result of his tactical success appears to be under-appreciated, or if another member is given credit.

As an over-arching example for the role of the maintenance sub-system, al Qaida relies on local *imams* of mosques and *madrassahs* to recruit potential militants. Maulana ul Haq, the head of the most famous *madrassahs* in Pakistan, Jaamiah Darul Uloom Haqqania, presided over 2,800 students, many of whom moved on to training camps in Afghanistan during the 1990s.[58] Other militants self-select, like Mohammad Rashed al 'Owhali, who participated in the 1998 U.S. Embassy bombing in Nairobi, Kenya. Al 'Owhali attended religious school in Riyadh where he was further exposed to *jihadist* value. This value was most likely operationalized, becoming a norm, while he was learning hijacking and kidnapping at the Khaladan training camp in Afghanistan.[59] The norm was reinforced on the battlefield, where he was distinguished in fighting with the Taliban. Based on his performance, he was rewarded with selection to special instruction on cell operations, including intelligence, administration, planning, and execution—essentially, he was taught how to replicate the VNSA system at a smaller scale.[60] The reward reinforced his commitment to the values of the system, resulting in a decision to charge him with executing an attack on the Embassy. Interestingly, there is some evidence to suggest that socialization was not fully achieved in al 'Owhali's case. When the massive bomb exploded on August 7, 2003, al 'Owhali had fled the scene when the plan to kill the gate guard failed—he had forgotten his gun![61] Clearly, his socialization was not strong enough to overcome a plan gone awry. His behavior, despite being the cell leader, is dramatically juxtaposed with the other terrorist, who stayed with the explosive-laden truck and subsequently killed 220 and injured more than 4,000.

III. Cognitive Sub-system

A spy gathers intelligence, key leaders meet to plan a series of urban bombings, a cell structure is implemented to ensure secrecy, and directions are issued for acquiring nuclear materials. These are sample activities of the cognitive sub-system. This sub-system's primary functions are learning, strategy, and control. Together, they comprise the decision-making structure of the VNSA, which is responsible for "controlling, coordinating and directing" the other sub-systems."[62] The system dynamic of decision-making may be the most difficult to diagnose, but it is also the most important for a coercive strategy that requires the VNSA to retain cognitive capacity. Where defeat is the goal, undermining the cognitive sub-system is certain to induce uncertainty, incongruence, and ultimately, system failure.

A. Learning

The VNSA learns through intelligence collection, analysis, and dissemination. VNSAs are cybernetic systems; they have a reflexive feedback capability that enables correction and in some cases self-awareness.[63] Although an organism can survive without learning when the environment is static, turbulence in the system generates a requirement for at least simple learning in order to survive. VNSAs, like organisms, develop regulatory mechanisms early in development. The most basic form of learning, which dominates the gestation and early growth period, is known as single-loop learning or simply as cognition. Developed by Chris Argyris and Donald Schon, single-loop learning involves learning from the consequences of previous behavior, resulting in changes in "strategies of action or assumptions underlying strategies in ways that leave the values of a theory of action unchanged."[64] We learn from mistakes and new information.

The Islamic Army of Aden (IAA) in Yemen provides an example of changing behaviors based on experience while still clinging to an underlying value of battling Westerners, particularly Americans, as part of a global *jihad*. In 1998, the IAA kidnapped sixteen western tourists, including twelve Britons, two Australians, and two Americans.[65] Led by Abu Hassan, the group's purposes included protesting the 1998 U.S. military operation in Iraq known as Desert Fox and seeking the release of three colleagues being held by the Yemeni government on bombing charges.[66] A rare attempt by Yemeni security forces to rescue the hostages initiated a two-hour firefight, leaving four hostages and three kidnappers dead. No prisoners were released, and Abu

Hassan went to prison with two henchmen. Having failed to secure their objectives through kidnapping, the IAA changed tactics. In January 2000, an attempt to bomb a U.S. warship failed when the explosive-laden raft sank immediately after being launched. This feedback did not cause a change in tactics, but there was a re-engineering of explosives on the raft. On October 12, 2000, a second raft blew a massive hole in the destroyer USS Cole, killing seventeen and injuring thirty-nine.[67]

As in this example, single-loop learning is sufficient when changes in strategies and tactics can satisfactorily correct errors in performance or improve effectiveness. It is not always sufficient, however, when the environment is turbulent or when the organization must change the values and norms that girder culture. The ability to adapt, to not only correct behavior but determine what behavior is correct, is essential for surviving crises.[68] It is a form of negative entropy known as double-loop learning. The double-loop refers to two feedback interfaces that link the intelligence about performance or the environment to strategies as well as to the values served by those strategies.[69] The VNSA learns to learn. Returning to the IAA, the value of attacking Westerners was never abandoned even though strategy and tactics changed. A redefinition of values in terms of a shift to non-violent protest would have been an example of double-loop learning; it is a fundamental shift in some or all underlying values. It might be argued, however, that the shift from kidnapping to suicide bombings was a lesser form of double-loop learning, because a group norm shifted from one of surviving an operation to one of dying while executing the attack. Since double-loop learning provides negative entropy, a counter-VNSA strategy must seek to drive groups to single-loop learning if defeat is the goal. If coercion is the goal, however, our strategy should seek to enhance double-loop learning so that the cognitive sub-system can affect changes in underlying values and norms.

Diagnosing single- and double-loop learning to support a C-VSNA (counter-VNSA) campaign demands pattern analysis over time. It also requires an investigation of the mechanisms for collecting, analyzing, and processing intelligence throughout the system. All sub-systems participate in learning through their interactions with the environment, and every individual, whether trained to collect intelligence or not, is a sensor. Distributed, informal intelligence collection is more likely during gestation and early growth, while it is likely to find formalized training and structures in late growth and mature VNSAs. Many mature groups, including al Qaida, IRA, and FARC, provide expert training in intelligence collection as well as specific individuals or sub-units that conduct reconnaissance and surveillance. Once the intelligence is collected, it must be analyzed and disseminated. Above the tactical level of operations, analysis is normally an aspect of the strategy development function, while dissemination is a control function.

Strategy

Strategy is an output of the cognitive sub-system, reflecting efforts of VNSA leadership to influence organizational outcomes by managing its relationship with the environment.[70] A successful strategy matches the competencies of the organization to the demands of the environment, and, in so doing, the VNSA gains resources, operational success, legitimacy, and negative entropy for survival. According to organizational expert Mary Jo Hatch, "when the competencies of the organization fit the demands of the environment, then the organization is selected and retained (the population ecology view), provided with resources (the resource dependency view), and legitimized (the institutional view)."[71] A good strategy crafts a congruent system. Diagnosing strategy is analytically challenging because you cannot simply rely on the statements of leadership or members—strategy is emergent, not directed. It is nonetheless essential to accurately diagnose strategy since undermining the decision-making capacity will deliver a system-crippling blow.

The strategy function is traditionally equated with rational decision making by leadership. According to the rational model, as articulated by Henry Mintzberg and as explained later in our discussion of ecological deterrence in chapter 7, strategy is created based on a careful examination of (1) threats and opportunities in the environment and (2) strengths and weaknesses of the organization.[72] Strategies and associated goals are identified to leverage opportunity and close performance gaps and then implemented by a mechanistic organization.[73] Rationality is achieved through defined rules and highly institutionalized relationships, which allow the entire structure to become subject to manipulation—an instrument of rational action.[74] To achieve this high degree of control and coordination, the formal organization is treated as a closed system. It is seen as a self-contained unit, functioning independent of changes in its environment.

The rational model is insufficient due to three reasons outlined earlier: (1) The formal structure never fully succeeds in "conquering the non-rational dimensions of organizational behavior"; (2) VNSAs are also open systems and subject to environmental effects; and (3) VNSAs have life cycles, resulting in a changing cognitive capacity relative to the phase of development.[75] Thus, it is more appropriate to think of strategy as the direction the organization takes, regardless of whether it is intentional.[76] With this perspective, strategy is something that emerges as a function of system dynamics. Strategic planning may occur under conditions of bounded rationality by the VNSA leaders, but it is also greatly influenced during development and implementation by individuals, the sub-systems, and the environment.

Diagnosing strategy begins by comparing the publicly disclosed strategy as reflected primarily in leadership statements and communiqués with the observed strategy. There are many public strategies in circulation, ranging from the Maoist insurgency to a contemporary global *jihad*.[77] Observed strategy is assessed based on pattern analysis of past activities and operations. Inventorying, assessing, and prioritizing the range of influences at each level of our framework can explain the delta between "stated" and "observed." Linking these dynamics to the VNSA's life cycle allows us to forecast alternative futures for the group.

In some cases, such as the many armed groups in Georgia and Azerbaijan that emerged in the early 1990s, initial "stated" strategies demanded little more than a degree of local autonomy. Warlords, such as Akaki Eliava in the Mingrelia area of Georgia, sought to retain power after the end of the 1993 Georgian Abkhaz civil war.[78] Over the 1990s, warlords in the Svaneti region of Georgia and the north of Azerbaijan shifted their strategies to include the accumulation of wealth through illegal activities and the adaptation of more radical religious agendas. Although the change was never "publicized," it can be assessed by observing the activities of the support, maintenance, and conversion sub-systems. Explaining it begins at the super-system level. In both countries, the conditions of violence have deepened, and the government's impotence increased during the period. Moreover, illegal trade prospered with the demise of the Soviet Union, and refugee flows from Chechnya brought weapons and conflict. In Azerbaijan, inroads by Islamic groups, including Egyptian Islamic Jihad, the Hizb ut Tahrir al Islami, and others, radicalized existing identity cleavages.[79] Looking inward, the support sub-system most likely placed demands for new sources of revenue to cover weapons acquisition, and new stakeholder associations with *jihadist* groups brought pressures for strategy change. Subsequently, the maintenance sub-system socialized recruits based on these new radical influences. In turn, these dynamics contributed to the emergence of new strategies, including goals aligned with Hizb ut Tahrir al Islami, whose aim is to

> resume the Islamic way of life and to convey the Islamic *da'wah* to the world. This objective means bringing the Muslims back to living an Islamic way of life in *Dar al-Islam* and in an Islamic society such that all of life's affairs in society are administered according to the Shari'ah rules, and the viewpoint in it is the *halal* and the *haram* under the shade of the Islamic State, which is the Khilafah State. That state is the one in which Muslims appoint a Khaleefah and give him the *bay'ah* to listen and obey on condition that he rules according to the Book of Allah and the Sunnah of the Messenger of Allah and on condition that he conveys Islam as a message to the world through *da'wah* and jihad.[80]

Even when Georgian warlords foreswear an endorsement of *jihadist* principles, observation of stakeholder associations, religious practices of key leaders, or even changes in the treatment of prisoners in line with Islamic practices (the laws dealing with prisoners are part of a sub-set of the *shari'a* known as *siyar*), can provide insight into the growing influence of Islamic groups. As with this abbreviated example, the key lesson is to ensure that analysis goes beyond rhetoric to examine real actions.

C. Control

Strategy is implemented by the control function, which attempts to align individual actions and functions with the strategy. Many of the mechanisms of control are carried out by other sub-systems, including socialization and rewarding/sanctioning by the maintenance sub-system, learning by the cognitive sub-system, and training by the conversion sub-system. Two additional aspects of control deserve our attention: social structure and communications.   I.)Support

Social structures are formal and informal. The traditional organization chart provides a skeleton of the formal hierarchy for the distribution of cognitive as well as roles and responsibilities. This is a useful starting point for determining whether the VNSA uses a simple, functional, matrixed, network, or hybrid structure to coordinate and communicate. A more difficult task is to figure out the informal associations, which interlace the formal structure. These can be investigated by inquiring as to the pattern of relationships as well as exchanges between sub-systems and individual members—essentially a fourth level of analysis.

For both types of social structures, three measures allow us to determine the extent to which the organization is mechanistic or organic: complexity, centralization, and formalization. *Complexity* is a measure of the horizontal or vertical differentiation.[81] Complexity is advantageous in a dynamic, hostile environment, but it suffers from increased communication and resource demands. *Centralization* refers to the diffusion of decision-making authority. Decentralized VNSAs empower members, pushing at least operational decision-making to the boundaries of the system, or the periphery of the network—al Qaida became highly decentralized after U.S. operation Enduring Freedom in Afghanistan. *Formalization* refers to the extent to which norms are explicitly laid out in directives, *fatwas*, etc. Formalization discourages innovation but has the benefits of increasing control.[82] Mechanistic organizations are complex, formal, and centralized, while organic organizations are informal, decentralized, and often simple, although complexity has increased due to improved forms of communications.

Communication is the essence of the system—"the exchange of information and the transmission of meaning."[83] As the VNSA grows, communication will become increasingly complex due to differentiation of work, necessitating restrictions to prevent system "noise," or information that distracts and misleads.[84] Without going into information theory, it is sufficient to say

that a robust countering strategy will generate system "noise" to increase uncertainty. Disrupting communications also undermines system congruence,
making it difficult for sub-systems to interact.

Achieving these effects requires an evaluation of the VNSA communication
network. Even though all VNSA continue to rely on couriers and face-to-face
interactions to ensure security, sophisticated information technologies have
improved communication in three ways: reduced transmission time, reduced
costs, and increased scope and complexity of information.[85] Many VNSA are
known to rely on satellite phones and computer networks. To avoid detection,
al Qaida and others have adapted common web-based communication systems with increased cleverness. For example, Microsoft Network's Hotmail
e-mail system is used to communicate, not by sending messages, but by
preparing messages and saving them in the "draft" folder, where they sit until
another operative logs on using the same account name—the message is never
actually sent and is thus less susceptible to interception. The ideological group
Animal Liberation Front communicates between cells in the United States and
Europe using an encryption program, Pretty Good Privacy (PGP), to send
coded e-mails.[86] These mechanisms and others are not error free, particularly
when combined with the misunderstanding inherent in human communication, and where possible, these vulnerabilities must be understood and exploited as part of a countering strategy.

IV. Conversion Sub-system

Child soldiers learn to shoot AK-47s, health services are delivered to a community, a suicide bomber records a martyr's video, underground bunkers are
built, guerrilla forces ambush a convoy, a politician is kidnapped, or aircraft
are used as missiles to attack landmarks. These functions and others constitute the dynamics of the conversion sub-system. This sub-system's primary
function is task accomplishment, converting energy within the system and
outputting a product to the environment.[87] In the case of VNSAs, the product
of most concern is collective violence; however, our C-VNSA strategy is also
concerned with other products that sustain the organization, such as social
services and those that reinforce the system of violence, such as illegal goods.

A. Operations

Operations can take many forms and do not always involve violence. Non-
violent operational activities, such as reconnaissance to gain intelligence or
public demonstrations to spread messages, demand more attention by intelligence analysts, as they are often important pre-cursors to violence. Surveillance is a particularly telling indicator, as it not only identifies likely targets

but it is often the only time an organization comes "above ground." In analyzing operational activities, each identified activity must be linked to other supporting operational activities and to the sub-systems involved. For example, surveillance is an operational activity that is also carried out by the cognitive sub-system to enable learning. Finally, the criticality of the linkages must be assessed to support the prioritization of actions intended to disrupt operations. Criticality can be assessed in terms of resource, stakeholder, and knowledge dependency as discussed earlier. Given the importance of collective violence to an overall discussion of the VNSA challenge, it earns additional focus in chapter 6.

B. Training and production

Training converts the recruits of the maintenance sub-system into militants, terrorists, criminals, logisticians, accountants, propagandists, etc., while production converts resources into useful materials, including drugs (cocaine, heroin), weapons (vehicle-borne improvised explosive devices, suicide vests), or social services, to name a few. Both processes are analyzed similarly and provide parallel relationships for exploitation. Inputs can be identified and linked to their appropriate source in the environment or one of the other system functions. Activities and associated infrastructure for each conversion can also be dissected. Most VNSAs, particularly mature groups like al Qaida, LTTE, IRA, and FARC, have well-developed and documented training programs. Al Qaida's training programs in Afghanistan prior to the fall of the Taliban in 2001 were even video-taped and globally dispersed for recruitment. Gestating and growing VNSAs are unlikely to have sophisticated programs for training and production; however, they are also inclined to acquire the skills or materials directly from government and non-government sources until they are sufficiently differentiated to conduct home-grown conversions. Many militia organizations in the United States and elsewhere are known to import skills by gaining recruits with prior military experience—these individuals then form the backbone of training programs.

Another important output is ideology in all its forms, ranging from communism to fascism to extremist religion. At its most basic level, ideology is "a set of core philosophical principles" that a group collectively holds about politics.[88] Ideology is not found lying on the street, it too must be converted from a variety of inputs including history, dogma, and social convention. These inputs are transformed by members of the organization into an ideological program. In recent history, al Qaida has proven the most adept at exporting ideology, evidenced by the highly influential *fatwas* issued on behalf of Osama bin Laden and Ayman al-Zawahiri. Among many, one of the earliest appeared on February 22, 1996, when bin Laden announced the formation of the *World*

Islamic Front for the Jihad against the Jews and the Crusaders. In this statement, bin Laden and cohorts set the agenda for the extended global *jihadist* insurgency that continues as of the time of this writing:

> Based upon this and in order to obey the Almighty, we hereby give all Muslims the following judgment: The judgment to kill and fight Americans and their allies, whether civilians or military, is an obligation for every Muslim who is able to do so in any country. . . . In the name of Allah, we call upon every Muslim, who believed in Allah and ask for forgiveness, to abide by Allah's order by killing Americans and stealing their money anywhere, anytime, and whenever possible.[89]

Conversion activities and associated facilities are often the main focus of current counter-insurgency, -narcotic, and -terrorism campaigns: destroying cocaine production facilities in the jungles of South America, raining cruise missiles on terrorist camps in Afghanistan, protecting facilities against guerrilla attacks in Baghdad, or fighting Islamic militants in the Pankisi Gorge of Georgia. While a conversion-centric approach may be necessary, the most effective strategy targets all sub-systems, recognizing that conversions do not have to occur for the VNSA to survive. Conversions do contribute to negative entropy by providing a surplus of trained members and products, and successful operations can produce internal and external support; however, the VNSA can survive an extended period of dormancy if other functions remain active. For example, Hamas can hold off on suicide operations for years and still prosper, as long as it continues to recruit, socialize, maintain stakeholder relations, and learn.

Life Cycle Vulnerabilities

In a mature VNSA, the sub-systems and associated functions outlined here are each generally well developed, inter-related, and are relatively equal in importance to system functioning. When mapped against life cycle phases of a specific VNSA, however, the extent of their development and their relative value will vary substantially, presenting a unique VNSA signature. A sub-system's value, or criticality, is assessed in terms of its contribution to reducing uncertainty and increasing negative entropy, which combine to sustain congruence. Armed with this knowledge, a refined counter-VNSA strategy will target the critical sub-system and take advantage of life cycle transitions.

Earlier, we introduced four life cycle phases: gestation, growth, maturity, and transformation.[90] These phases, although suggestive of linear development similar to the human life, manifest in a non-linear fashion. In some cases, two or more phases may occur simultaneously, as in a mature VNSA that continues to grow. The phase shift is most often a result of group's changing relationship to the environment; however, a change in strategy by group leaders or an effective counter-VNSA campaign may be the cause. The transformation phase can take many forms, including duplication, dormancy, or death.

During the 1980s, the Sendero Luminoso (Shining Path), for example, was a mature VNSA. Former university president Abimael Guzman, led a cognitive sub-system with a well-developed culture based on the extreme elements of values and norms associated with Mao Tse Tung and Che Guevara. Even while the conversion sub-system waged collective violence in the form of murders, bombings, and assassinations, the support sub-system was still pursuing the growth of the organization through an increasingly unsuccessful recruiting campaign that involved killing those who refused to join.[91] It can argued that the fear-based mechanisms employed by the agents of the conversion system directly contributed to decline by undermining the success of the support sub-system to gain resources and sustain stakeholder associations, particularly with the very peasants Guzman was "saving." Recalling the discussion of niche construction earlier, the Shining Path undercut its own environmental space. With negative entropy depleted, the capture of Guzman in 1992 initiated system disintegration, forcing a transition to a dormant gestation phase. Of note, the failure of the Peruvian government to satisfactorily alleviate the conditions of violence in the ensuing decade contributed to the Shining Path's survival and a minimal resurgence in 2000.

As in the example, specific sub-systems tend to "lead," or be the most critical, during each life cycle phase. During gestation, for example, the VNSA is a primitive collective response to a common problem—the conditions of violence.[92] At gestation, the idea is no more than an embryo in the minds of one or several identity entrepreneurs who are part of an at-risk identity cleavage. In order for a group to form, the identity entrepreneur and his/her nucleus of founders must be linked to resources, stakeholders, and future members. Embedding the primitive VNSA in the environment through a network of critical relationships is the responsibility of the support sub-system. Until the support sub-system does its work, maintenance and conversion sub-systems will lack the people and tools required for socialization, sanctioning, training, production, and operations. Although the support sub-system is most critical during gestation, it is guided by a basic cognitive sub-system. Decision-making and control are not the result of an elaborated, participatory process at this point. Rather, the identity entrepreneur can easily set the agenda and control functions due to his familiarity with all group members.[93]

The growth phase is entered when all sub-systems initiate activity or total system activity increases; however, the relevant importance of the sub-systems varies with VNSA. In early growth, the support sub-system continues to lead, but is increasingly interlaced with the development of specific maintenance and conversion functions. Maintenance functions are likely to dominate in VNSAs that stress a transcendental agenda, such as the Islamic Jihad in Palestine or the Kahane Chai in Israel. These groups and others place a greater premium on loyalty and commitment to the religious or ideological goals of the group. Conversion functions will dominate in VNSAs that pursue a more pragmatic agenda, such as the Chinese Triads or the warlords of Afghanistan, where the accumulation of wealth or consolidation of power requires the production of drugs or the training of guerrillas to hold territory and extract resources.

The growth phase is characterized by high levels of uncertainty related to the idiosyncratic behaviors by group members, doubt about reliability of resources and stakeholders, and the evolving character of the organization. In an effort to increase stability and survivability, the growth phase will increasingly reflect efforts to differentiate and enforce roles and responsibilities. Therefore, the cognitive sub-system will assert itself during growth by clarifying goals and establishing more formal structures. Differentiation generates pressure to integrate functions, a task carried out by the control function.[94] Additionally, the VNSA leadership will recognize the importance of continued environmental scanning through intelligence collection activities as a means to reduce uncertainty and harmonize the fit of its sub-systems to the opportunities and constraints of the environment. In the most adept VNSAs, learning will gain prominence—the earlier it does in the life cycle, the more successful the VNSA is likely to be in a turbulent environment. Finally, sporadic violent acts can be expected during the growth stage; however, these are more likely to be for reasons articulated earlier, including establishing legitimacy, enhancing recruiting, collecting intelligence, and testing tactics than they are for achieving overarching VNSA goals.

Closing

For the mature VNSA of the world, all systems perform in concert; congruence is achieved, uncertainty is managed, and negative entropy is built. Based on this ideal system type, each function is fully articulated in terms of sustainable, adaptable patterns of activity, the culture is strong, the decision-making process is based on double-loop learning, control is efficient, training has efficacy, and operations achieve goals. We are fortunate that this ideal rarely exists. Yet, even growing VNSAs trapped in single-loop learning, or lacking sanctuary for training, or failing to attract new recruits, or running short of funds, are tough to defeat. With our systems-based, diagnostic tools presented here, the strengths and the weaknesses of the VNSAs can be exposed for exploitation by a counter-VNSA strategy.

The systems approach allows us to approach geographically and even temporally disparate groups like Kumpulan Mujahidin Malaysia (KMM) or Colombia's ELN within a common framework. Each operates within a similarly structured environment, exhibits common system properties like negative entropy, and progresses through comparable life cycle stages. In the case of the KMM and ELN, both prosper in regions where the roots of violence are strong, failures in government are prevalent, and identity mobilization extensive. Moreover, both are mature VNSAs engaging in environmental scanning, converting inputs in the form of recruits, money, and weapons, and exporting violence. Levels of analysis provide the scaffolding on which we build the distinctive signature of each group. A VNSA's signature is a function of its unique interactions or patterns of activity, within and across the levels of the analysis. By way of example, the KMM's interactions with the environment in the form of identity mobilization and resource acquisition are constrained by a more capable Malaysian government, which has successfully detained 48 alleged members of the KMM under the Internal Security Act and limited overall group membership to 70–80 assessed members.[95] The ELN, on the other hand, prospers in the northeast of Colombia with a membership of 3,000–5,000 fighters due in part to Bogota's inability to control the Antioquia region.[96] The dynamic of "governance" in relation to critical VNSA functions is only one of several dimensions of the group's signature. Signatures enable our counter-VNSA strategy to retain its global consistency using a menu of transportable instruments and effects while still being tailored to the challenges of a particular region or group.

Notes

1. For a discussion of the Basque region, which includes insight into ETA's development, we recommend Mark Kurlansky's *The Basque History of the World* (New York: Penguin Books, 1999). Insights for this vignette were also derived from the author's visit to the Basque province in December 2003, which involved informal discussions with members of the ruling Basque Nationalist Party as well as leaders of several non-governmental social organizations pursuing nonviolent solutions to the Basque conflict.

2. Richard L. Daft provides a good summary of the evolution of organizational theory in *Organization Theory and Design* (Mason, OH: Thomson South-western, 8th ed., 2004), 25–27.

3. Ibid., 14.

4. Daniel Katz and Robert L. Kahn, "Organizations and the System Concept," in their *The Social Psychology of Organizations* (NY: John Wiley and Sons, 1978). Reprinted in *Classics of Organization Theory*, eds. Jay M. Shafritz and J. Steven Ott (Fort Worth, TX: Harcourt College Publishers, 5th ed., 2001), 262.

5. Ibid., 262.

6. Michael I. Harrison and Arie Shirom, *Organizational Diagnosis and Assessment: Bridging Theory and Practice* (Thousand Oaks, CA: Sage Publications, 1999), 52.

7. Ibid., 54.

8. Ibid., 301.

9. Philip Selznick, "Foundations of the Theory of Organization," *American Sociological Review* 13 (1948), Reprinted in Shafritz and Ott, *Classics of Organization Theory*, 125.

10. Ibid., 125.

11. Ibid., 125.

12. Ibid., 126.

13. Ibid., 128.

14. Shafritz and Ott, *Classics of Organization Theory*, 257.

15. Ibid., 260–65.

16. Ibid., 260–63.

17. Ibid., 262.

18. For a complete explanation of the rational choice model and critiques by Graham Allison and others, see "Understanding the Role of Power in Decision Making," in *Power in Organizations* by Jeffrey Pfeffer (Marshfield, MA: Pitman Publishing, 1981). Reprinted in *Classics of Organization Theory*, 304–18.

19. John Hill, "China's Turbulent Backyard," *Jane's Intelligence Review* (June 2002, Vol. 14, No. 6), 48–49.

20. Shafritz and Ott, *Classics of Organization Theory*, 264.

21. Ibid., 264.

22. From Ludwig von Bertalanffy, *General Systems*, Yearbook of the Society for the Advancement of General Systems Theory (1956), reprinted in *Classics of Organization Theory*. 265.

23. Katz and Kahn refer to equifinality as the ability of a system (organization) to reach the same final state (mature VNSA) from different initial conditions (system of violence) and by different paths of development. Ibid., 267.

24. David Eshel, "The Rise and Fall of the Al Aqsa Martyrs Brigades," *Jane's Intelligence Review* (June 2002, Vol. 14, No. 6), 20.

25. Ibid., 21.

26. Chapters included Nablus, Jenin, Tulkarm, Ramallah, Bethlehem, and Hebron. Ibid., 23.

27. Ibid., 22.

28. Katz and Kahn, *The Social Psychology of Organizations*, 52.

29. According to NPR reporter Emily Harris, "Some 90 U.S. troops have been killed by hostile fire since May 1 (2003), when President Bush announced an end to major combat. Many of the attacks on American forces appear to be coming from Iraqis loyal to Saddam Hussein's regime." From "U.S. Troop Toll Mounts in Iraq," *NPR Morning Edition*, October 2, 2003.

30. Katz and Kahn, *The Social Psychology of Organizations*, 84.

31. A comprehensive examination of typical forms of support for insurgents, which also applies to other VNSAs, is offered in Daniel Byman, Peter Chalk, Bruce Hoffman, William Rosenau, and David Brannan, *Trends in Outside Support for Insurgent Movements* (Santa Monica, CA: RAND, 2001), 83–99.

32. Angel Rabasa and Peter Chalk, *Colombian Labyrinth: The Synergy of Drugs and Insurgency and its Implications for Regional Stability* (Santa Monica, CA: RAND Project Air Force, 2001), 26.

33. Suzanne Lassen, "Drug Trafficking and Terrorism in Colombia," in Barry Rubin, ed., *The Politics of Counter Terrorism: The Ordeal of Democratic States* (Washington, DC: The John Hopkins Foreign Policy Institute, 1990), 112.

34. Rabasa and Chalk, *Colombian Labyrinth*, 24.

35. According to Rabasa and Chalk, the FARC "took advantage of a cease fire with the government of President Belisario Betancur from 1984 to 1987 to expand and consolidate its operations in resource rich areas," including cattle in the eastern plains, agriculture in Uraba and Santander, oil in the Magdalena valley, and gold in Antioquia. Ibid., 25.

36. I. M. Jawahar and Gary L. McLaughlin, "Toward a Descriptive Stakeholder Theory: An Organizational Life Cycle Approach," *The Academy of Management Review* (Briarcliff Manor, NY: July 2001, vol. 26, issue 3). Obtained through ProQuest (no page number available).

37. Rabasa and Chalk, *Colombian Labyrinth*, 26.

38. Mary Jo Hatch, *Organization Theory: Modern, Symbolic, and Postmodern Perspectives* (Oxford, United Kingdom: Oxford University Press, 1997), 79–80.

39. Katz and Kahn, *Social Psychology of Organizations*, 84.

40. Cited in Augustus Richard Norton, *Amal and the Shi'a: Struggle for the Soul of Lebanon* (Austin, TX: University of Texas Press, 1987), 168–69.

41. Hatch, *Organization Theory*, 65.

42. The full extent of diaspora support to the LTTE is superbly detailed in Byman et al., *Trends*, 42–55.

43. Ibid., 51.

44. Ibid., 45.

45. Ibid., 46.

46. Approaches for dealing with stakeholders are adopted from research by several organizational theorists into understanding stakeholder salience to a given company throughout its development. Stakeholder dependency theory is admirably discussed in Jawahar and McLaughlin, "Toward a Descriptive Stakeholder Theory."

47. Ibid.

48. During the 1990s, the LTTE assassinated leading moderates and scholars in Sri Lanka. Byman et al., *Trends*, 47.

49. Katz and Kahn, *Social Psychology*, 84–85.

50. Katz and Kahn, *Social Psychology*, 53.

51. Ibid., 53.

52. Ibid., 53.

53. Katz and Kahn, *Social Psychology*, 385.

54. Ibid., 386.

55. Ibid., 385.

56. Ibid., 388.

57. Thomas G. Cummings and Christopher G. Worley, *Organization Development and Change* (Cincinnati, OH: South Western College Publishing, 1997), 480.

58. Peter L. Bergen, *Holy War, Inc.: Inside the Secret World of Osama bin Laden* (New York: The Free Press, 2001), 149.

59. Ibid., 107.

60. Ibid., 107.

61. Ibid., 108.

62. Ibid., 55.

63. Hatch, *Organization Theory*, 371.

64. Chris Argyris and Donald Schon, *Organizational Learning II: Theory, Method and Practice* (Reading, MA: Addison Wesley Publishing Company, 1996), 20.

65. Bergen, *Holy War*, 176.

66. Ibid., 181.

67. Ibid., 167.

68. Hatch, *Organization Theory*, 372.

69. Argyris and Schon, *Organizational Learning*, 20.

70. Hatch, *Organization Theory*, 101.

71. Ibid., 103.

72. Explained by Hatch, *Organization Theory*, 105–10, drawing on Henry Mintzberg, *The Design School: Reconsidering the Basic Premises of Strategic Management* (New York: John Wiley and Sons, 1990).

73. Ibid., 108.

74. Selznick, "Foundations of the Theory of Organization." Reprinted in Shafritz and Ott, *Classics of Organization Theory*, 125.

75. Ibid.

76. Hatch, *Organization Theory,* 113.

77. Typical insurgent strategies are expertly discussed by Bard E. O'Neill in *Insurgency in the Modern World* (Boulder, CO: Westview Press, 1980), 141.

78. The status of non-state armed groups in the Caucasus region is well covered in Anna Matveeva and Duncan Hiscock, eds., *The Causcus: Armed and Divided,* (London: Saferworld, 2003), 62.

79. Ibid., 62.

80. Extracted from the official website of *Hizb ut-Tahrir,* accessed on December 27, 2003, at www.hizb-ut-tahrir.org.

81. Ibid., 168.

82. Ibid., 170.

83. Katz and Kahn, *Social Psychology,* 428.

84. Ibid., 430.

85. John Arquilla and David Ronfeldt, *Networks and Netwars* (Santa Monica, CA: RAND Corporation, 2001), 35–36.

86. Ibid., 37.

87. Katz and Kahn refer to this as the "production" sub-system; however, this label is too limited for the varied tasks associated with it. *Social Psychology,* 84.

88. Charles W. Kegley and Eugene R. Wittkopf, *World Politics: Trend and Transformation* (New York: Bedford/St. Martins, 2001), 12.

89. Quoted in Bergen, *Holy War, Inc.,* 95–96.

90. There are numerous alternatives to these labels; however, there is some general agreement on changes in differentiation and integration during the course of a VNSA's life. For alternatives to life cycle constructs, we recommend reviewing the following: Richard L. Daft, *Organization Theory and Design* (Mason, OH: Thomson South-western, 2004); Robert E. Quinn and Kim Cameron, "Organizational Life Cycles and Some Shifting Criteria of Effectiveness" (*Management Science,* 29, 1983); John R. Kimberly, Robert H. Miles, and Associates, *The Organizational Life Cycle* (San Francisco, CA: Jossey Bass Inc., Publishers, 1980); and Larry E. Greiner, "Evolution and Revolution as Organizations Grow" (*Harvard Business Review,* July–August, 1972).

91. Clifford E. Simonsen and Jeremy R. Spindlove, *Terrorism Today: The Past, the Players, the Future* (Upper Saddle River, NJ: Prentice Hall, 2000), 60–61.

92. Katz and Kahn, *The Social Psychology,* 71.

93. Based on Larry Greiner's model of organizational life cycles. Evaluated in Hatch, *Organization Theory,* 174.

94. Katz and Kahn stress the importance of coordinating the inputs, productions, and outputs so that "correct levels of raw materials are brought into the organization" and so outputs (sales in the case of businesses, but violence in the case of VNSAs) are in balance with planned production. Discussed in Hatch, *Organization Theory,* 178.

95. See the U.S. Department of State report *Patterns of Global Terrorism 2002.*

96. Rabasa and Chalk, *Colombian Labyrinth,* 30–31.

5

Violent Non-State Actors

Standing among heavily laden fruit trees with the murky waters of the Syr Darya flowing nearby, it is difficult to envision the fierce fighting that occurred in November 1998 between Tajik government forces and the private army of a renegade Uzbek warlord. Taking advantage of a puzzle-work of borders that delineate the Ferghana Valley, Colonel Makhmud Khudoiberdiyev led nine hundred armed militia in a raid into Tajikistan from Uzbekistan, seizing security installations in the northern town of Khujand. As many as 200 were killed and 500 injured, including innocent civilians, in the two weeks of fighting. Colonel Khudoiberdiyev recruited locally from a growing pool of disaffected young men, gained training and weapons from fighters in Afghanistan, and took advantage of Dushanbe's inability to secure its northern region.

COL. KHUDOIBERDIYEV IS CHARACTERISTIC of many similarly aggressive and disproportionately strong warlords in the region and around the globe. But warlords with private militias are only one type of VNSA in the region, which includes militant religious movements, ethno-political groups, and transnational criminal organizations (TCO). The Islamic Movement of Uzbekistan (IMU), for example, represents a hybrid VNSA. It brought considerable instability to Central Asia in the late 1990s. Fighting during 1999 and 2000 in the Pamirs and Ferghana Valley resulted in the deaths of approximately twenty-seven Uzbek and fifty-five Kyrgyz soldiers. Once operating from mountain bases in Tajikistan, the IMU engaged in terrorist and guerrilla tactics in a self-proclaimed effort to establish an Islamic state in the Ferghana. Ostensibly motivated by faith, the IMU financed operations with funds from the Taliban in Afghanistan, narco-trafficking, small arms proliferation, and probably human smuggling. Prior to their defeat during the U.S. military's operations in Afghanistan, the IMU epitomized the character and activities of a VNSA system at the nucleus of regional and transnational security challenges.

This chapter breaks out and examines the many VNSA found across the geo-political landscape with two inter-related typologies—one general, one specific. Open systems theory provides the skeleton on which we can flesh out several "species" of VNSA based on broadly similar identity-driven strategies and functions, providing rules of thumb for determining key properties like negative entropy and congruence. As we mine the functions of each VNSA type, we unearth highly specific patterns of activity that pertain only to a single group. Generally, VNSA are oriented toward either a transactional or a transcendental agenda, coloring every function with its priorities and culture. More specifically, VNSA can be broken out in terms of functional continuities into warlords, TCO, militant religious movements, ethno-political groups and ideological or interest-based groups. In reality, most VNSA are hybrids, reflecting both types of strategies and functional aspects of multiple group types.

Transcendental VNSA build group cohesion and purpose around a value system with emphasis on ideology, religion, the supernatural, or some type of existential moral code. The transcendental VNSA inculcates a value system that encourages its members to embrace a subjective reality. Inculcating members to a transcendental value system is slow; however, once embraced, these value systems are robust and maintain loyalty of individual members against long odds and in tough times. It is ideal for sustaining role behaviors. It is for this reason the most violent, unconstrained VNSA typically are transcendental in nature—if their action is sanctioned by the divine, concerns over a low probability of success, breaking human laws, or even losing one's life are minimized. In fact, the very rejection of these normal constraints on behavior can become a sacred duty.

Transactional VNSA, on the other hand, operate for more pedestrian reasons. Typically, these types of VNSA exist for the purpose of making money, acquiring resources, or expanding a base of power. Purely transactional VNSA have value systems that encourage utility-maximizing behavior within organizational boundaries. An organization based on transactional values, such as making money, can be built quickly; however, undermining the ability of the organization to acquire resources and provide tangible rewards easily impacts them. As a result, internal discipline is often required to manage utility-maximizing behavior. Essentially, the odds of defection are higher if profit or power is available elsewhere with acceptable risk.

Knowing the type of VNSA one is facing—transactional versus transcendental—is key to a countering strategy. Transactional VNSA, for example, build negative entropy primarily through resource acquisition. Hence, the

United States enjoyed considerable initial success against various drug cartels by interrupting financial resources.[1] Targeting the financial assets of al Qaida—clearly a transcendental VNSA—may not be met with the same success, as that group acquires much of its negative entropy from the socialization of its members to the value system. The most effective VNSA combine transactional and transcendental approaches to gathering negative entropy. Should the VNSA enter a financially challenging period, for example, faith will help keep the VNSA together. Conversely, should the VNSA go through an ideological crisis, transactional rewards and sanctions will bolster the organization.

Combining transcendental and transactional methods is useful in more than just crisis—an ability to appeal to a broader array of potential stakeholders increases the VNSA's ability to grow more quickly and acquire more resources. In the absence of any crisis, a "double-barreled" VNSA has greater potential to overshadow any competitors it may have. Hamas is a classic example. Hamas has substantial financial support as well as a deep ideological commitment from its members. Thus, this group has far greater stores of negative entropy—even in the face of an aggressive Israeli response—than does a similar group in the region, the Al Aqsa Martyrs' Brigade.

The most common types of VNSA are warlords with private militias, TCO, militant religious movements, and a potential new breed of VNSA—interest-driven violent opposition groups, such as anti-globalizationists and eco-terrorists. Although more detailed case studies of specific groups is warranted, our initial application of the systems approach to these categories offers insights that we hope will shape a nested strategy focusing on VNSA generally, categorically, and specifically. Of note, we intentionally do not consider that "terrorist groups" as an organizational type—terrorism is a form of warfare and tactic. While a group like the IMU is clearly a "terrorist group," the moniker is of limited value—it is more than an organization that uses terrorism to pursue its goals. Big difference b/w Hoffman J&NYPD

I. Warlords

The opening vignette draws attention to Colonel Khudoiberidyev, a warlord in Central Asia who briefly seized the Tajik town of Khojand in 1998. He is representative of most warlords, which are defined as leaders of armed groups that control territory locally and at the same time act "financially and politically in the international system without interference by state(s) in which [they are] based."[2] A warlord can also be viewed as a military commander exercising civil power in a region, whether in nominal allegiance to the national government or in defiance of it. Warlords and their private armies are mature gangs with memberships ranging from around one hundred to several thousand. They are also distinct from insurgents. Where the insurgent draws support from the local population, the warlord preys on the population. Although the warlord recruits from the community, he does not ultimately depend on its popular support for any political end game.[3]

Environmental Predators

The warlord exists in an environment where state power is weak, or more likely, non-existent. Warlords in Central Asia, the Horn of Africa, and even western Africa thrive in terminally ill states or in the absence of any sort of notion of statehood, state power, or state identity. Next, they are likely to emerge where the roots of violence run deep, the transformational engines are strong (especially the presence of competing identities), and control by the state is sketchy at best. The individuals living in these failed states would not refer to themselves as "Afghanis" or "Somalis"; rather, they would refer to themselves as Pashtun, Dir, Isaaq, or in some cases, Muslim. The identities can be reinforced along exclusionary lines and/or manufactured into something new and symbolic, giving the outsider—few of which would have any reason to identify with the state anyway—a reason to desire membership. Warlords typically have some type of revenue-generating scheme that is usually parasitic on the environment, be it imposing taxes on goods traversing their territory, drug sales, protection rackets (to include protecting drugs, for example), or other type of extortion.

Thuggish Systems

The warlord himself is leader, commander, dictator, judge, and jury. While he has lieutenants to help him carry out functions, his word is final. The warlord combines charisma with cunning opportunism—the consummate identity entrepreneur. Through membership in his private army, he uses his recruitment and socialization functions to offer valuable incentives that the state typically cannot offer, such as a small paycheck and shelter. Discipline is harsh. Recruits are paid, but are expected to be absolutely loyal. In this regard, the warlord generates a sense of purpose and belonging. He is able to exploit existing identity cleavages, most often capitalizing on socio-economic disparities along ethnic and/or regional lines as well as tribal and clan loyalties.

The warlord typically has some form of professional military or at least extensive paramilitary experience. He tends to be highly fluid, moving in and out of government as a function of shifting alliances, power struggles, and often greed. More often, a warlord will pursue an alliance with the state based on control over some type of economic activity that will generate revenue. In the most lucrative of situations, warlords are given control over casinos, drug routes, industries, or trade. When government cooperation or cooptation is not sufficiently profitable, warlords often turn to overt criminal behaviors. As an organized and relatively capable military unit, local police or civilians are not likely to offer much resistance.

Additional characteristics of private armies ensure their elusiveness as a potential adversary. They rarely wear uniforms or display rank, making it difficult to distinguish them from civilians. Control functions are usually driven by personal relationships. Unit size is not standardized, rendering unit designation useless as a means of assessing movements, personnel, and equipment numbers. This ambiguity extends to the rank structure. Non-commissioned officers are an extreme rarity. Rather, there is usually a single officer commanding an indistinguishable band of irregulars. The officers are often chosen based on clan structures rather than on merit. Among the Tajik forces that compromised part of the Northern Alliance in Afghanistan, a fifteen-year-old boy—the youngest commander in the Afghan civil war, led one unit of approximately three hundred men. Mohammed Aqa Humayun Khadim took command of his unit upon the death of his father, an ethnic Uzbek chieftain of Bolak Kushlaq. Rising every morning at 0500 to pray, Humayun issued orders to soldiers well beyond him in age and experience. As the soldiers moved out to man the six tanks and truck-mounted BM-21 rocket launcher under his command, Humayun was quoted as saying, "they were my father's soldiers and now they belong to me."[4]

Most VNSA do not have the attitude, structure, or effectiveness of professional military units.[5] Instead, they are "organized around the magnetism of their leaders" and rely on "their frightening behavior and appearance."[6] The warlord relies on collective violence to sanction uncooperative communities, collecting taxes by generating fear of lost limbs, slain family members, or destroyed property. As asymmetric warriors, these private armies rarely engage government forces or other warlords in open battle, although the most successful private armies are "capable of absorbing defeat in one district and executing revenge at another venue."[7] Tactically, the First Brigade mentioned at the beginning of the chapter demonstrated greater combat capabilities than most private armies—yet, even it was defeated by a rag-tag Tajik army.

Kahn's charms

Ismail Kahn, one of the warlords in post-Taliban Afghanistan, personifies the charming thug sketched here. Kahn controlled most of western Afghanistan from his seat of power in Herat where he was once the governor and has amassed a considerable following. His personal charisma was boosted by his history of fighting the Soviets and the Taliban. He personally listened to the needs and complaints of his populace. He, like his followers, is Tajik, a very distinct ethnic group in Afghanistan differentiated by language, geography, and their version of Islam. Herat lies about as far away from Kabul as one can go, and the exceptionally poor state of the transportation network magnifies the geographic distance. It is the perfect setup for a warlord—a charismatic leader coupled with a country conditioned to violence, multiple identity cleavages, and a central government that is nearly powerless outside the capital.

Kahn's job of making Herat his fiefdom was made easier by the fact that Herat is the most economically prosperous province in Afghanistan; the local roads are mostly paved, the city is generally clean, and there is, relatively speaking, security. The province's position near the borders with Iran and Turkmenistan helps bring millions of dollars in tax revenue every month, little of which is sent to Kabul. Almost a darling of the western press, Kahn referred to himself as the Emir of Herat. Popularity aside, Kahn is like most warlords in having an exceptionally strong maintenance sub-system, and he was not hesitant in handing out harsh sanctions to defectors and violators of group norms. Kahn's conversion sub-system was impressive as well. Training and production functions created a private army that was outfitted and armed from suppliers in Iran. Khan was ultimately unable to adapt his VNSA to a changing environment, resulting in his ultimate removal by the central government in 2004.

Somali warlordism

The warlords in Somalia represent perhaps the worst in warlordism. Shifting alliances between the Soviets and the West, nepotism, corruption, and authoritarianism during the 1960s, 1970s, and 1980s progressively weakened the Somali state and undermined the notion of Somali citizenship; individuals increasingly looked to their local clans for governance. By the 1980s, various clans attempted to overthrow President Siad Barre, and a variety of clan-based organizations existed outside of Somalia with the intent of overthrowing his government. When President Barre was forced from Mogadishu in 1991, the country of Somalia was thrown into a state of anarchy. Literally dozens of warlords vied for influence, tens of thousands of Somalis were killed or starved to death despite United Nations armed intervention, and hundreds of thousands of refugees fled to other areas in and outside the would-be country. To this day, despite several valiant attempts by well-intentioned organizations and individuals, no strong central government exists that can exert control over Somalia's clan-based warlords.

In late 2003, two important news headlines captured the violence in a telling way. Eight people were killed and ten wounded in the southern port of

Marka, ostensibly controlled by the Habar Gedir clan. The apparent cause of the violence stemmed from a decision from the leader of the Ayr sub-clan (of the Habar Gedir) in the region to impose taxes on the export of bananas through the port—a resource acquisition and disposal function. The businessmen running the port, all from the Sa'd sub-clan (also Habar Gedir), would end up paying these taxes. When the two sub-clans could not reach an amicable agreement, they both sent in their private militias to fight it out, and eight people were killed.[8] The second headline concerned a recently released United Nations report indicating that the terrorists responsible for the November 2002 bombing of the Paradise Hotel in Kenya used Somalia as a training ground, transit point, and escape route.[9] Both events—one resulting in a local shootout, the other an international terrorist incident—have the same roots: warlordism run amok.

A final vignette perhaps best captures the depth of power and influence warlords exert. In 1992, reports ran in the European press of "unnamed European firms" contracting with local warlords to dump toxic waste both in Somalia and off Somalia's shores. The United Nations Environment Program was called in to investigate, and the Italian parliament issued a report later in the decade. Several European "firms"—really front companies created by the Italian mafia—contracted with local Somali warlords to ship hundreds of thousands of tons of toxic industrial waste from Europe to Somalia. The warlords would typically claim to be legitimate representatives of Somalia, but usually were little more than petty sub-clan leaders who managed to make contact with the representatives of these front companies. Put differently, one type of VNSA signed a multi-million dollar contract with another type of VNSA to ship a tightly controlled substance from one continent to another—all outside the auspices of the international system.[10] The incongruity is striking: two VNSAs consummated an illegal operation by signing a legally binding contract. While appropriate, "honor among thieves" is simply inadequate to fully capture the mockery this particular transaction makes of international norms and conduct.

Alive and Killing

As a transactional VNSA, warlords build negative entropy by acquiring resources and sustain congruence by providing tangible value to stakeholders. Warlords themselves largely define their strategies as the pursuit of resource capture—acquiring money, controlling markets (especially illegal ones), expanding power or territorial control. Member loyalty is purchased, and it is for sale. A quick review of the warlord dynamics in Afghanistan illustrates this well—shifting alliances, purchased armies, and fleeting loyalty were hallmarks of both the civil war and the U.S.-led Operation Enduring Freedom.

II. Transnational Criminal Organizations

In Colombia, a load of coca leaf imported from Peru is changed to coca paste in a jungle laboratory controlled by the FARC. In China, a shipload of counterfeit cigarettes made in the hinterlands is being shipped to Canada under the watchful eye of the Chinese Triads. In Romania, a young girl is kidnapped on her way to school and sold into sex slavery as part of a deal with the Russian Mafia. Several tons of small arms and ammunition make their way to Albania, amalgamated from all over the world in order to fulfill an order from the Kosovo Liberation Army. These are but a small handful of the transactions that occur outside state control by the prototypical transactional VNSA—the TCO.

TCO are transnational groups with a corporate structure whose "primary objective is to obtain money through illegal activities, often surviving on fear and corruption."[11] Like multinational corporations, TCO operate in several states simultaneously. Unlike multinational corporations (MNCs), they do so illegally. In this regard, Phil Williams suggests they are "transnational organizations par excellence" since they "operate outside the existing structures of authority and power in world politics and have developed sophisticated strategies for circumventing law enforcement in individual states and in the global community of states."[12]

Environmental Exploitation

TCO, unlike warlords, cannot exist exclusively in failed or failing states. Indeed, TCO often need successful states in order to operate effectively. These needs are multi-dimensional. First, the TCO support sub-system must leverage the transportation, communication, financial, and other infrastructures of successful states. To do this, TCO create legitimate "front" businesses,[13] or simply corrupt those who control legitimate ones. TCO have interesting stakeholder associations in that they also need the consumer demand generated by citizens of prospering states. Without a significant market demand for opium in Europe, poppy crops in Afghanistan could not be a lucrative investment for warlords and TCO.

Successful TCO take advantage of their environment, applying their adaptive and innovative organizational networks to a relationship with the global marketplace. Essentially, TCO link regions where failures in governance can be effectively exploited with regions where income levels can sustain consumption.[14] Failures in governance create political and economic space for growth.[15] Sanctuary is typically needed to produce illicit goods; it can come in the form of either a thoroughly corrupted government or an impotent one. Indeed, at the environmental level, TCO need a portfolio of conditions to most effectively carry out their functions. They thrive at niche construction.

Further, a fluid, networked control function allows the TCO to interact, responding quickly to local conditions while avoiding any concentration of resources or capability. The distributed quality of the TCO control networks makes them particularly difficult to assess, monitor, and attack.

Explanations for the existence of TCO are varied. A common perception of TCO is that they are merely powerful black marketers; economists have led the analytic pack in developing theory and analyzing these groups. Economists generally analyze organized crime—a representative but not exhaustive element of TCO—with criminal monopoly. That is, a criminal organization takes over an illegal market in a region and earns income persistently greater than could be earned by other activities, legal or illegal.[16] Thomas Schelling updated this idea by pointing out that organized crime can also be an extortionist of legitimate providers of goods and services, especially where the organization had been able to corrupt legitimate state functions.[17] Criminologists also use a market-oriented approach. For example, Gresham Sykes makes the argument that if organizations can cheaply use violence to establish a monopoly over a lucrative illegal market, they will do so:

> The existence of a strong and persistent demand for such illegal goods and services as illicit sex, drugs, and gambling presents an opportunity to make enormous profits. The cost of providing such goods and services is low, and the price can be set high by those able and willing to circumvent the law in creation of a monopoly based on the intimidation of small operators and competitors.[18]

Sociologists explain organized crime as a "way up" for those elements of society that are closed off to legitimate paths to success. For example, Daniel Bell described the phenomenon as a "ladder of social mobility" in America. Italian and Irish immigrants arriving in the first quarter of the twentieth century, for example, often turned to gangs and other organizations involved in illegal activities for status and economic gain, as other ethnic groups controlled legitimate organizations. A similar explanation is often given for inner-city gangs in modern America.

Criminal Systems

At the system-level, TCO are transactional organizations that acquire, produce, and distribute illegal goods and services. Criminal groups typically do not start out as TCO, but may develop into sophisticated transnational players over time. The evolutionary process can be understood in three phases, which parallel the organizational life cycle. In the first, the predatory stage, localized gangs use violence to control turf.[19] These gangs gain recognition from other power brokers, including legitimate authorities as well as influential VNSAs. For example, gangs in the Batken oblast of southern Kyrgyzstan probably controlled localized heroin distribution networks, drawing the attention of more dominate actors like the IMU or possibly corrupt Uzbek and Kyrgyz governmental security forces. A parasitical stakeholder relationship develops in which the more powerful state and VNSAs manipulate the gangs to their own purposes. Over time, a symbiotic relationship forms with "the host itself dependent on the parasite" for sustainment.[20] In the Osh and Batken oblasts as well as tribal areas of Turkmenistan, major Russian and Afghan narco-traffickers need local markets to not only move product across frontiers, but to develop local clientele.

TCO activity is of more importance than the vast amount of ordinary criminal activity that goes on within states on a daily basis for three primary reasons. First, a TCO has well-developed sub-systems; the level of organization, capacity and sophistication needed by an organization to transport large amounts of material across such great distances requires greater functional differentiation and sophistication. Organizations with these attributes are typically powerful enough to directly challenge, successfully evade, undermine, or corrupt the state. As a result, the very existence of such organizations weakens the state system itself. Second, the production function enables the TCO to provide goods and services that the state typically refuses to provide or has refused to allow the free market to provide—illegal arms, prostitution, drugs, and human smuggling. Since the state typically has deemed such goods and services to be socially, politically, or economically harmful, their introduction undermines the goals of the state. Furthermore, TCO often introduce counterfeit legitimate goods including money itself, electronics, digital media, or an increasingly common example, prescription drugs. The introduction of counterfeits distorts the free market and undermines legitimate businesses. Third, economic transactions controlled by TCO deprive legitimate businesses of revenue and the state of associated taxes. The large amount of goods and services controlled by TCO represent significant amounts of money. Moreover, when a TCO controls all or a portion of a given market, that market becomes criminalized, with all the associated negative externalities—increased violence, increased law enforcement and prosecution costs, and an increase in the destabilization of the state system.

The TCO is distinguished from localized warlords by its stakeholder relationships; TCO typically use strategic alliances with other criminals as a means of increasing profit and reducing risk;[21] for example, narco-traffickers in Central Asia are tied in to the Russian mafia and the Chinese Triads. Others point to the role of Iranian drug lords, such as Hajj Bhulam Baloch. That said, Iran is responsible for more than 80 percent of the global seizures of opium due to an extensive interdiction effort that involves concrete dam barriers, observations posts, 30,000 law enforcement personnel, and the death penalty for narcotics possession.[22]

Like warlords, crime bosses and drug lords capitalize on the conditions of violence to aid recruitment. While not necessarily charismatic leaders, they do offer membership in a group that is often defined along family, clan, or ethnic lines. Most importantly, they offer steady income. The IMU reportedly offered new militants up to $100 a day, with commanders receiving up to $500.[23] When compared to $1–$3 per day for most rural people, the risk of being arrested is assessed as worth taking for a larger number of individuals. Even though traffickers get 90 percent of the "value-added" for heroin in a producer country, farmers still get a 6 percent cut, processors 2 percent, and traders 2 percent.[24] In terms of specific membership, reports indicate that 65.3 percent of the region's drug traffickers are Tajik citizens, 10.8 percent are Russian citizens, 9.2 percent are Kyrgyz citizens, and 8.2 percent are Turkmen citizens.[25] Looking behind the numbers, it is interesting to note the growing role of women in narco-trafficking. Based on drug arrests, women in Kazakhstan have increased their participation from approximately 3 percent in 1996 to 12.2 percent.[26] This figure is up to 35 percent for Tajikistan.[27] According to Martha Brill Olcott and Natalia Udalova, women accept less pay, are more protective of their sources, and generally receive more lenient sentences.[28] The TCO in the Central Asian region recognize this and use it to their advantage. Women have a lower potential cost for participating in narco-trafficking and are thus turning to them to maintain their activities.

Criminal Aggression

TCO are the masters of collective violence at the low end of the conflict spectrum, applying lethal force in a highly organized, selective, and compartmented manner. Widespread street knowledge of the murders, kidnappings, and gunfights associated with organized crime is enough to maintain discipline and usually deter would-be competitors. Violence can also be used for other purposes, especially if the VNSA is not purely a TCO. For example, a string of high-profile kidnappings by the IMU in the so-called "Osh Knot" of the Ferghana Valley, including Japanese and American tourists, were largely for ransom. When one combines criminal intent with the political and religious motivations of hybrid VNSAs like the IMU, collective violence can take various forms, to include terrorism and guerrilla attacks.

Drawing again on the pioneering work of Phil Williams, there are three general types of violence associated with TCO. Although he focuses on narco-trafficking, our research suggests equally valid application to networks associated with other illegal commodities. First, there is violence to protect profits and turf.[29] Turf fights are typically between TCO, while the government is more likely attacking profits. While violence may be used against the government, TCO often rely on bribes and payoffs to secure an official blind eye. Indeed, Professor Anara Tabyshalieva of the Institute for Regional Studies in Kyrgyzstan describes the Central Asian drug mafia as a "model of inter-ethnic cooperation,"[30] suggesting violence within the drug mafia is quite low. For example, many experts regard the IMU raids into the Ferghana Valley of Kyrgyzstan and Uzbekistan in 1999 and 2000 as primarily for protecting drug routes. But true to the TCO's creed, co-optation is preferable to violence; indeed, the border raids appear to have been limited after 2000 because the IMU was able to co-opt the border guards. Additionally, most experts accept that the Russian 201st Motorized Rifle Division along the Tajikistan border and other Russian border troops are co-opted as well, and in on the trade. Among the more damaging reports are accusations that Russian military aircraft are used to move drugs from Tajikistan to airports outside Moscow.[31]

An additional type of violence is a tool found in the maintenance subsystem, specifically for rewards and sanctions. TCO are notorious for using violence within their own ranks to maintain discipline, enforce contracts, and address overly ambitious individuals in their own ranks. Again, this type of violence is very measured; the threat of violence is often all that is needed to ensure such internal discipline is maintained. The last type of violence involves drug addicts committing crimes to support their habits and users perpetrating violence while under the influence of mind-altering substances.[32] There is strong evidence that drug-related crimes are climbing steadily upward, catching the West and Russia.[33] As isolated behaviors, these acts of violence do not contribute to our understanding of VNSAs; however, we consider growing drug use by VNSA members to be both likely and dangerous. Even with religious prohibitions, addiction is on the rise, especially among the dispossessed youth that are ripened by the roots of violence.[34] For relief organizations and military operators alike, countering the threats posed by civilian-clothed, networked irregulars that are simultaneously intoxicated will be a significant challenge.

Dark Dynamics

The dark dynamics of globalization are contributing to the rapid proliferations of TCO. Again, we turn to Central Asia to provide illustrations. According to the UNESCO, the Kazakh Security Committee recently identified more than 125 organized crime groups in Central Asia.[35] Thirty of these groups, and possibly another ninety or more identified by Kyrgyzstan, are directly tied to the drug trade. The rise of transnational economic activity has made it significantly easier to disguise illicit sales, launder money, transfer product, and communicate with strategic allies.[36] This dynamic has also resulted in the emergence of several global commodities—the most destructive and lucrative of which are narcotics. Indeed, their raison d'être is controlling black or gray economic markets, the ultimate expression of transactional values. Weakening the resource acquisition function is among the best ways to weaken TCO. In the United States, taking down organized crime involved seizing assets and convictions on minor financial transgressions.[37]

III. Militant Religious Movements

The call to prayer resonates throughout the bazaar in Andijan, a leafy provincial capital in the Ferghana Valley. A diverse array of men stream through the market stalls and pile out of Daewoo mini-vans. Some wear heavy beards and flowing robes while others are clean-shaven and sport western attire. The former take greater risks since the Uzbekistan security services are known to monitor this mosque and keep records of men that "appear" to have connections to militant religious movements like the IMU. The main Friday mosque, or *Juma* Mosque, quickly overflows, leaving many to unroll their prayer rugs on the surrounding streets. The strong showing is not surprising given the Ferghana Valley's reputation as a center of Islamist activity. Militant religious movements such as those born in the Ferghana Valley, the jungles of Southeast Asia, or the streets of Western Europe, pose a grave threat to security.

Environmental Callings

Militant religious movements have received increasing global attention, largely as a result of the September 11, 2001, terrorist attacks on the World Trade Center and the Pentagon. However, those attacks only punctuated a trend toward increased religious extremism that began decades earlier.[38] There is no clear consensus on what specific environmental factors are contributing to the rise in militant religious movements, only that such a rise is in fact occurring. That said, the most militant and dangerous organizations appear to emerge and thrive where the conditions of violence are potent and strength in governance is insufficient to curb radicalism. Islamic militants are the most obvious of such movements; however, Hindus, Christians, Jews, and other religions suffer their own militant offspring.

A common environmental explanation for the rise of militant religious movements is the increased contact between cultures and religions as a result of globalization. This contact comes in the form of greater access to all forms of information. Greater contact with outside cultures and religions may be perceived as threatening to cultural purists or fundamentalists, leading some elite to demonize the alien believers. For example, many of Osama bin Laden's speeches point to the threat Christianity, Judaism, and Western culture pose to the Islamic world and criticize the Saudi royal family for cooperating with associated countries like the United States. Bin Laden was especially angry at the House of Saud for allowing non-Muslim soldiers to be based in Saudi Arabia throughout the 1990s.

A related set of theories suggests that religion is often a cover for the other causes of conflict outlined in our framework. Despite the religious-laced language and rhetoric, the amount of Sikh violence in India is often blamed on political, economic, and social factors, rather than explained as religious-based violence.[39] In one of the few empirical studies of religious violence, RAND analyst Heather Gregg found that once other significant factors were controlled, religion per se failed to show a statistically and practically significant influence on the presence of violence.[40] Rather, individuals rooted in certain circumstances related to our conditions of violence often decided to use religion as a pretext for conflict. This seems to support our argument that identity shapes but does not cause conflict.

A third explanation that also fits with our framework suggests religion is manipulated by those seeking power. Asahara, the spiritual leader of Aum Shinrikyo, reportedly had desires to be Japan's prime minister, and his organization actually ran in parliamentary elections in 1998. Indeed, extensions of this idea essentially argue that violence actually needs religion; those who have decided to use collective violence as a tool to achieve their goals may need to exploit religion and religious symbols in order to create the necessary level of emotional commitment needed to incite such violence.[41] Moreover, religion is manipulated to give a divine sanction to behaviors that run counter to social norms, or are strictly illegal.

Of particular concern are those militant religious organizations that have been smoldering for years unbeknownst to the state where they reside. While certainly not an armed group, the Falun Gong's ability to hide from Chinese authorities and shock the government with a massive collective "sit-in" in July 1999 illustrates the ability to take even an authoritarian state by surprise.[42] The complexity of militant religious VNSA and their sub-system functionality has certainly increased with time. Enabled by the Internet, the Christian Patriots, for example, appear to have used a "leaderless resistance" organizational typology to communicate, or at least give suggestive guidance to those who follow its ethos. The 1996 bombing in Oklahoma City by Timothy McVeigh illustrates the power of such communication, despite obscurity.[43]

Given the lack of clarity regarding the environmental effects, it is difficult to shape the environment in a way that discourages militant religious movements from emerging. Indeed, attempting to do so can backfire; perceptions of the state "meddling" with religious issues can quickly give rise to the very violence the state is attempting to prevent. President Karimov of Uzbekistan is currently facing this dilemma; in an attempt to prevent the IMU from gaining too much support or influence in his country, he cracked down on Islam in general—and is now viewed as an enemy of Islam rather than a protector of the state.

Indeed, militant religious movements may prove to be the greatest challenge to the state system. At the state level, many religious militants do not wish to be ruled by apostates or those who do not share their beliefs—illegitimacy. For example, it was not enough for the Islamic Jihad to overthrow what it saw as an insufficiently Islamic government in Egypt; it must help redraw the map in the Middle East altogether. To do that, it merged with a global Islamic fundamentalist umbrella organization, the al Qaida network. Presently, Islamic Jihad helps recruit, train, and equip militants to attack on continental fronts.

The September 11, 2001, attacks zeroed the world's attention in on Central Asia and the Middle East, where the phenomenon of religious conflict is far from new. Assuming all militant religious movements are Islamic in nature, however, is a mistake. The Christian Patriotic Union in the United States, Aum Shinrikyo in Japan, Kach in Israel, and various Hindu groups in India earn membership in this notorious club. Other militant organizations, such as the Irish Republican Army and the Kosovo Liberation Army, have religious undercurrents. Indeed, one can make the argument that many eco-terrorists are following a religion of sorts, whereby "earth-worshippers" resort to violence to combat what they see as defilements of their goddess.

With these caveats, it is a mistake to underestimate the proliferation of Islamic militant movements. At the great risk of over-simplifying, these groups spring from several conditions. As mentioned earlier, the Muslim Brotherhood, the father of the Egyptian Islamic Jihad, owes its creation partly to poverty in Egypt and the ideological formulations of Sayyid Qutb. The Palestinian Liberation Organization was created partially in response to socio-economic conditions and the Zionist movement. In fact, the creation of the state of Israel contributed to the formation of a variety of religious militant organizations, both Jewish and Muslim—an environmental response. The legacy of that conflict is two of the most developed and deadly religious VNSA in the world—Hezbollah and Hamas. Al Qaida raised the bar by going global. By rejecting the western notion of the state as a secular entity, al Qaida is the latest organization to try to create a collective, perhaps a modern *dar al Islam*,[44] the equivalent of an Islamic state, or possibly even the re-establishment of the Islamic Caliphate as it existed in A.D. 600–1200.[45]

Interestingly, the West has underestimated religious militant organizations over the past few decades. For example, the United States was caught by surprise when Islamic militants stormed the American Embassy in Tehran and the Shah fled into exile as part of the 1979 Iranian revolution. Although the world was shocked by Islamic Jihad's assassination of Anwar Sadat on October 6,

1981, the event was not generally perceived as a threat to non-Muslim governments. Even in 1991, a mere three years before the Taliban emerged, Graham Fuller wrote about Afghanistan:

> But the *mujahideen* almost surely will not be able to remain united, and the Islamists will be unable to control the country any more firmly than past Afghan regimes, including the communists, have been able to do. Any Islamic republic that might ever come into existence in Afghanistan will not replay the virulence and xenophobia of Iran, nor will it devote itself single-mindedly to opposition to the United States as Tehran has done.[46]

Further, Richard Betts argued in 1994: "Islam, for example, is a political force in countries as disparate as Egypt, Nigeria, Pakistan, and Indonesia. There is no evidence yet, however, of globally or even regionally coordinated action on the basis of religious motivation."[47] Attacks conducted by al Qaida and its related organizations since then highlight how very difficult it is to accurately forecast the threat.

Militant Believers

Looking again to the rich kaleidoscope of Central Asia, we can contrast some of the aspects of non-violent and militant religious organizations. Religious VNSA must be distinguished from non-violent, politically active religious movements. In addition to avoiding misguided generalizations, these groups warrant our consideration because the potential exists for currently peaceful movements to resort to violence in response to excessive state coercion or other failures in governance.

Religiously political

Political religious movements in the Central Asian region are currently entirely Islamic. Islamic nationalists have their roots in the Soviet era when unregistered mullahs led underground communities of believers. Great risks were taken to operate illegal mosques, open religious schools, and perform life cycle rituals.[48] Their activities tended to revolve around holy places, which provided a forum for the religious leaders, or *mullahs*, to address the *umma* outside of "official" mosques controlled by the Soviet state. By some estimates, there were over 1,800 clandestine mosques in 1987 as compared to 365 official ones.[49] Thus, the past half-century put the state in an adversarial position in relationship to the believer.

Independence brought an overt attempt by the clandestine Muslim community to integrate Islam with the emerging political system. For these emergent groups, Islam is an all-encompassing faith that cannot be divorced from the political, social, and economic life of the state. Among the several Islamic republican parties that emerged, the most organized and active is the Islamic Revival (or Renaissance) Party (IRP), which ultimately fractured into state-specific parties throughout Central Asia and the Caucasus. The general goals of the IRP include:

(1) Explain to the people the real meaning of the holy Koran and *hadith* (traditions of the prophet) and call the people to live and act according to the Koran and *hadith*;

(2) Fight national and racial discrimination, impudence, crime, alcoholism, and all other things forbidden by Islamic law (*shari'a*) through understanding and appeal;

(3) Educate young people in the principles of Islam and create instruction and training centers and *madrassahs* for this purpose;

(4) Ensure that the rights of all Muslims are exercised according to the Koran;

(5) Strengthen Islamic brotherhood, develop religious relations with the Muslim world, and seek a relationship of equal rights with representatives of other religions;

(6) Cooperate with other democratic parties and state organizations in all fields;

(7) Create philanthropic funds that will support anyone in need of help;

(8) Strengthen the family according to the principles of Islam and ensure the rights of women and children;

(9) Ensure the principles of Islamic economy and regain economic purity;

(10) Solve the problems of the people according to the holy Koran and *hadith*.[50]

Notably, these goals do not call for the dissolution of the secular state or establishment of an Islamic state. That said, achieving these objectives is only feasible in the context of an Islamic republic, or at least creating links between Islamic communities both inside and outside the auspices of the state system. The IRP also avoids calls for immediate violent action.[51] Thus, the Uzbek IRP works out of its Ferghana Valley strongholds, like Andijan, to train and socialize new clerics and renew adherence to Islam among the population. As articulated by Imam Abdul Ahmad in Namagan, associated with the IRP, "first Ferghana, then Uzbekistan and then the whole Central Asia will become an Islamic state."[52]

The IRP and other Islamic nationalist parties face significant obstacles to their long-term goals. Most importantly, the authoritarian regimes of the region have banned all Islamic political parties, resulting in thousands of Uzbeks crossing the border to the Kyrgyz side of the Ferghana Valley. The lone exception is Tajikstan where the IRP holds a role in government as a result of the peace accords. Second, government security services actively monitor suspected Islamists, accusing IRP members of being terrorists. Whether the label is warranted is a matter of some controversy. It is widely known that law enforcement officials consider a beard to be a sign of membership in the Islamic opposition, sufficiently telling of one's political views to warrant listing, harassment, arrest, or "disappearance." The first to go was Abdullo Utaev, the leader of the IRP in Uzbekistan. He was abducted in 1992 during the first year of independence and remains missing.[53] Since then, several additional waves of arrests targeting "Wahhabists" in Uzbekistan have occurred, although no reliable numbers on those arrested or missing are available.

In addition to state coercion, the IRP faces challenges from militant groups who accuse IRP leaders of cooperating with the government and of being co-opted by the official, state-controlled Islamic institutions. A fourth obstacle is the general political passivity of the region's Muslims, which is reinforced by a personal faith tradition. Given these trends and the persistent sources of tension outlined in chapter 2, we expect there to be increasing defections and fissures with the Islamic nationalist movement.

Militantly religious

Militant Islamists benefit from the continued failings of the moderate Islamic nationalists. They too have their roots in the Soviet period. The Basmachis, for example, resisted the early years of Soviet rule in the 1920s and 1930s. With some 20,000 fighters spread across the region, local *mullahs* led guerrilla operations against an ultimately more powerful Soviet Red Army. Today's militant Islamists share characteristics with extreme militant religious movements around the world.[54] Richard Shultz and William Olson summarize these characteristics in their 1994 work, *Ethnic and Religious Conflict: Emerging Threat to U.S. Security:*

(1) Militant religious political movements tend to view existing government authority as corrupt and illegitimate because they do not uphold religious values;
(2) They attack the inability of government to address the roots of violence;
(3) They are universalists, seeing their views as part of an inheritance for all believers, which orient them toward transnational activities and disregard for national boundaries;
(4) They are exclusionists, relegating all conflicting opinions to the margins or excluding them all together;
(5) They are willing to use coercion to achieve their true ends—compromise is unacceptable.[55]

In Central Asia, these qualities are primarily associated with a "purist" religious movement known locally as Wahhabism, or Salafism.[56] Originating in the harsh deserts of Najd, Saudi Arabia, Wahhabism arrived in Central Asia around 1912 by way of India and Afghanistan. Espousing a strict, puritanical version of Islam, Wahhabis are unwilling to entertain the theologies of the other four main Sunni schools of thought: Hanafi (the school of most Central Asian Muslims), Maliki, Shafi'i, and Hanbali.[57] The Wahhabi movement does have a doctrinal connection with the Hanbali School, which also emphasizes the Koran and *hadith* as the definitive sources of Islamic law. Such a rigorous interpretation leaves little room for cooperation with the state, Islamic institutions set up and managed by the state, or other faiths—any such cooperation is seen as violating stakeholder agreements. Indeed, it is not an exaggeration to declare that there is an evangelical war being waged between Christian missionaries and Wahhabi *mullahs* on the streets of Bishkek.

Wahhabi intolerance is compounded by a *jihad* culture that embraces a strict interpretation of the so-called verse of the sword, which translates "when the forbidden months are past, then fight and slay the Pagans wherever ye find them" (9:5).[58] Wahhabis believe this verse commands Muslims to attack disbelief until it is eradicated from the earth.[59] Placed in context, as argued by the Islamic scholar Mohammad Ali, the verse takes on a different meaning. Indeed, one finds that it is directed against those that initiate an attack on Muslims, and the idolatrous tribes that broke treaties with Muslims (IX: 13, VIII: 56).[60] A broader interpretation, based on Shaybani's *The Islamic Law of Nations*, suggests *jihad* to be a struggle to both improve and expand Islam, but not necessarily through violent means.[61] The Wahhabi reject these more "liberal interpretations." The Wahhabis are ready to fight to see the Islamic Caliphate restored on earth. As articulated by a leading Wahhabi *mullah*, "the IRP wants to be in parliament. We have no desire to be in parliament. We want a revolution."[62] Wahhabis are also willing to die for their cause. Indeed, one the first martyrs of Islam in the modern era was Bahauddin Vaissov, a Wahhabi teacher in Ferghana who in 1950 was imprisoned where he later died.[63]

The movement spreads at the grass roots level, fueled by charismatic leadership and external support. *Mullah* Abdul Kehi and Abdulwali Qari are especially well known for their persuasive sermons in footholds throughout the Ferghana Valley, particularly in Namangan and Ferghana, Uzbekistan, and Osh and Jalalabad, Kyrgyzstan. But fiery rhetoric is rarely sufficient. As part of the conversion sub-system, Wahhabi provide social services the state fails to deliver. They build schools and mosques. In Namangan, a multi-story Islamic education complex was built in the mid-1990s, rumored to have cost over $127,000. Islamic centers have also been built in Osh, Jalalabad, Andijan, and Margilan.[64] Rather than bribing for books and marks, students are given books, literature for their parents, and free lunches. In return, they proselytize with the *mullahs* in local villages on the weekend, and when older, they might join a VNSA.[65]

Stakeholder associations are key to Wahhabi success. The Saudi Arabian Wahhabi movement, known as *Ahl e-Sunnah*, was the principal benefactor. Within two years of independence in 1991, *Ahl e-Sunnah* had set up offices in Margilan, and funneled over $1.3 million to new construction and social services. Despite U.S. efforts, the flow has not substantially subsided.[66] Other important benefactors were the Taliban, Osama bin Laden, and the *Jamaat-i-Islami* out of Pakistan. In the face of government crackdowns on mosques and schools, prospective students often traveled to Afghanistan and Pakistan for education. They were sponsored by the Taliban, with bin Laden backing, and ultimately recruited for their *jihad* against corrupt Arab regimes and the West. Since the global war on terror began in 2001, this orderly flow of funds and students was disrupted; however, other, less efficient systems of money transfer and training are being created.[67]

The IMU, also known as the *Harakatul Islamiyyah*, was the most organized and violently active of the Wahhabi groups.[68] It earned worldwide notoriety and a fourth-place ranking on the State Department's Foreign Terrorist Organizations List in September 2000 after the kidnapping of four U.S. mountain climbers. The IMU's political leader is Takhir Yuldash and its military commander was Juma Namangani. Namangani brought a warlord's character to the movement. His military background included service as a Soviet paratrooper in Afghanistan and commander of approximately of one thousand irregulars during the Tajik civil war. After the end of the civil war, he capitalized on the thousands of unemployed former fighters and the resource backing of the Wahhabi movement to expand IMU operations.

Recruiting was heaviest in the Batken region of Kyrgyzstan. The region was and remains desperately poor and packed with mercenaries, ready to accept the regular wages that come with joining the *jihad*. Islam is probably not the only motivating factor in their service. Among IMU members were also Tajiks, Uzbeks, Chechens, Uighars, and Afghans, many of whom were seasoned veterans from the civil wars in Afghanistan and Tajikistan. The link to Afghanistan remained strong with these fighters; indeed, many of the al Qaida members and their affiliates shared a common link in their experiences in Afghanistan. The IMU was no different; Namangani and his fighters received sanctuary and training in Afghan camps.

Tactically, the IMU embraced the full range of collective violence. In addition to the high profile kidnapping in 2000, the IMU raised $3 million from the kidnapping of four Japanese geologists in 1999 and $50,000 for three Kyrgyz district officials. Assassinations and bombings were also part of IMU arsenal. The Uzbek government holds the IMU responsible for a series of

Tashkent bombings in 1997, which missed their target, Islam Karimov, but left 16 dead and 128 wounded.[69] Additional assassination attempts on Karimov as well as bombings in 1997 and 1999 resulted in a government crackdown that continues today.

Namangani also commanded guerrilla and conventional forces, which conducted a series of cross-border raids from Tajikistan in recent years. In 1999, approximately 800 IMU guerrillas launched an unsuccessful attack near Batken with the intent of establishing a permanent base from which to launch assaults on Uzbekistan.[70] A smaller force of approximately 100 guerrillas tried again in August 2000, attacking Kyrgyz security forces and seizing several villages in Uzbekistan, where 27 soldiers were killed. The latter become the subject of the popular government-created music video showing an Uzbek soldier battling for his freedom from an IMU camp. A third round of attacks was expected in 2001, particularly when Yuldash announced during a BBC interview on August 3rd, that several thousand IMU fighters had established a base in Batken.[71] Yuldash certainly exaggerated, as no attack materialized. The IMU as an operational VNSA was essentially destroyed in Operation Enduring Freedom, with Juma Namangani assessed as being wounded in an aerial bombardment of Mazar-e-Sharif in early November 2001, and eventually dying of his wounds.[72] Despite this setback, stores of negative entropy in the form of a socialized radical theology and the persistent conditions for violence ensure the IMU has at least a modest future.

Raging Religion?

In Central Asia, nationalist Islam is more dominant on the political landscape, but is also constrained by institutional and cultural obstacles to generating enthusiasm for its agenda. That said, Islamic VNSA do have a solid foothold in the Ferghana Valley and are able to move with relative ease across the border between Tajikistan and Afghanistan. Persistent socio-economic deprivation, resource scarcity, and demographic pressures are certain to expand the recruiting pool. State coercion, charismatic identity entrepreneurs, and resource access are strong transformational engines. The defeat of the Taliban regime and eradication of the al Qaida network dealt a significant blow to the IMU in particular, which is heavily dependent on these relationships for financial backing, training, and safe haven. Even with such a defeat, Islamic VNSA will persevere. While they will likely not achieve their primary goal of a new caliphate in the near term, they will continue to pose a challenge to the existing world order in general and the West in particular.

Militant religious groups are the penultimate transcendental VNSA. They obtain their authority—and therefore their negative entropy—by invoking the divine. No higher authority is possible, and no lower authority can countermand or overrule. Leaders of militant religious groups typically claim to have a special connection with God, and serve as a conduit to pass instructions from God to the members of the VNSA. Those members who are also true believers, those who are truly inculcated with the transcendental values of the VNSA, can be compelled to do nearly anything in his name.

Transcendental VNSA often attract those who already have a disposition toward their belief system. Typically, some sort of additional socialization is required to deepen the ideological convictions; further, isolation from the rest of the world is coupled with this additional indoctrination in order to ensure the individual does not have their beliefs "polluted" by family pleadings, media reports, etc. Al Qaida, Hamas, the LTTE, Aum Shinrikyo, and even Jim Jones's Jonestown cult all have or had spiritual advisors, spiritual training, and elements of isolation for their operatives. The socialization function of the maintenance sub-system is where militant religious organizations build up their stores of energy to survive crisis and create congruence among functions. Against all logic, reasoning, or utility calculations, members thoroughly indoctrinated are likely to stay committed to the transcendental value system. Targeting this function may not re-convert those members who are already thoroughly indoctrinated, but it may engender role deviation, disrupt recruiting, or prevent individuals outside the group from developing sympathetic beliefs with the militants in the first place.

IV. Ethno-political Militants

The ethnic component of warlords, TCO and militant religious movements is important but not always the uniquely defining characteristic. Therefore, we also examine the potential rise of violent ethno-political groups pursuing ethnic-based agendas. Unlike the warlord pursuing power and prestige, the TCO chasing profit, and the militant religious group following a mangled theology, ethno-political groups strive for ethnic consciousness and rights to be validated in the form of political power.

Ethnic Environments

Militant ethno-political groups arise in an environment where perceived ethnic differences exist. "Perceived" is a key word, as ethnic groups often co-exist with one another without incident until minor differences are exploited (such as the variety of ethnic groups on the pre-colonial Indian sub-continent), or no such ethnic divisions actually exist but are created by those who would benefit from the resulting division (such as the Hutus and the Tutsis in Rwanda and Burundi). Multiple influences can heighten this level of perception, including media statements and stories, elite rhetoric, policies exacerbating social, economic, and political differences between ethnic groups, and identity entrepreneurs who make it a point to aggravate, intensify, or create disagreements between such groups. The greater the number of divisions between ethnic groups—social, informational, economic, political—the greater the probability an "us" versus "them" stage will be set, and the greater chances an ethno-political VNSA will emerge.[73]

Ethnically-aware Systems

Ethno-political groups grow into VNSAs relatively slowly. Reinforced identity cleavages coupled with reduced efficacy of the state or low state identification will accelerate formation and growth. An ethno-political process that VNSA may follow as an aspect of their life cycle is: (1) become ethnically aware; (2) become ethnically organized, which includes sub-system development and specification; (3) develop goals which primarily or exclusively help one's own ethnic organization, which includes developing a viable strategy; and (4) using violent means to achieve ethnically-based goals.

Several ethnic identities compete with the five Central Asian states for attention. Most Central Asian peoples were not ethnically aware prior to Russian colonization. Soviet disintegration, coupled with nation-building programs by the five Central Asian republics at independence, and more recently Afghanistan and Pakistan, ensure that nearly all peoples are now aware of their ethnicity. The number of political parties, non-governmental groups, and informal (and often illegal) groups based on ethnic lines is large and growing.[74] Paradoxically, all five Central Asian republics recently cracked down on almost all political actors (the press, political parties, and NGOs); thus, the likelihood of such ethno-political actors going underground is growing as well. Actions likely to encourage the creation of additional ethnic organizations include nationalizing policies, perceived favoritism of certain ethnic groups or clans, and economic disparities along ethnic divides. Some ethnic organizations have reached the third stage in the process by developing the strategy function, illustrated by their willingness to define their goals exclusively for their own ethnic group. A handful of groups are at the extreme end of the spectrum, using violence to accomplish their goals. While some of these groups form in an ad hoc manner (such as Uzbek farmers in Osh resorting to violence over perceived favoritism for their Kyrgyz peers), others exist for the primary purpose of advocating violence to pursue ethnic goals.

An important fact resulting from an application of this model to Central Asia is that only a paltry handful of ethnic organizations are transforming away from ethnic mobilization. The vast majority of ethnic groups are gaining momentum in their upward march toward ethnic-goal setting and violence, including

Karakalpaks, Tajiks, Kyrgyz, Kazakh, Uighars, Afghani, and Pamiris. The primary reason Turkmen clans are not moblizing is President Niyazov's exceptionally heavy-handed tactics in repressing any political or organizational expression other than adoration for his own regime. This stalled movement is temporary— once the aging and unhealthy Niyazov passes on, such clan-based identity will likely come back with a vengeance, especially if the lesser clans believe that the dominant Tekke clan was unfairly privileged or were repressive to other clans under Turkmenbashi's rule. Two prominent examples serve to highlight the process by which a group emerges and moves toward the cusp of becoming a VNSA—Uighars and Karakalpaks.

Worth fighting for

The recent history of the Uighar (and the Uighar Diaspora in Central Asia) begins with China's absorption of Eastern Turkestan (an infant state created during World War II) in the late 1940s. Fleeing the communist government, tens of thousands of Turkic-speaking Uighars fled west from China, which had expanded its Xinjiang province to include Eastern Turkestan. As a result, every Central Asian republic, in addition to India, Pakistan, and Afghanistan, have a noteworthy Uighar population; Kyrgyzstan and Kazakhstan especially have significant Uighar presence.[75] The resulting Diasporas retained their ethnic and cultural identity during Soviet times. With the collapse of the Soviet Union came the concurrent irredentist desire to regain a Uighar homeland. China quickly established diplomatic ties with the Central Asian republics; however, this left the Uighar nation divided by the complicated and (still) unsettled borders of the region.

The Uighars, much like their Muslim brothers to the west, identified themselves along religious lines prior to the Chinese arrival. Just as Russian colonization introduced national identity to many of the Central Asian peoples, Chinese occupation and subjugation made the Uighars ethnically aware as well. Thus, for the Uighars, the first step toward becoming a VNSA was taken nearly fifty years ago. Under strict communist rule by both the Soviet Union and the People's Republic of China, organization for the Uighar community was difficult. However, soon after the collapse of the Soviet Union, several Uighar-based organizations emerged in Central Asia, reflecting the desire of at least a portion of the Uighar population to have their own country. The Chinese partially placated this desire for independence by establishing the Xinjiang Uighar Autonomous Region (XUAR).[76] Thus, the next two steps up the ethnic motivation process can reasonably be estimated as complete in the early 1990s.

Chinese President Jiang Zemin announced his "Go West" policy in 1996, largely to develop the desolate western portions of China. As a result, tens of millions of ethnically Han Chinese are expected to move to XUAR in the next two decades. This massive demographic shift has created significant resentment with the Uighar population; the Chinese are quickly changing the cultural trappings of the area (not the least of which is consuming massive amounts of pork—an insult to that Muslim population).[77] Although Uighar separatists have waged a campaign of sporadic violence since the late 1980s (which is, ironically, when a great deal of inter-ethnic violence in the rest of Central Asia erupted), the level of violence increased with the increasing number of Chinese.[78] This violence has included planting bombs, killing Chinese police and soldiers, robbing banks, etc. Furthermore, anti-Chinese rioting in the region's capital of Urumqi, Kashgar, and Yining left some Chinese dead.[79] Following one particular 1997 riot in Yining that left at least ten dead and a bomb attack in Beijing the same year, China cracked down on the Uighars and began passing a series of bilateral understandings with Kyrgyzstan and Kazakhstan in an attempt to get those governments to do the same.[80]

More recently in early 2001, Uighar separatists conducted yet another bombing campaign. The response from the Chinese government was swift—in the resulting wave of arrests, called Operation Strike Hard, more than two hundred Uighars were sentenced to death and many more were handed lengthy prison sentences.[81] Furthermore, as several Uighars were among those captured in Afghanistan in 2001, the Chinese government is using the global war on terror as a pretext to increase aggressive policing in XUAR and to change a variety of laws specifically aimed at its own "domestic terrorists," which is a euphemism for Uighar separatists. Indeed, since December 2001, several thousand Uighars have been detained as a result of these actions.[82]

How the violent relationship between the Uighars in XUAR and the Chinese government affects Uighar mobilization in Central Asia is clear—the structural coercion extends beyond China's borders to those Central Asian governments as well. Uighar separatists and Kazakh authorities in Almaty waged a tit-for-tat battle in September of 2000.[83] Kyrgyz authorities branded the Uighars as Muslim extremists and actively tried to link them to the Khizb-ut-Takhrir, an active Islamist militant organization. Further, most avenues of Uighar protests against any government, including the Chinese and Kyrgyz, are closed.[84] Thus, the state is now viewed as an obstacle toward Uighar expression.

As a result, several Uighar organizations exist in the Central Asian Republics, some of them devoted to the violent creation of a Uigharstan. These groups include, but are not limited to, the Uighar Ozatlik Tashlakhty (bases in Kazakhstan, fighting for an independent Uighar enclave in Xinjiang), the United National Revolutionary Front of Turkestan, the Organization for the Liberation of Uigharstan, and the International Committee for the Liberation of Turkestan and Yana Ayat. Although the focus of these groups' violence is primarily China, actions since 2000 illustrate that Central Asian governments are considered legitimate targets.

Some Central Asian authorities believe any independent homeland for the Uighars will negatively affect them as well. According to a representative of the Kazakhstan Foreign Ministry, "It should be remembered that the aim of the Uighur separatists is to create an independent Uighur state, not only on the territory of Sintszyan-Ugursk [Xinjiang] but also in parts of Kazakhstan."[85] At this point, the political boundaries between China and Central Asia become less relevant for all sides—Uighar separatists attack both Central Asian and Chinese targets, Central Asian regimes fear increased Uighar influence both in their own homelands and in China, and China convinced the Central Asian states to adopt oppressive measures against their Uighar populations.

The future for the Uighars and the Uighar movement is cloudy. While the majority of Uighars are not violent, both Central Asian and Chinese authorities are fearful of outside Islamic influences radicalizing the Uighar population. For example, in 1997 the French newspaper *al-Watan al-'Arabic* erroneously reported that Osama bin Laden had intentions of moving to Xinjiang to start a *jihad* against Chinese rule there.[86] This greatly worried Chinese leaders, who were concerned about conditions in Afghanistan due to the flow of drugs and other illegal goods.[87] This last point should not be lost. One of the more influential sources of VNSA incubation may be outside actors. The ranks of the Taliban are depleted due to international action and cooperation. The remnants of the Taliban and al Qaida may look beyond Afghanistan and Pakistan for new recruits.

Emergent Karakalpaks

Karakalpakstan, literally meaning the "land of the black hats," is an autonomous region at the extreme western end of Uzbekistan, bordering on the Aral Sea and the Amu and Syr Darya Rivers. The Karakalpaks history in the region goes back at least to the sixteenth century. Having always been at least autonomous, the Karakalpaks fought against the Mongols, the Khiva, and Kazakh Khanates, and later the Russian encroachment. The Karakalpak history becomes complicated after the Soviet Revolution. In 1924, the region was awarded autonomous status under the administration of Kazakhstan. In 1930 it became a part of the Russian Federation, and on March 20, 1932, it was reformed as the Karakalpak Autonomous Soviet Socialist Republic. On December 5, 1932, Karakalpakstan became a part of the Uzbek Republic, a status that remained until the break-up of the Soviet Union. In December 1991 the Karakalpak Republic was announced as an autonomous republic in Uzbekistan.[88] With this status came its own constitution, parliament, capital, and other structures associated with government. Given this long tradition of independence and some level autonomy under the Soviets, the Karakalpaks have a level of ethnic awareness.

The most striking thing about Karakalpakstan is not its political status, but the wretched conditions in which that region exists. It is home of one of the greatest environmental catastrophes in the world—the dying of the Aral Sea. Fishing villages that fifty years ago rested on the lapping shores of the Aral, now lie over one hundred miles away from the poisoned water. Vast dry flats are suggestive of former placid waters—now replaced with barren soil mixed with harsh chemicals and salt, constantly whipped by the wind, sending noxious dust clouds for hundreds of miles. The only place where many of the Aral Sea fish (which once sustained the Karakalpaks) now exist is in the Karakalpak museum in Nukus.

The health catastrophe is as bad as the environmental collapse. Anemia among women is nearly universal. Most Karakalpaks show signs of malnutrition. Children below the age of fifteen, who make up 40 percent of the population, show signs of scurvy and liver and kidney problems. Infant mortality in some areas is 50 per 1,000. Birth defects, which match the startling figure, are five times the rate in Europe. The list of depressing statistics could continue, but the point is made—the Karakalpaks are an exceptionally unhealthy population.[89]

It is not a leap to suggest the Karakalpak's health woes are linked to the environmental ruin in their homeland. Indeed, a comparative analysis with other population groups in the region with similar dietary and living habits show that those populations in the Aral Sea region suffer greater health problems than those further away (such as Turkmen or Uzbeks from the eastern half of the country).[90] A temporal analysis, comparing what few statistics on the health of the Karakalpak population earlier this century with that populations' current health, suggests the same thing—this population began getting sick approximately two decades ago, as the Soviet agricultural practices of the region were beginning take a toll on the environment.

Given the ethnic awareness and organization, the poverty, resource shortages, and other conditions conducive to VNSA incubation, why are the Karakalpaks still peaceful? According to Thomas Szayna, a RAND Corporation expert on Central Asia, the answer contains many dimensions.[91] First, the problems facing the Karakalpaks are similar to the problems facing all Uzbeks—only far more severe—thus negating perceptions of relative deprivation. With an extensive drought hammering western Uzbekistan (because of weather patterns but also largely because the Amu and Syr Darya Rivers are fully exploited before they reach western Uzbekistan) new disparities are likely to emerge. With a shortage of potable water, many are drinking from poor sources of water, creating a surge in infectious diseases. As of 2001, approximately 48,000 are without their main source of income, as crops have withered. No rice was harvested in Karakalpakstan at all in 2000. With up to 90 percent of Karakalpak's agriculture destroyed in both 2001 and 2002, the Karakalpaks may be at the breaking point.[92]

A second reason Karakalpakstan is still reasonably stable is that no charismatic leader has emerged willing to directly challenge Tashkent. Two events could change that. The first is a continuing rise in Karakalpak identity awareness. Although Karakalpak ethnic awareness can be traced back several decades (possibly centuries), it is not exceptionally deep. With less than 40 percent of Karakalpakstan's population actually being Karakalpak (Uzbeks outnumber the Karakalpaks), a penetrating and uniform ethnic awareness is difficult to accomplish. With more and more Uzbeks moving east due to the drought and health problems, these population dynamics will change, increasing the probability that an ethnic Karakalpak "entrepreneur" may emerge.

The second potential "trigger event" is the Uzbek state being fully occupied with other challenges to its authority, such potential protests in major cities as continued U.S. military presence, increased underground opposition to the current administration, or the re-emergence of Islamic activists. These events could force the central government to pull the limited resources directed to the Karakalpak region into other areas such as internal policing or defense. Should that occur, the Karakalpaks might begin adopting a victim mindset, creating a growing list of grievances against the central government. Additionally, the central government may be perceived as too occupied with other challenges to worry about its far western province. Such a window of opportunity may be what Karakalpak nationalists are waiting for.

The Karakalpak issue must be described as latent, but it should not be dismissed. If some kind of stasis or slight improvement is achieved, the likelihood of the Karakalpaks transforming into a VNSA in the near future is unlikely. Should any of several triggering events develop, however—VNSA uprisings elsewhere, conditions getting comparatively worse, or a charismatic leader emerging—this dormant issue has the foundation to incubate violent groups with the goal of independence from Uzbekistan.

Ethnic Myths

Ethno-political groups typically rely on some level of transcendental values in order to create negative entropy. Referring back to some earlier mythical hero usually augments identity creation with the hero's actual accomplishments embellished or completed fabricated. An ethno-political group often resorts to the rallying cry of "Remember the greatness of our past!" For example, the Sendero Luminoso, whose followers were largely the *campesino* of Indian descent, aggressively marketed the notion of the Golden Age of Peru's history when the Inca Empire was at its peak; ignoring some of the more brutal aspects of Incan rule, Sendero stressed the benevolence of the Incan rulers—and then link the greatness of the Incans to the justification of their attacks on the "non-native" political and economic elites in the cities.[93] Attacking or weakening socialization and effecting learning are key to weakening and eventually defeating ethno-political VNSA. Creating an alternative appeal or nostalgia for a non-violent course of action will help counter the VNSA's appeal for a violent one.

Eco-warriors, Millenarian Groups, and Other VNSA

An interesting milieu of VNSA has begun emerging in just the past decade. Eco-terrorists, anti-globalizationists, millenarian groups, and other assorted "interest-association" VNSA are marks of an increasingly complex world. These phenomena are sufficiently emergent that few definitive statements can be made about them. For example, at anti-globalization rallies around the world, young anarchists wearing black protest side-by-side with labor union members; environmental advocates hold signs next to fisherman; and indigenous peoples are arrested just like the blue-collar workers whose jobs were recently exported to a developing country.

As might be expected, these groups reflect various phases in the VNSA life cycle. Earth First! and the Earth Liberation Front are clearly mature VNSA—they conduct sophisticated attacks, destroy a great deal of property, and exhibit adaptive skills. Anti-globalizationists, on the other hand, do not represent such a clear case. Indeed, some elements within these planned protests do engage in violence; however, the majority of the protestors are not—they simply oppose certain government policies. A defining and common identity does not exist—yet. Anti-globalizationists may represent the beginning of a new type of VNSA, one where the membership is not defined, control structures are developed only to the point of notifying disgruntled individuals when protest opportunities are available, and formalized conversion functions for directing the violence to a strategic purpose are non-existent; indeed, the purpose of the VNSA may be to simply be violent as a method to register their displeasure with their economic and political elites.

These more spontaneous organizations are possible only through the advent and proliferation of information technology. By way of example, the social unrest and limited violence in Peru in May 2003 was remarkably shaped by information technology. The president of Peru, Alejandro Toledo, recently concluded a summit of all South American heads of state in the small Andean town of Cuzco. In an effort to raise visibility to the problems at home rather than prestige abroad, a number of Peruvian groups attempted to protest during the summit. The response was rapid and decisive—Cuzco was shut down, the army and police were deployed, and many protestors were arrested. In the small ("primitive" is only a slight exaggeration) towns, villages, and cities all over Peru, farmers dressed in traditional Andean garb and the unemployed with a week's worth of dirt caked on their fingers were hunched over achingly slow computers in internet cafes sending and receiving e-mails planning the next day's nation-wide strikes—which were stunning in their coordination and effectiveness.

There is no tradition in Central Asia of violent environmental organizations such as the Earth Liberation Front or Earth First! Indeed, although environmental degradation in the region is pervasive and substantial, no concomitant environmental consciousness, such as that compared to western societies, yet exists. This said, environmental awareness is on the rise for a variety of reasons. Educated individuals (particularly university professors) are beginning to speak out on the issue. The large increase of NGOs working in Central Asia has increased both local and world awareness of the catastrophes in the region. With the exception of Turkmenistan, "home-grown" NGOs, many of them based on environmental awareness, have sprung up since 1994. Websites, newsletters, conferences, and grassroots projects all mark the arrival of this new voice of civil society.

Supporting the assessment that an eco-warrior VNSA could emerge is the Nevada-Semey movement. Founded in 1989 by Olzhas Suleymenov, a Kazakh poet and politician, the Movement's original goal was to stop nuclear testing at the Polygon, located in northeastern Kazakhstan, the largest such testing facility in the world. After two particularly massive tests that created huge shock waves and a radioactive plume over much of northern Kazakhstan, Suleymenov organized a grassroots campaign that collected over one million Kazakh signatures demanding an end to the testing. Eight months later, the Kazakhstan Communist Party called for closure of the Polygon, and no additional tests occurred. After Kazakh independence in 1991, the Polygon was permanently closed. Such a massive demonstration of discontent with government policies empirically suggests that Central Asians *will* take action based on purely environmental concerns.

This history, coupled with the rapidly expanding awareness of environmental issues provides grounds for VNSA creation in two ways. First, eco-warriors may actually develop indigenously—albeit for resource scarcity issues rather than for the aim of simply protecting the environment. For example, in 1992 and 1993, due to the severe water shortages Uzbeks and Turkmen communities near Dashoguz sent raiding parties across the common Amu Darya in order to destroy the other community's pumping stations and canals.[94] A more troubling question is how long until organized groups, who would not directly benefit from such destructive activity, begin using violence to oppose government or social group activity based on their own singular environmental concerns.

A second incubation route involved external factors such as outside actors, possibly Diasporas, attempting to influence events. An example is the organization Eastern Turkestan. This organization claims that a large swath of western China, roughly encompassing the Xinjiang province and parts of Tibet, was illegally invaded by the Chinese Army and is now illegally occupied. Its goals include secession from China and creation of an independent Eastern Turkestan. This organization began beating the environmental drum in 1993 in response to Chinese nuclear testing at Lop Nur. Its on-line newsletter reported a large protest at the Chinese embassy in Almaty, Kazakhstan, which was in support of the victims in Eastern Turkestan.[95] Perhaps more ominous, the World Tibet Network described in detail the ecological disaster and the health impacts on the citizens of Eastern Turkestan due to Chinese testing at Lop Nur. The press release ended with the following suggestive statement: "The peaceful demonstrations of the peoples of Eastern Turkestan living at home and abroad demanding the closure of the nuclear testing site have so far achieved no results."[96] The point here is that a group with political aspirations may turn to environmental issues to find resonance within its local populace, its Diasporas, and possible sympathetic environmental organizations outside the region.

In a similar vein, it is also possible that Western militant environmental and/or anti-globalization groups could infiltrate the region and organize violent attacks or protests against various symbols of environmental abuse. While unlikely, perusing many websites published by these groups results in stories such as the U.S. government secretly developing a killer fungus in state laboratories in Uzbekistan in an attempt to destroy the poppy fields in the region.[97] As these groups of protesters have illustrated a remarkable mobility and global presence, it is possible that such groups could organize violent activities even in the tightly controlled republics of Central Asia. The U.S. military seems to be taking the potential of emerging eco-warriors/terrorists seriously as well. U.S. Central Command, in cooperation with the Woodrow Wilson Center's Environmental Change and Security Project, listed the emergence of eco-terrorists as one of seven key environmental security issues to be watched in Central Asia.[98]

Closing *Transnational / Transcendental*

VNSA typologies are useful—in this chapter, we presented merely two. Open systems theory enables the analyst to create typologies that serve purposes and goals of the analyst. A military commander, for example—especially if they are in charge of protecting a base or installation—may want to group VNSA by the form of violence they use. A business expanding into an area with VNSA influence may be more interested in classifying VNSA according to what markets they own or have infiltrated. Of the major typologies, understanding the differences between transactional and transcendental VNSA is perhaps the most important. All VNSA must have negative entropy to survive and congruence to perform. Knowing what functions are responsible to each is essential to formulating strategy. Additionally, understanding the difference offers insight into what types of violence VNSA will pursue and why they pursue it. At a minimum, approaching VNSA in this manner opens a wider range of questions, avenues of analysis, and understanding of the VNSA phenomenon.

Notes

1. Unverified stories abound of drug kingpins having millions of dollars of cash that they were unable to put into the financial system. The reporting requirement for any deposit or withdrawal of $10,000 or more apparently put a significant crimp in the drug cartel's ability to use the considerable wealth gained from their nefarious trade.

2. John Mackinlay, "Defining Warlords," *Monograph 46: Building Stability in Africa: Challenges for the New Millennium* (Peoria, South Africa: Institute for Security Studies, February 2000), 1.

3. Mackinlay goes on to assert that the warlord is a "wholly negative phenomenon. There is, so far, no mitigating Robin Hood tendency which might show him to be a redresser of global inequality." Ibid., 9.

4. Tim Judah, "Afghan Boy Takes on Taliban," Institute for War and Peace Reporting, *Reporting Central Asia* 78, October 25, 2001.

5. Mackinlay, "Defining Warlords," 7.

6. Ibid.

7. Ibid.

8. Integrated Regional Information Network of the United Nations, "'Banana War' Leaves Eight Dead," as carried on the Awdal Somaliland News website. Accessed on November 26, 2003 at www.awdalnews.com/wmview.php?ArtID=1767.

9. As reported by the *New York Times*, "The Lesson of Somalia: Just a Humpty Dumpty Story?" November 26, 2003. Accessed on-line on November 26, 2003. query.nytimes.com/gst/abstract.html?res-F40A13F6345F0C758EDDA80994DB404482&incamp-archive:search

10. Several accounts of this story exist. For the best accounts, see the Italian newspaper *Famiglia Christiana*, which ran a series of articles in 1998 regarding the whole episode. The Trade and Environmental Database of the American University offer an excellent legal analysis of the episode. Accessed on November 24, 2003. Available at www.american.edu/ted/somalia.htm.

11. Per Fenton Bresler, *Interpol*, referenced in "Organized Crime and the Illegal Market in Weapons in Southern Asia," Tara Kartha, *Strategic Analysis: A Monthly Journal of the IDSA* 24, no. 2 (May 2000).

12. Phil Williams, "Transnational Criminal Organizations," in *In Athena's Camp: Preparing for Conflict in the Information Age*, ed. John Arguilla and David Ronfedt (Santa Monica, CA: RAND, 1997), 321.

13. Al Qaida is successful in creating front businesses. Osama bin Laden created several successful businesses and companies in Sudan, many of which were used to fund the August 7, 1998,

bombings of the U.S. embassies in Kenya and Tanzania. See Rohan Gunaratna, *Inside Al Qaeda: Global Network of Terror* (New York: Columbia University Press, 2002).

14. Phil Williams adapts the idea of "zones of peace" and "zones of turbulence" to this relationship. "Transnational," 332.

15. Ibid.

16. See, for example, Robert Kelly, Ko-lin Chin, and Rufus Schatzberg, eds., *Handbook of Organized Crime in the United States* (Westport, CT: Greenwood Press, 1994), 91–120.

17. Thomas Schelling, "Economic Analysis of Organized Crime," President's Commission on Law Enforcement and the Administration of Justice, *Task Force Report: Organized Crime* (Washington, DC: U.S. Government Printing Office, 1967).

18. Gresham Sykes, *Criminology* (New York, NY: Harcourt Brace Jovanovich, 1978), 194–203.

19. Adapted from Tara Kartha, "Organised Crime and the Illegal Market in Weapons in Southern Asia," *Strategic Analysis* 24, no. 2 (May 2000).

20. Ibid.

21. A useful examination of strategic alliances, particularly for narco-traffickers can be found in Paul R. Viotti and Mark V. Kauppi, "Terrorism, Crime and Weapons Proliferation" in their *International Relations and World Politics: Security, Economy and Identity* (Upper Saddle River, NJ: Prentice Hall, 1997), 173–78.

22. Martha Brill Olcott and Natalia Udalova, "Drug Trafficking on the Great Silk Road: The Security Environment in Central Asia," Working Paper 11 for the Russian and Eurasian Program, Carnegie Endowment for International Peace, March 2000, 8.

23. Tamara Makarenko, "Terrorism and Religion Mask Drug Trafficking in Central Asia," *Jane's Intelligence Review* 12, no. 11 (November 1, 2000). Accessed through the LEXIS-NEXIS Database.

24. Olcott and Udalova, "Drug Trafficking," 13.

25. Ibid., 12.

26. Ibid., 18.

27. Ibid.

28. Ibid.

29. Williams, "Transnational," 329.

30. Nancy Lubin, Keith Martin, and Barnett R. Rubin, *Calming the Ferghana Valley: Development and Dialogue in the Heart of Central Asia* (Washington, DC: The Century Foundation, 1999), 72

31. Reported by Olcott and Udalova, "Drug Trafficking," 18.

32. Williams, "Transnational," 329.

33. In 1998, Kyrgyzstan reported 3,295 drug-related crimes and Kazakhstan 18,479 drug-related crimes (702 and 1,193 crimes per million people respectively) as compared to about 1,261 per million in Russia for 1997. Olcott and Udalova, "Drug Trafficking," 17.

34. Rates are roughly equivalent to the United States and higher than Europe. Kazakhstan has the highest rate with 12.3 addicts per thousand in 1998. Ibid, 15.

35. Olcott and Udalova, "Drug Trafficking," 18.

36. See Williams, "Transnational," for a more complete discussion, 316–20.

37. The classic example of this is the conviction and imprisonment of Al Capone, who served 11 years in prison for income tax evasion—despite being responsible for several dozen murders. See the Chicago Historical Society's account of Capone, available on line at www.chicagohs.org/history/capone/cpn4.html as of January 7, 2004.

38. Goldstein, Joshua, *International Relations* (New York, NY: HarperCollins College Publishers, 1996), 204–5.

39. Mark Juergensmeyer, "The Logic of Religious Violence," in *Inside Terrorist Organizations*, David Rapoport, ed. (London, UK: Frank Cass Publishers, 2001), 173.

40. Heather Gregg, "The Causes of Religious Wars: Holy Nations, Sacred Spaces, and Religious Revolutions," Ph.D. Dissertation, Massachusetts Institute of Technology, February 2004.

41. Juergensmeyer, "The Logic," 181.

42. "Thousands Protest Beijing's Crackdown on Meditation Sect," CNN On-line July 21, 1999. Available on-line at www.cnn.com/WORLD/asiapcf/9907/21/china.protest.02/index.html as of January 6, 2004.

43. McVeigh, for example, openly admitted to interviewers his belief in Christian Patriotism and involvement in Patriot activities, thus tacitly admitting his adherence to that theological belief system. See Tim Kelsey, "The Oklahoma Suspect Awaits Day of Reckoning," *The SundayTimes* (London), April 21, 1996. See also Bruce Hoffman and Ian Lesser's *Countering the New Terrorism* (Santa Monica, CA: RAND Corporation, 1999). Also available on line at www.rand.org/publications/MR/MR989/ as of November 25, 2003.

44. Literally interpreted, this phrase means land or abode of Islam. However, in this context, it refers to the legalistic interpretation, which is that land which is governed by a just Muslim ruler and is ordered by *shari'a* law. For further explanation and detail, see Rudolph Peters', *Islam and Colonialism: The Doctrine of Jihad in Modern History* (New York: Mouton de Gruyter Publishers, 1984).

45. Other ideologies and organizations have already called for such a "post-state" social structure. The Muslim Brotherhood in the 1930s wanted to restore the Caliphate; indeed, even in the 1920s a very active movement in South Asia, Malaysia, and elsewhere attempted to stop the breakup of the caliphate. Even an anti-religious ideology—that of communism—called for the dissolution of states in order to create a worldwide commune. Therefore, al Qaida's call for redrawing the map in such a "post-state" way is not new or creative.

46. Graham E. Fuller, *Islamic Fundamentalism in the Northern Tier Countries: An Integrative View* (Santa Monica, CA: RAND Corporation, 1991). Quoted in Richard Betts, *Conflict after the Cold War: Arguments on Causes of War and Peace* (Upper Saddle River, NJ: Allyn and Bacon Publishers, 1994), 389.

47. Ibid., 383.

48. For analysis of the role of Islam in political life during the early 1990s, see Troy S. Thomas, "The Central Asian Umma: Composition and Prospects," unpublished paper, 1992.

49. Alexandre Bennigsen, "Islam in Retrospect," *Central Asian Survey* 8 (1989), 101.

50. Mehrdad Haghayeghi, *Islam and Politics in Central Asia* (New York: St. Martin's Press. 1996), 89–90.

51. The exception is the IRP of Tajikistan, which moved in and out of government and conflict during Tajikistan's civil wars. For a complete description of the IRP's role, see Ahmed Rashid, *The Resurgence of Central Asia: Islam or Nationalism* (Karachi, Pakistan: Oxford University Press, 1994), 159–86.

52. Poonam Mann, "Fighting Terrorism: India and Central Asia," *Strategic Analysis* 26, no. 11 (February 2001): 102.

53. Ibid.

54. We use the worlds violent, militant, extreme, and radical interchangeably to represent the willing use of force to coerce and attack those that do not share their outlook and agenda. The term "Islamist" refers to Muslims who embrace a political program for the state.

55. Richard H. Shultz Jr. and William J. Olson, *Ethnic and Religious Conflict: Emerging Threat to U.S. Security* (Washington, DC: National Strategy Information Center, 1994). Explained by Kegley and Wittkopf, *World Politics*, 220.

56. This term is also used derogatively by governmental officials and others that consider the Wahhabis a threat to stability.

57. See also Haghayeghi, *Islam and Politics*, 95.

58. Abdullah Yusuf Ali, trans., *The Meaning of the Glorious Qur'an* (London, UK: Nadim and Co., 1976), 248.

59. Maulana M. Ali, *The Religion of Islam* (Lahore, Pakistan: The Ahmadiyya Anjuman Isha'at Islam, 1983), 540.

60. Ibid., 540–41.

61. Mian R. A. Khan, *Islamic Jurisprudence* (Lahore, Pakistan: Sh. Mohammad Ashraf, 1978), 199.

62. Quoted in Haghayeghi, *Islam and Politics*, 95.

63. Rashid, *The Resurgence*, 92.

64. Haghayeghi, *Islam and Politics*, 94.

65. Rashid, *The Resurgence*, 78.

66. Council on Foreign Relations, *Terrorist Financing*, October 20, 2002. Available on line at www.cfr.org/pub5080/william_f_wechsler/terrorist_financing.php as of January 6, 2004.

67. Steve Kiser, "Offense versus Defense: What's Best in the War On Terror?" RAND Corporation unpublished manuscript, November 2003.

68. Although discussed here as a militant religious movement, the IMU is a hybrid VNSA, as it is also assessed as participating in narcotics and weapons trafficking.

69. Poonam Mann, "Fighting," 8.

70. Kenneth Katzman, "Terrorism: Near Eastern Groups and State Sponsors, 2001" (Congressional Research Service Report for Congress, Library of Congress, September 10, 2001), 16.

71. Reported by Sultan Jumagulov and Kubat Otorbaev for the Institute for War and Peace Reporting (IWRP) in "Kyrgyz IMU Fears Mount," August 3, 2001. Available at www.iwpr.net/index.pl?centasia_200108.html as of January 9, 2004.

72. Associated Press, November 25, 2001. As reported by UzLand On-line. Available on line at www.uzland.uz/2001/november/26/03.htm as of January 6, 2004.

73. A more comprehensive discussion of the "narcissism of minor differences" is beyond the scope of this book, but we recommend two key texts for helping understand the manufacture of hate. Willard Gaylin, MD, *Hatred: The Psychological Descent into Violence* (New York: Public Affairs, 2003), and Michael Ignatieff, *The Warrior's Honor: Ethnic War and the Modern Conscience* (New York: Henry Holt and Company, 1997).

74. The number of NGOs registered with the Ministry of Justice in Kyrgyzstan stood at three thousand at the end of 2000; while the majority of these NGOs work in the social sector (largely addressing poverty, unemployment, women's issues, etc.), a significant number work ethnic issues. It is important to note that some of these NGOs exist in an effort to improve inter-ethnic relations, not simply to advance the cause of a single ethnic group. "Kyrgyzstan at Ten: Trouble in the 'Island of Democracy,'" *ICG Asia Report* No. 22, August 28, 2001. Available at www.crisisweb .org/home/index.cfm?id=1433andl=1 as of January 6, 2004.

75. Igor Grebenshchikov, "Kyrgyz Exploit Uighar Minority," IWPR, 27 April 2001. Available at www.iwpr.net/archive/rca/rca_200104_49_5_eng.txt as of January 6, 2004.

76. Mark Burles, *Chinese Policy Toward Russia and the Central Asian Republics* (Santa Monica, CA: RAND Corporation, 1999), 8–9.

77. Ruth Ingram, "Uighars Defy Beijing," IWPR, 19 July 2001. Available at www.iwpr.net/index.pl?archive/rca/rca_200107_61_4_eng.txt as of January 6, 2004.

78. Dimitry Balburov, "China's Wild West," *World Press Review,* August 1997. As quoted by Burles, *Chinese,* 8–9.

79. Anthony Davis, "Xinjiang Learns to Live with Resurgent Islam," *Jane's Intelligence Review,* September 1996.

80. "A Bomb in Beijing," *The Economist,* March 15, 1997, 37–38. See also "Xinjiang Conference on Separatism, Religious Activities" (Xinjian Ribao, Urumqi, May 7, 1996), 74. Appearing in Foreign Broadcast Information Service—China, May 22, 1996.

81. Ingram, "Uighars."

82. Amnesty International, "China's Anti-terrorism Legislation and Repression in XUAR," January 2002. Available on line at www.amnesty.ca/library/asa1701002.pdf as of January 6, 2004.

83. Aidar Kaliev, "Almaty Fears Uighar Militants," IWPR, November 10, 2000. Available at www.iwpr.net/archive/rca/rca_200011_29_2_eng.txt as of January 7, 2004.

84. Grebenshchikov, "Kyrgyz Exploit."

85. Ingram, "Uighars."

86. Burles, *Chinese Policy*, 18.

87. Ibid.

88. "History of Karakalpakstan." Karakalpakstan Online. Available at karakalpakstan.freenet .uz/English/English percent20HC/English percent20History.htm as of August 21, 2001.

89. Sascha Gabzion, ed., *Sustainable Water for Karakalpakstan*, WECF, Utrecht, November 1998. Full report available from: WECF, PO Box 12111, NL-3501 AC Utrecht, The Netherlands. e-mail: wecf@antenna.nl. Selected statistics available at karakalpakstan.freenet.uz/English/English percent20HE/English percent20Health percent20Problems.htm.

90. Ibid.

91. Thomas Szayna, RAND Corporation, Santa Monica, CA. Personal interview conducted by Steve Kiser on September 27, 2001.

92. Vladimiar Davlatov, "Drought Devastates Region," September 22, 2000. Available at www.iwpr.net/archive/rca/rca_200009_22_1_eng.txt as of January 4, 2004.

93. Luis Maza, McNair Scholar, Berkeley University, "The Emergence of Sendero Luminoso in Peru," Available on line at www.mcnair.berkeley.edu/uga/osl/mcnair/94BerkeleyMcNairJournal/ 19_Maza.html as of January 7, 2004.

94. Adrian Hyde-Price, "Eurasia," Caroline Thomas and Darryl Howlett, eds., in *Resource Politics, Freshwater and Regional Relations*, (Philadelphia, PA: Buckingham Publishers, 1993), 166. As referenced by Stefan Klotzli, "The Water and Soil Crisis in Central Asia—A Source for Future Conflicts?" *ENCOP Occasional Paper No. 11*, Center for Security Policy and Conflict Research/ Swiss Peace Foundation, Zurich/Berne, May 1994.

95. *Eastern Turkestan Information Bulletin* 3, no. 5 (October 1993). Availabe at www.caccp .org/et/etib3_5.html as of September 26, 2001.

96. *World Tibet Network News*, October 8, 1994. Available at www.tibet.ca/wtnarchive/ 1994/10/8_1.html as of September 26, 2001.

97. "Are We Having Fungus Yet?" *Earth Island Journal*, Fall 1998. Available at www.earthisland .org/eijournal/fall98/departments/ecoMole.html as of January 9, 2004.

98. Woodrow Wilson Center, "Current Events Archive." Available at ecsp.si.edu/archive/ central_command.htm as of September 20, 2001.

6

Collective Violence

"We have come here to die, we all want to go to Allah, and you will be going with us." Not long after speaking these words, the masked Chechen female notices a caustic green gas starting to fill the Dubrovka Theater in Moscow, followed quickly by rapid gunfire from storming Russian Special Forces. In less than two hours, the 50-odd Chechens and over 110 of their 800-plus civilian hostages lay dead. Eight months later, in June 2003, a young Chechen woman wrapped in loose, traditional clothing approaches a bus, which has stopped at a railway crossing in the province of North Ossetia. It is not clear whether she boards the bus or crawls underneath, but in either case, she detonates her hidden explosives, killing seventeen Russian Air Force personnel. She is the third female suicide bomber in just three weeks and reportedly one of over twenty "black widows" trained by Shamil Basayev and associated with his group, the Riyadus-Salikhin Reconnaissance and Sabotage Battalion of Chechen Martyrs. Basayev's links to collective violence extend well beyond these two notorious acts to include hijacking a plane in 1991 and seizing a hospital in 1995. Claiming lineage through a lieutenant to the Chechen rebel Imam Shamil, who was tenacious in his fight against the tsar's army throughout the mid-nineteenth century, Basayev and his followers employ a striking array of violent tactics in their decade long war for the establishment of an independent state in Chechnya.[1]

THE WARS OF CHECHNYA HAVE INVOLVED brutal acts of violence that reflect a transformation of war to what has been variously termed asymmetric, informal, fourth generation, post-heroic, and post-modern warfare.[2] Whether by the state or by any of the several rebel groups that are party to this fight, the belligerents have waged, and the civilians experienced, a war that involves the full spectrum of collective violence, ranging from violent crime to conventional warfare. In this respect, the mountainous battlegrounds of the Caucasus are not unlike fights being waged in the jungles of Southeast Asia or the ghettos of West African mega-cities. While a VNSA's unique violence signature can be distinguished by its specific targets, tactics, and chosen weapons, generalizations about contemporary non-state violence can be made to gain greater insight into the system. Moreover, conflicts involving VNSA challenge western notions of warfare, which are founded on a construct of the state wielding the instruments of coercion in the furtherance of policy. The VNSA of our globalized era, however, exist outside this international system of nation-states and often export violence for non-traditional reasons in non-traditional ways.

Collective violence is not the only output of the VNSA system, but it is the export of violence to the environment that draws our attention; it moves the group out of civil society to a society of violence where lethal force takes the place of dialogue. It is the violent act that usually triggers the first response from the state or another armed non-state group, and it is the termination of violent activity that normally marks transformation or death. The assassination of Anwar Sadat on October 6, 1981, drew immediate attention to the Egyptian Islamic Group, whereas the incarceration of Aum Shinrikyo leader Shoko Asahara in 1995 signaled the transformation of the group into the ostensibly non-violent Aleph under its new leader Fumihiro Joyu. Although collective violence may not be the most critical to building reserves (negative entropy), its presence always earns recognition for the group as a security challenge.

This recognition often comes too late. Small acts of violence, whether as an enabler to criminal activity or directed inward to maintain role behaviors, are generally managed at the law enforcement level without consideration of their contribution to VNSA development or their potential strategic consequences down the road. Since they occur outside the arena of what we call war, they are not always appreciated as a precursor to war or an aspect of an existing but unrecognized war. Knowledge of war's shifting threshold helps structure our understanding of VNSA strategy and opens the door to a broader range of policy options. Importantly, understanding that collective violence has crossed war's threshold does not obligate a military response, particularly when political considerations, domestic and international laws, and moral concerns argue for a more limited response. That is, the objective reality of war does not necessitate warfighting. Rather, understanding whether a security challenge involving VNSA is a war ensures that policy does not underestimate the intentions of the adversary or artificially constrain the full range of national power instruments.

From Sun Tzu to Carl von Clausewitz to this writing, the most important analytical task is to understand the war we are in. Clausewitz asserts in his treatise *On War (Von Kriege):*

Now, the first, the grandest, and most decisive act of judgment which the States-
man and General exercises is rightly to understand in this respect the War in
which he engages, not to take it for something, or to wish to make it something,
which by the nature of its relations it is impossible for it to be. This is, therefore,
the first, the most comprehensive, of all strategic questions.[3]

While the diagnosis presented in this book seeks understanding of the VNSA
throughout its life cycle, this chapter focuses on the most challenging social
setting—war. Where we have previously discussed the reasons for resorting to
violence, we now look at the forms it is likely to take. This evaluation of collective violence is not only essential to achieving a fuller appreciation of the
non-state adversary, but to understand the environment and how it shapes a
response to the VNSA challenge. It is common to frame a strategic response
in terms of the forms of warfare. Counter-terrorism seeks to defend against
and defeat terrorists; counter-insurgency has the same aims against guerrillas.
These labels mask a more complex reality. As revealed in Chechnya, Colombia, Iraq, and elsewhere, most VNSA engage in the full spectrum of collective
violence simultaneously—another aspect of their hybrid character. Like the
FARC or al Qaida, the most challenging VNSA are simultaneously criminals,
terrorists, guerrillas, and soldiers. Focusing a strategy on tactics alone, therefore, fails to appreciate VNSA complexity and may artificially limit strategic
options.

We examine non-state violence in this chapter by first defining collective violence and relating it to VNSA development. Our next task is to clarify the
conditions under which VNSA violence moves beyond criminal behavior into
the realm of war. To this end, we dust off the military theorist Clausewitz to
draw out and characterize warfare involving VNSA in terms of the three core
criteria of purpose, engagement, and force. The reasons VNSA fight, today
and in the past, stretch a narrow understanding of war as an instrument of rational policy. The engagement focuses attention on the relationships among
belligerents. Finally, force takes many forms depending on VNSA capabilities
and the demands of the environment. This examination generates a clearer
picture of the conflict as well as greater insight into an adversary's strategy and
capabilities. It also sets the stage for a more robust and tailored counter-VNSA
strategy.

To distinguish wars between states alone, which are sometimes known as formal wars, we embrace the term *informal war* to distinguish armed conflict
"where at least one of the antagonists is a non-state entity."[4] For example, the
United States was simultaneously prosecuting a formal war against the Taliban
and an informal war against al Qaida. Al Qaida and its associated groups like the
Abu Sayyaf and the IMU, are not strictly post-modern or pre-modern, but rather
reflect characteristics that precede the birth of the nation-state while embracing

elements of twentieth century total war. Informal war is less new than it is a resurgence of old methods shaped by globalization. VNSA are not states, nor do they mobilize the populace to serve in organized, hierarchical armies. They regularly operate in loose guerrilla bands and networked cells. They do not always wear uniforms or unit insignia. Most importantly, they do not always employ force to achieve political ends as conventionally understood. We call them informal for now in order to distinguish these confrontations from the more familiar construct of inter-state conflicts, but a future where informal wars are the norm and formal wars the rare species is on the horizon.

Collective Violence

Collective violence is *organized action that causes injury*. For greater rigor, we turn to Charles Tilly, who recently followed up his seminal work on collective action, *From Mobilization to Revolution*, with *The Politics of Collective Violence*. Arguing that gang brawls, car bombings, and the Cambodian genocide share commonalities, he offers the following standards for determining whether an observed social interaction is collective violence:

(1) It immediately inflicts physical damage on persons and or objects ("damage" includes forcible seizure of persons or objects over restraint or resistance);
(2) it involves at least two perpetrators of damage; and
(3) it results at least in part from coordination among persons who perform damaging acts.[5]

These criteria offer a good starting point, but they are limited in two respects. First, damage can be both physical and moral. Indeed, there is little controversy surrounding the idea that one of terrorism's goals is to generate fear, which can be experienced as a form of psychological damage. Additionally, the requirement for "immediacy" is unnecessary and fails to account for acts of collective violence that have both immediate and delayed effects.

With these caveats, our commonsense definition of collective violence scopes the problem. It rules out individual aggression. Thus, the burglar who stabs the hapless victim is not pertinent to this analysis. But it does include a broad range of collective activities often mapped against a linear continuum with absolute or total war at one end and violent crime at the other extreme. The linear approach appropriately captures the degree of collective violence involved but does not satisfactorily accommodate the salience of violence to the act and the extent of coordination required. For a more comprehensive approach and one that links up more directly with open systems we return to

Tilly, who maps forms of collective violence against two dimensions that helps to relate violent activity to non-violent politics.[6]

The first is known as the *salience of short-run damage*, which refers to the extent that damage is inflicted as a function of the activity:

> At the low extreme, damage occurs only intermittently or secondarily in the course of transactions that remain predominately non-violent. At the high extreme, almost every transaction inflicts damage, as the infliction and reception of damage dominate the interaction.[7]

Low salience acts include debates that involve incidents of physical confrontation, such as the shoving match that erupted in Japan's parliament in July 2003. High salience acts are inherently violent, such as the beheadings that occur in the central square of Riyadh, Saudi Arabia. The second dimension, *extent of coordination among violent actors*, marries well with the relationship between VNSA life cycle and progressive differentiation. At the low end of the spectrum, violence results from "common culture" or spontaneous signaling (as in, "Get him!"), while at the high end, growing and/or mature organizations "follow shared scripts [plans, routines, orders] as they deliberately guide followers into violence-generating interactions with others."[8] Bar room brawls are at the low end, and conventional war is at the high.

Using this framework of salience and coordination, Tilly builds a two-dimensional classification of violence that includes a variety of categories, including violent rituals, coordinated destruction, opportunism, brawls, individual aggression, scattered attacks, and broken negotiations.[9] Rather than detailing each, it is more useful to note that VNSA travel this two-dimensional map during their life cycle, but not always in a linear order. During gestation and early growth, violence may not be an output at all. When present, environmental and organizational constraints often limit it to scattered attacks and opportunism. The former occur within the context of "widespread small-scale and generally non-violent interaction" when members of the VNSA "respond to obstacles, challenges, or restraints by means of damaging acts."[10] They don't plan to be violent, but when their non-violent methods are frustrated, violence may spontaneously occur. Scattered attacks normally occur within the context of stable relations when two or more participating parties are evenly matched and their routine interactions generate occasional violence, such as skirmishes between transnational criminal organizations (TCOs) over turf.[11] Since VNSA are rarely evenly matched with the state, scattered attacks also occur when the participant with the "preponderance of force" (the state) uses violence to demonstrate its strength as in a show of force, or when the VNSA responds to this demonstration with resistance.[12] This is a case of a failure in governance due to excessive coercion. Or, at least, the VNSA hopes to create a situation where the state's action is perceived as failure, leading to a loss of legitimacy. Resistance can take many forms, including sabotage, arson, vandalism (symbolic destruction), or assaults on agents, but rarely does it reflect a coordinated plan of action.

Violence as a function of opportunism is also more likely early in the VNSA's ontogeny, although we cannot rule it out during all phases. Opportunistic violence occurs as "a consequence of shielding from routine surveillance and repression, individuals or clusters of individuals use immediately damaging means to pursue generally forbidden ends; examples include looting, gang rape, piracy, revenge killing, and some sorts of military pillage."[13] Essentially, the requirements for coordination are low to medium, but the salience of damage is high. Thus, opportunistic violence is often a byproduct of a coordinated plan of collective violence in a late growth or mature VNSA. During gestation and early growth, opportunistic violence, if it exists at all, is likely to be: (1) the purposeful output of a VNSA with limited capabilities, or (2) the near spontaneous output of a VNSA in response to a short-term need; a type of knee-jerk reaction. For example, the timing and specific targets of Abu Sayyaf kidnappings over the last few years is more likely a function of financial crisis and opportunity (bad luck for the tourists) than a function of a deliberate planning process. Kidnapping may be part of their overall strategy, but when and where to strike are opportunistic acts.

During late growth and in maturity, VNSA are more likely to export collective violence that is high in both salience and coordination. At the high-high end, we find violent rituals and coordinated destruction. Violent rituals are the output of a "well-defined and coordinated group" following a known script, or plan, "entailing the infliction of damage on itself or others as it competes for priority within a recognized arena."[14] According to Tilly, violent rituals are the most extreme form of coordination due to their highly scripted nature in which sharp distinctions are made between identity cleavages; identity entrepreneurs polarize the participants, thus simultaneously exaggerating and disciplining the features found in other forms of collective violence."[15] Examples include public executions and internally symbolic destruction such as acts of mass suicide by apocalyptic cults.

Less rare than violent rituals and more common to the mature VNSA is coordinated destruction—"persons or organizations specialized in the deployment of coercive means undertake programs or actions that damage persons and/or objects."[16] Tilly makes a distinction among conspiratorial terror, campaigns of annihilation, and lethal contests that is useful. As scattered attacks and opportunism become more organized and sustained, they take on the character of what is known as conspiracy violence, or highly organized violence with limited participation on a small scale.[17] Even during gestation, one must not ignore the potential for a VNSA to develop an elite cadre of specialists that can carry out attacks designed to demonstrate strength, gain legitimacy, or access resources. Given that surveillance of a target, building an improvised explosive, and delivering it to a hardened target can be carried out with only a few thousand dollars and four to five operatives, even fledgling VNSA are capable of serious violence. Campaigns of annihilation exist when "one contestant wields overwhelming force or the object of attack is not an organization specialized in the deployment of coercive means."[18] The most obvious example is genocide as most recently practiced in Kosovo and Rwanda. Finally, lethal contests come closest to war in which two organized groups of violence specialists (warriors) confront each other.[19]

Given the many categories of collective violence outlined by Tilly and others, it is clear that most collective violence is not war. Without further inquiry, we might conclude that only coordinated destruction, which involves a high salience of violence and extensive organizational resources, reaches the threshold of war. While this is generally true of conventional war, we contend that wars involving VNSA embrace many of the forms of collective violence outlined by Tilly, thus lowering or at least shifting war's threshold.

War

War is a powerful word with real consequences. When war is declared, restraints lessen, responsibilities shift, expectations change, and violence reigns. Asserting the existence of a war serves to mobilize public opinion and resources, trigger the jurisdiction of international laws pertaining to the justice of and in war, and legitimize the use of destructive military force. Reflecting on the revolutionary, citizen-based character of the Napoleonic wars of the late eighteenth century and the "skulking" tactics of the wild Cossacks of Russia, Carl von Clausewitz authored the most important study of war. *On War* (*Von Kriege*) is impressive in scope; among its many important ideas is an assessment of what war is. Insisting that theory pass the test of reality, Clausewitz began simply by declaring that "war is an act of force to compel our enemy to do our will."[20] Force is the means of war and to impose one's will on the enemy is its object; to "secure that object we must render the enemy powerless," which is in theory the purpose of war fighting.[21] Underpinning this simple definition are three criteria—identified by and adapted from Donald J. Hanle's *Terrorism: The Newest Face of Warfare*—that enable us to determine whether collective violence by a VNSA crosses war's threshold: political purpose, engagement, and lethal force. In Hanle's own words, these criteria, "were derived by analyzing war from its most basic level of abstraction and through the eyes of a wide spectrum of military thinkers," of which Clausewitz is dominant.[22] In the following pages, we look at each criterion in turn, analyzing it to determine whether collective violence by VNSA meets its requirements, and ultimately to determine the nature of the conflict.

Political Purpose

The first criterion is at the crux of contemporary debates surrounding the changing character of war, and it centers attention on the reasons for resorting to collective violence in the first place. Since the French Revolution and Napoleon's conquest of Europe, war has been subordinated to politics. In the words of Clausewitz, "war is not merely a political act, but also a political instrument, a continuation of political relations, a carrying out of the same by other means."[23] Or, as is often conventionally stated, "war is a continuation of policy by other means."[24] Policy uses war to its own ends, thus negating the idea of war for war's sake, or for any non-political reason. This view also sees war as a tool of the state, drawn upon when the other instruments of policy, such as diplomacy or commerce, fail, or when the use of lethal force is seen as the most expedient and justified means of achieving a political goal. As stressed by Clausewitz, policy

> makes out of the all-overpowering element of War a mere instrument, changes the tremendous battle sword, which should be lifted with both hands and the whole power of the body to strike once for all, into a light handy weapon, which is even sometimes nothing more than a rapier to exchange thrusts and feints and parries.[25]

The rapier is generally considered to be in the hand of the state. In this section, however, we challenge the received interpretation of Clausewitz to reveal the non-state actor's deadly hand.

Political ends

What then is a political end, and do the purposes of VNSA fit its mold? A strict interpretation of war as "a continuation of policy by other means" suggests war to be the rational expression of state interests.[26] In realist language, state interest is about power, and war is about the redistribution of power in an anarchic international system. Under these terms, the VNSA is never at war, since it is neither a state, and its purposes and actions are not always a rational expression of policy. Nor does this narrow interpretation help us understand war in the pre-Westphalia period when combat was often a self-fulfilling act, or the messy internal wars that have gained prominence in the last decades, such as the brutish conflicts in Sierra Leone and Rwanda, many of which seem to be fought for the base reasons of greed and hate.[27] And some people we call terrorists do it for the glory and adventure—Carlos the Jackal hired out his gang for any cause.

Military historian John Keegan argues that war can be divorced from politics. More directly, he opens his classic *A History of Warfare* with: "War is not the continuation of policy by other means. The world would be a simpler place to understand if this dictum of Clausewitz were true."[28] He continues, "war is almost as old as man himself, and reaches the most secret places of the human heart, places where self dissolves rational purpose, where pride reigns, where emotion is paramount, where instinct is king."[29] While many take Keegan's critique to mean that war can be apolitical, it is more appropriate to interpret his approach as speaking more directly to the human will to war. War is not just political; it is cultural. This is not to discount political motives by VNSA, since many pursue traditional goals, including a desire to access the halls of power. Even in the uncivil civil wars of sub-Saharan Africa, rebels leaders are rarely content to carve out a territorial repository of diamonds or oil—they want to sit on the throne, if only to legitimate their control over said resources to gain wealth. Rather, it is to argue that many groups and certainly many members of groups kill for reasons as basic as greed, emotions like hate, pride, and revenge, or even in the more enlightened sense of Homer's warriors in the *Iliad*, for self-knowledge and glory.[30]

More specifically to the global fight against terrorism, Clausewitz does not at first seem to help us understand or deal with an adversary that is not just seeking to shift power in the system but seeks to overthrow the entire system from outside that system. On one level, Osama bin Laden and other Islamist leaders may point to the previous U.S. military presence in Saudi Arabia or the U.S. role in the Israeli-Palestinian conflict as primary causes for global *jihad*. In fact, a *fatwa* entitled "Declaration of the World Islamic Front for *Jihad* against the Jews and the Crusaders," released on February 23, 1998, in the *Al-Quds al-'Arabia* newspaper (based in London), seemed to be calling for holy war in the furtherance of traditional political goals when it declared:

> to kill Americans and their allies, both civil and military, is an individual duty of every Muslim who is able, in any country where this is possible, until the Aqsa mosque [in Jerusalem] and the Har'm mosque [in Mecca] are freed from their grip, and until their armies, shattered and broken-winged, depart from all the lands of Islam, incapable of threatening any Muslim.[31]

But there is also strong evidence to suggest that bin Laden and other members of this global *jihadist* insurgency were not satisfied with the change in U.S. policy that came with the U.S. pull out from Saudi Arabia in 2003. On November 15, 2001, Taliban ruler Mullah Mohammed Omar told the BBC, "the current situation in Afghanistan is related to a bigger cause—the destruction of America."[32] This is what Michael Ignatieff, Director of the Carr Center for Human Rights Policy at Harvard, calls "apocalyptic nihilism." He argues, "The apocalyptic nature of their goals makes it absurd to believe they are making political demands at all. They are seeking the violent transformation of an irremediably sinful and unjust world."[33]

On the surface, these critiques of Clausewitzian war seem valid. It is true that even within the conventional military forces of the industrialized world individual soldiers speak of fighting not on behalf of a president or policy, but for their fellow soldier. At the organizational level of VNSA, it is often hard to immediately discern the policy of groups like the Chinese Triads, Somali warlords or the South African Hard Livings Gang. Nonetheless, this first test can remain a useful tool for understanding wars with VNSA if we embrace a broader and more accurate understanding of Clausewitz's word "politik." Rather than translating it as policy, we should read it as politics. This reading allows us to refer back to the classic formulation of politics by David Easton as "the authoritative allocation of resources,"[34] or frankly, any of several definitions of politics that imply conflict between socio-political entities, which VNSA are, over material (oil, land, people) and non-material (ideas, identity, psyche) goods. War may sometimes be an expression of rational policy, but even when it is not, it is still political in this sense. As argued by Clausewitz scholars Edward J. Villacres and Christopher Bassford,

> The only element of this political trinity that makes it unique to *war* is that the emotions discussed are those that might incline people to violence, whereas politics in general will involve the full range of human feelings. Thus Clausewitz tells us that the conscious conduct of war (strategy, etc.) *should* be a continuation of rational calculation and policy, but also that war *inevitably* originates and exists within the chaotic, unpredictable realm of politics.[35]

VNSA are at war as long as their reasons for using violence can be considered political. While this seems to rule out violence as a self-fulfilling act, it is rare to find such a pure expression. When it does occur, it is often only a few within an organization that is pursuing political goals. Rather, an investigation into the transcendental and/or transactional strategy of the system is likely to reveal goals that are articulated or at least emergent, and these goals are likely to be political in nature.

Political actors

Within the same intellectual framework of war being only an instrument of rational policy is the core idea that war only occurs between states, involving armies, and is being waged on behalf of or at the expense of the people. Together, the state, army, and populace make up what is known as Clausewitz's "remarkable trinity." In only four paragraphs on the trinity, Clausewitz establishes "an interactive set of three forces that drive the events of war in the real world."[36] Ignored for many years, the trinity emerged as a framework for understanding warfare with the publication of Harry G. Summers' *On Strategy: A Critical Analysis of the Vietnam War*. According to Summers, the three forces

are the people, the government, and the army.[37] The government, or nation-
state, engages in war as an expression of politics. The instrument of the state
is the army; organized, uniformed, and subordinate to political leadership.
The third element is the populace on whose behalf or at whose expense the
war is waged. Others, including preeminent military scholars John Keegan
and Martin van Creveld, pick up this line of interpretation. In Keegan's words
from *A History of Warfare*, war as policy was

> the compromise for which states he knew had settled. It accorded respect to
> their prevailing ethics—of absolute sovereignty, ordered diplomacy and legally
> binding treaties—while making allowance for the overriding principle of state
> interest.[38]

In *The Transformation of War*, van Creveld argues that in the Clausewitzian
universe, "where there is no state, whatever armed violence takes place does
not amount to war."[39]

Like the narrow definition of political ends, conflict involving VNSA also
challenges the trinitarian notion that war is wedded only to the state, which
has a monopoly on the legitimate use of force. This approach has further
backing in contemporary international custom and convention; the 1907
Hague Regulation III refers to war as a condition among states.[40] But clearly,
war pre-dates the Peace of Westphalia in 1648, which established the sovereign
nation-state, and VNSA are engaged in combat in modern times. Although
many of our examples are contemporary in nature, it is worth remembering
that the United States was in some respects a VNSA at its founding, and became engaged in conflict with VNSA in its first years. During the administration of Thomas Jefferson, for example, the Barbary States of North Africa employed pirates to seize cargo and scuttle trading ships. After languishing in
prisons, crews were ransomed or sold into slavery.[41] Jefferson responded in his
first State of the Union address to Congress,

> to this state of general peace with which we have been blessed, only one excep-
> tion exists. Tripoli, the least considerable of the Barbary States, had come for-
> ward with a demand unfounded either in right or in compact, and had permit-
> ted itself to announce war on our failure to comply before a given day. The style
> of the demand admitted but one answer. I sent a small squadron of frigates to
> the Mediterranean.[42]

If we cling to this restrictive interpretation of trinitarian war, then the United
States was not at war against the Barbary Pirates, the Viet Cong, the Habr
Gedir clan of Mohammad Farrah Aideed, or the *fedayeen* in Iraq. To the participants in these conflicts and others, it smelled, sounded, and felt like war. It
was war, and Clausewitz would agree. His discussion of the trinity actually

speaks to the irrational, non-rational, and rational fields of action present in all wars. The "people" of Summers's and van Creveld's interpretations experience the irrational, or the violence and passion of war, while the army deals with the uncertainty, chance, and probabilities of war.[43] The rational field is the "business of government alone."[44]

Recasting the trinity in these more accurate terms, the people involved in VNSA conflict continue to experience the horrors of war. With VNSA, however, it is not always necessary to distinguish between the army and the government, although this can be done in a mature organization where the conversion sub-system serves as a military wing and the cognitive sub-system as the governing entity. In either case, the VNSA deals with the non-rational dimensions of conflict just like the state. This is entirely consistent with our argument that the system can only survive turbulence in its environment if it reduces uncertainty through the activities of its sub-systems. Moreover, the VNSA system also deals with the rational to the extent that its development and the cognitive sub-system's capacity allows rational decision-making to occur. Thus, VNSA pass the first and most important test of determining war—they are social entities fighting for political reasons.

Engagement

The second test springs from the "immutable factor of war" known as the engagement, which is the focus of Clausewitz's fourth book of *On War*.[45] He asserts, "the essential military activity, fighting, which by its material and psychological effect comprises in simple or compound form the overall object of war."[46] To put it more simply, "war is nothing but a duel on an extensive scale."[47] A common mistake of military analysts is analyzing the belligerents in isolation. Since war is relational, a more accurate depiction of the engagement requires the conflict to be examined as the interaction between two opposing systems in a competitive environment, remembering of course that the "fog" of war always limits accuracy. When the engagement involves VNSA against states, a defining characteristic will be its asymmetry. In terms of both its type and the forms of collective violence employed, fights between states and VNSA lack "a common basis of comparison in respect to a quality, or in operational terms, a capability."[48] Asymmetry does equate to newness or something that is surprising, but rather the often-dramatic differences between the state and VNSA in terms of a broad range of qualities. The best definition of asymmetry came out of the U.S. Army War College in 2001:

> In the realm of military affairs and national security, asymmetry is acting, organizing, and thinking *differently* than opponents in order to maximize one's own advantages, exploit an opponent's weaknesses, attain the initiative, or gain greater freedom of action. It can be political-strategic, military-strategic, opera-

tional, or a combination of these. It can entail different methods, technologies, values, organizations, time perspectives, or some combination of these. It can be deliberate or by default. It can be discrete or pursued in conjunction with symmetric approaches. It can have both psychological and physical dimensions.[49]

At its core, asymmetry is about *difference*. The most challenging informal wars will exist when there is a dramatic dissimilarity between opponents in several key areas, particularly when the belligerents are fighting different types of wars. For example, the Iraq War initially pitted the United States against the Iraqi conventional forces in a contest that was generally symmetric in terms of doctrine, weaponry, organizational structure, etc., but that also reflected war-defining asymmetries in training, technology, and cohesion to name a few. The asymmetries played to the U.S. advantage through the fall of Baghdad on April 9, 2003. As the war transitioned to an insurgency, the asymmetries grew, particularly in terms of strategy, weaponry, and tactics. Asymmetry does not mean that one side is necessarily advantaged, but it does have real consequences for the way the VNSA will employ collective violence and how the state should confront it.

Among the various qualities that might form the basis for an asymmetry, VNSA most often rely on an asymmetric strategy, which links means to ends. VNSA excel in "poor man's warfare." It relies on what military strategist Liddell Hart calls the *indirect approach*, attacking vulnerabilities while simultaneously avoiding direct physical engagements.[50] VNSA complicate the contest further by mixing unconventional tactics and weaponry with their strategy; in fact, the one influences the other. Rather than fielding a mechanized infantry unit to fight the British Dragoons Guards in Basra, Iraq, former regime loyalists employed small cells using improvised explosive and standoff mortar tubes. In many cases, the weapons are among the most out-dated and cheapest on the black market, including Strella and Stinger man-portable surface-to-air missiles and anti-personnel mines. In one example of low-tech weaponry as part of an indirect approach, U.S. soldiers captured a donkey cart mounted with rocket-propelled grenades used against the Iraqi Oil Ministry building and two hotels in November 2003.[51] Many other examples of innovative and unconventional tactics and weaponry exist, including cyber attacks and weapons of mass destruction. However, these methods and others are likely to be an aspect of more general approaches, and probably more important to the overall character (duration, intensity, scope, etc.) of the engagement, asymmetries in objectives, and methods.

Donald Hanle distills a rich body of literature on types of wars into a classification scheme based on objectives, political and military, and methods to further qualify the asymmetric relationship between two belligerents.[52] Starting with the political component, political objectives are either total or limited. A *total* objective seeks the complete destruction of the enemy as a political entity, while the *limited* objective seeks only the abandonment of or a change in policy.[53] Examples of the former can be found in the early positions of the Palestinian National Authority toward Israel, or more recently in the tapes of Osama bin Laden and *fatwas* of other extremists toward the United States. A total military objective of *annihilation* pursues the destruction of the adversary's armed forces in decisive battle, and the limited objective of *attrition* leverages time to erode the enemy's will to fight.[54] Finally, military methods are either *positional*, using maneuver to seize or hold terrain (conventional war), or *evasive*, using maneuver to avoid the enemy's strength (guerrilla war and terrorism).[55]

Applying this framework to the insurgency in Iraq, the former regime loyalists and foreign *jihadist* fighters were fighting a limited war of attrition using evasion. That is, they were seeking the limited objective of causing the United States and its allies to leave the country by eroding cohesion and will through a sustained series of knife cuts with car bombings, ambushes, and seemingly random attacks. As the weaker political entity, the VNSA of the Iraq War are forced to "employ security and maneuver to evade the enemy's [U.S.] stronger armed forces, hitting only when and where local superiority can be assured."[56] Understanding that the Iraq War is informal and limited both in terms of political and military objectives provides insight into the key to VNSA victory. In informal, limited wars, VNSAs win by "making the cost of victory greater than the opponent is willing to bear."[57] Where the objectives are limited, the VNSA is most likely expending energy to other non-violent projects, which in the long term may be more important than the violence itself. The social services of groups like *Hezbollah* or *Hamas* exemplify this approach, where violence is just one of several important outputs.

If it is correct to conclude that al Qaida is fighting a total war of attrition using evasion against the United States as part of its global *jihadist* insurgency, then the key to VNSA victory shifts. Drawing on Clausewitz, Hanle argues correctly that "in total war you erode your enemy's power base so that he becomes unable to fight, and in a limited war you maximize the cost(s) until he becomes unwilling to fight."[58] Of note, it is rare to find a VNSA pursuing a total war of annihilation given the limited ability of VNSA to generate the physical (more so than the moral) force required to defeat a state's armed forces in open battle. This is not to say it is impossible, but it is rare. As an example, an exception might be the Zulu of southern Africa. Shaka, chief of the Zulu, "became the commander of an army of savagely disciplined regiments that waged battles of annihilation."[59]

When up against a strong state, as in the case of the Afghan *mujahideen* against the Soviet Union, positional methods were rarely used, since the Afghan resistance lacked the forces to hold terrain. While not embracing Mao Tse-Tung's ideology, they did rely on evasive methods that hearken to his famous slogan: "When the enemy advances, we retreat. When the enemy halts, we harass. When the enemy seeks to avoid battle, we attack. When the enemy retreats, we pursue."[60] Regardless of the military strategy, positional or evasive, victory always hinges on "destroying the enemy's will to resist" by employing the force available.[61]

Lethal Force

The final test relates to the goal of compelling an enemy to do one's will through the employment of force. For war to exist, lethal force must be employed, and if it is to be successful, it must target the adversary's will. Since war is essentially a social exchange, force is directed against will on both the physical and moral planes. Physical force compels by "removing all alternatives and options the target body may be considering, compelling it to act in accordance with the force-wielder's will."[62] More simply, physical force is the ability to fight. A VNSA employs physical force when it can fire a mortar or when it can build and plant an improvised explosive. Some form of physical force is nearly always retained even when the battle is lost. In contrast, moral force is exerted at the psychological level, and it "represents the ability to animate physical force, converting it from potential to kinetic energy and equally important, the ability to resist demoralization in the face of the enemy's physical force."[63] It is the will to fight. A VNSA retains moral force when it continues to conduct ambushes against government forces even after terrific combat losses in physical terms: insurgents killed, weapons captured, bases destroyed. Moral force is built by all the sub-systems working in concert and with the maintenance subsystem socializing members and ensuring cohesion through rewards and sanctions. In this respect, moral force is simultaneously a key contributor to congruence and a source of negative entropy. The relationship between physical and moral force on the battlefield is important and best described by Hanle:

> The reason moral force enjoys such predominance over physical force can easily be seen by examining how physical force actually functions on the battlefield. As mentioned earlier, physical force is manifested in combat by disabling the enemy: that is, by destroying or damaging his means to fight and by killing, wounding, or capturing the enemy's combatant. Physical force confronts physical force until one of the other is expended. In combat, however, the total annihilation of one of the contending forces is a relatively rare phenomenon, since the combatants on the losing side usually perceive what is happening long before the final blow and attempt to disengage. In this situation, physical force begins to exert extreme psychological pressure upon the side that perceives it is losing, and that side becomes demoralized. Demoralization, of course, immediately affects the physical force available to the demoralized army since the combatants lose courage and willingness to fight. In short, there is nothing with which to animate the physical force necessary to defeat the enemy.[64]

Even though moral force is the stronger of the two forms of collective violence, Hanle argues that the engagement must occur on the physical plane for war to exist.[65] This is consistent with our definition of collective violence, which requires some form of damage or injury to occur. Thus, it is not sufficient to hurl propaganda or electrons at one another and call it war; something must break, or someone must get hurt. When VNSA attack on the physical plane, the war threshold is crossed; however, it is not until the VNSA attacks on both the moral and physical planes that it has any hope of success. Thus, VNSA are most likely to rely on forms of "coordinated destruction" that attacks on both planes, primarily guerrilla warfare and terrorism, and where possible and productive, conventional war. Together, these three are "forms" of warfare, which can be "viewed as a variety of organized violence emphasizing particular armed force, weapons, tactics and targets."[66] Forms of war are distinct from strategies and are often confused with concepts like revolutionary war, insurgency, *jihad*, preemptive war, etc. These concepts refer to politico-military constructs that will employ one or more of the forms of collective violence as warfare described here.

Conventional warfare

Even though there are few examples of VNSA fielding large, mechanized conventional forces, they do exist. In the 2001 war in Afghanistan, bin Laden fielded an "elite" force of Arab fighters with mechanized equipment as the 55th Arab Brigade. Other VNSA, such as the Liberation Tigers of Tamil Elan (LTTE) in Sri Lanka or any of the many rebel groups in Africa, have occasionally fielded armies, small though they were. Indeed, Mao's strategy ultimately calls for a transition out of guerrilla war into pitched conventional battles as the final stage of the "People's War." These rare occasions aside, a conventional VNSA force capable of force-on-force engagements is a rarity for three principal reasons relating to our open systems scaffolding. First, the building and deploying of a conventional force requires geo-political space or the environmental niche to build and sustain it. The VNSA must carve out the territory for force development from the state. In the case of al Qaida, the Taliban offered the space. In the case of the FARC, former Colombian president Andres Pastrana actually ceded territory as part of a peace process, allowing the FARC to consolidate its forces. In most cases, the VNSA must wrestle the space from the state, an approach that has proven successful after initial successes in internal wars. Even when space is obtained, the VNSA must be sufficiently developed to recruit, train, equip, and feed a conventional force. Given the limited resources and soldiering skills of most VNSA, building a conventional force that is certain to lack the capabilities of the state's forces is an unwise investment. This, of course, is the final reason for the infrequency of conventional VNSA armies. States can build and sustain conventional forces that VNSA find difficult to rival. Moreover, by building a conventional force, the VNSA is playing to the state's asymmetric operational advantages and thus setting itself up for easier defeat. Against an industrialized foe, concentrating one's forces is an invitation to summary destruction. Given these few reasons and many others, guerrilla and terrorism strategies are far more popular forms of collective violence by VNSA at war.

Guerrilla warfare

Guerrilla warfare is war by the weak against the strong, and at its core is the avoidance of direct confrontation. The guerrilla's only chance of winning is to survive, preserving his smaller forces while simultaneously wearing down his adversary. Small, persistent attacks on the physical plane are intended to compel the enemy's will on the moral plane. It takes advantage of the asymmetries of informal war by directing what lethal force is available to the VNSA against the state's vulnerabilities. In the words of one of guerrilla warfare's primary architects, Mao Tse-tung, "the strategy of guerilla [sic] war is to put one man against ten, but the tactic is to pit ten men against one."[67]

Like the difficulty we face in drawing out a single definition of war and later terrorism, the U.S. Department of Defense (DoD) offers a definition that is only partially helpful: "military and paramilitary operations conducted in enemy-held or hostile territory by irregular, predominantly indigenous forces."[68] This definition correctly gets at the military aspect of the operation, the obvious geo-political space (hostile) in which operations occur, and the irregular nature of the forces. Moreover, guerrillas are principally indigenous forces; however, conflicts have witnessed a significant increase in the participation of non-indigenous forces ever since the Afghan *mujahideen* welcomed the participation of Arabs in their fight against the Soviet Union. With victory against one of the world's superpowers in 1989, foreign fighters were emboldened and unemployed. Like the roving mercenaries of the pre-Westphalian period or contemporary West Africa, they embraced bin Laden's call for a global *jihad* and fanned out across the globe to support a perceived defensive struggle by the Islamic community, or *umma*, against infidels and apostate regimes in the Balkans, Chechnya, Afghanistan again, and now Iraq, among others. On the eve of the Iraq War of 2003, Syrians, Afghanis, Yemenis, Chechens, Saudis, and others rushed to Iraq to join the fray.

Where the DoD definition comes up short is in its failure to address the distinctive targets and tactics of guerrilla warfare. In terms of targets, guerrilla warfare is distinguished from terrorism by its focus on the government rather than innocents. Gray areas exist. Whereas most guerrilla operations throughout history have centered targeting on the state's military, it is not uncommon to see guerrillas go after other government officials and related support facilities. In the eyes of the guerrilla, these are legitimate targets, given their association with the state's instruments of coercion, but the further removed the target is from the causal chain of coercion, the more likely the attack is going to be perceived as terrorism. Of course, even when the targets are considered legitimate, the state is likely to employ the rhetoric of terrorism in an effort to discredit the guerrillas.

Strategy and tactics are certain to see unique application in different periods and environmental settings; however, guerrilla warfare has remained throughout its long history a strategy that focuses on eroding the enemy's will and capability.[69] In systems terms, it is a strategy of creating positive entropy or disorder, to slowly and deliberately undermine the performance of government forces, creating incongruence and depleting its stores of negative entropy. In the case of the VNSA confronting the state, the state's negative entropy is likely to be popular support and its associated legitimacy. By demonstrating the state's incapacity, the VNSA hopes to induce a failure in governance; it is simultaneously constructing and expanding its environment niche and increasing its support in the populace. This strategy is being played out in the so-called Sunni Triangle of Iraq where insurgents sought to demonstrate the inability of the U.S.-led coalition to provide security and basic services by attacking police stations, pipelines, non-governmental organizations (Red Cross), inter-governmental organizations (United Nations), and the coalition military forces.

The history of guerrilla warfare is replete with well-known theorists and practitioners, including Sun Tzu, Clausewitz, T. E. Lawrence, Col. Charles Callwell (author of the influential *Small Wars: Their Principles and Practice*), Che Guevara, and General Vo Nguyen Giap.[70] All contributed to its development, but for the best articulation of its overall strategy and tactics we return to Mao as quoted in Bard E. O'Neill's *Insurgency and Terrorism*:

> What is the basic guerrilla strategy? Guerrilla strategy must be based primarily on alertness, mobility, and attack. It must be adjusted to the enemy situation, the terrain, the existing lines of communication, the relative strengths, the weather, and the situation of the people.
>
> In guerrilla warfare, select the tactic of seeming to come from the east and attacking from west; avoid the solid, attack the hollow; attack; withdraw; deliver a lightning blow, seek a lightning decision. When guerrillas engage a stronger enemy, they withdraw when he advances; harass him when he stops; strike him when he is weary; pursue him when he withdraws. In guerrilla strategy, the enemy's rear, flanks and other vulnerable spots are his vital points, and there he must be harassed, attacked, dispersed, exhausted, and annihilated.[71]

Mao's emphasis on environmental conditions reflects his sophisticated, yet not explicit, understanding of open systems theory as well as the organizational limitations of a growing non-state actor. Of course, Mao also sees guerrilla warfare as a set of tactics to be employed as part of a broader revolutionary struggle that will ultimately transition to mobile war; this is recognition of the life cycle. If we embrace Mao's thinking, all wars involving VNSA will be protracted for two reasons: (1) to permit the guerrillas to gain strength to reach equilibrium with the adversary; and (2) to allow external and internal political and economic pressure to build on the adversary to erode his ability and will to continue the war.[72] Both reasons reflect the inevitability of an organization to seek balance or congruence with its environment.

There are many reasons why guerrilla warfare is likely to be the strategy of choice for the VNSA. The most obvious is that it is within their grasp. Although gestating and early growth VNSA may not be able to develop or sustain guerrilla-size units, the late growth and mature VNSA can muster small units of ten to twenty, provide basic training and weapons, and orchestrate a strategy involving multiple hit-and-run attacks. Witness the expansion of guerrilla attacks by the Iraqi insurgency in 2003–2004, which grew as the organization took form, marshaled the cash resources and developed a strategy. Guerrilla warfare may also reflect the VNSA's read of the environment. Given its emphasis on strategic defense and tactical offense, the guerrilla strategy is one of essentially waiting out and wearing down the state. Based on perceived environmental changes, such as deteriorating socio-economic conditions or political elections, the VNSA may conclude that conventional war is not necessary even if it is within the organization's capability. That said, the choice between guerrilla warfare and conventional war is largely one of capability, whereas the choice between guerrilla warfare and terrorism is largely one of popular legitimacy. The guerrilla seeks to preserve popular support by not intentionally killing civilians. The terrorist, as we shall set forth in the next section, kills civilians to either eradicate the enemy, which includes the civilians, or force a change in policy without regard to popular support.

Terrorism

Terrorism is the ultimate form of asymmetric informal war. Even in the midst of a global war against terrorism, however, debate surrounds whether terrorism is crime, war, or both. In this section, we explore and, it is hoped, resolve this dilemma in order to understand terrorism as form of criminal warfare, which allows but does not necessitate a warfighting response. A quick scenario sets up the discussion. Shortly before 10:00 p.m. on Tuesday, June 25,

1996, a fuel truck parked next to the northern perimeter of the housing complex in Dhahran, Saudi Arabia, known as Khobar Towers. Within minutes and before the nearest apartment tower could be fully evacuated, a powerful blast shattered the still night. The entire northern face of the closest tower was erased, windows blew out in surrounding buildings, and the sound rumbled for miles across the desert. As the dust cleared and the attacker sped away, nineteen American airmen lay dead in the ruins. Were these victims of crime or casualties of war? The same question can be asked of thousands killed in other attacks, including the 1993 World Trade Center bombing (6 killed, 1,000 plus wounded), the 1998 American Embassy bombings in Kenya and Tanzania (224 killed, 4,000 plus wounded), the 2000 USS Cole bombing (17 killed, 33 wounded), and of course, the attacks of September 11, 2001, where the death toll centers around 3,000. The answer is not simple, nor can it be readily discerned by past and present responses to terrorism by the United States and others. Looking only to the United States, Washington responded to the 1998 embassy bombings with cruise missile attacks on al Qaida camps in Afghanistan and a suspected chemical factory in Sudan. Initial U.S. response to the Khobar and USS Cole bombings were to pursue criminal investigations, although military options were considered. As a result of this crime fighting, approximately 17 people were convicted; this is clearly insufficient to bring terrorism to its knees. When terrorism was treated as war after September 11, 2001, the arrest and capture totals rose dramatically.

To resolve the crime-versus-war dilemma, we must first come to grips with the definition of terrorism. What is terrorism? Violent theater?[73] Like the concept of war, the problem with defining terrorism is that the word has been abused and overused. As pointed out by Bruce Hoffman, author of *Inside Terrorism*, "virtually any especially abhorrent act of violence that is perceived as directed against society—whether it involves the activities of anti-government dissidents or governments themselves, organized crime syndicates or common criminals, rioting mobs or persons engaged in militant protest, individual psychotics or lone extortionist—is often labeled terrorism."[74]

Indeed, terrorism may be even more difficult to define than war, as evidenced by the varying definitions used by the United States. The FBI, for example, emphasizes the criminal aspect of terrorism as the "unlawful use of force or violence against persons or property to intimidate or coerce."[75] The State Department on the other hand, draws our attention to the political character of the actor and the non-combatant status of the target. The Department of Defense ignores the actor entirely and focuses on the act, which is unlawful and can be motivated by "political, religious, or ideological objectives."[76] The current body of international law proscribes certain targets and specific tactics, thus whittling away at terrorism but never attacking it head on.[77] In the absence of definitional consensus, we need to at least identify terrorism's core elements.

A survey of definitions suggests the following key elements: political objectives; violence or the threat of violence; psychological effects beyond the victim or target; and organized perpetrators. Bruce Hoffman pulls these elements together in a widely accepted definition: *the deliberate creation and exploitation of fear through violence or the threat of violence in the pursuit of political change.*[78] This is a good definition, but it casts the net too wide. Without knowing we were examining terrorism, one might conclude that this definition also works for other forms of force employment. That is, guerrillas also seek to induce fear in the conventional force they confront for the purpose of demoralizing the unit as a means to its ultimate defeat, and eventually, political change. Returning to the work of Hanle and many others, we should incorporate the idea of "abnormal force." Terrorism got its name because of the terror aspect, and terror occurs when the normative values, or expectations, of the target and/or audience is violated.[79] The abnormality of the act of collective violence can be assessed in terms of the target and tactics. Regarding the former, there is general consensus on the prohibition against intentionally targeting innocents. In fact, the intentional killing of innocents is the most direct way of distinguishing terrorism from other forms of warfare, and it immediately justifies a strong moral condemnation of the act. In terms of the latter, tactical abnormality equates to criminal violence; terrorism involves criminal tactics.

With these caveats, we are left with a more useful definition: *the deliberate creation and exploitation of fear through the use or threat of collective violence against innocents in the pursuit of political change.* This definition is consistent with our revised definition of war. It is purposeful force by political entities, including non-state actors, to achieve broadly defined political goals. Terrorism seeks to achieve a psychological effect on a target audience, which is most often separate from the victim. The target audience of the September 11, 2001, attacks was not the passengers or the employees of the World Trade Center, but the American public. In this respect, it is the most sophisticated form of warfare, attacking on both the physical and moral planes.[80] Thus, "terrorism represents a clash of wills," and if the participants employ force to resolve this clash and they both seek a political outcome "then war exists, and the terrorism used by either belligerent constitutes a form of war."[81]

The suicide bombing of the USS Cole on October 12, 2000, offers an interesting test case as well. Strategically located near the mouth of the Red Sea, Aden was undergoing a modest revival as a refueling stop when the USS Cole made its visit. Around noon, the USS Cole was in the middle of the harbor preparing to refuel at a floating station while small rubber boats secured the massive destroyer to the surrounding buoys with mooring lines. Two men in one of the boats apparently smiled and waved as they returned to its side. As sailors continued in their work, an unexpected explosion tore a twenty-by-forty-foot hole in the hull near the engine room and adjacent to eating and living quarters. Throughout the night and into the next day, sailors fought to save their mates and their boat. In the end, seventeen sailors were killed and thirty-nine injured.

Was it terrorism? Even with our definitions, the answer is not clear. Based on target criteria, the answer seems to be no. Although it involved the deliberate creation and exploitation of fear through the use or threat of collective violence in the pursuit of political change, the attack was not directed against innocents. One might argue, however, that the sailors of the USS Cole were not part of a logical causal chain designed to harm someone, and it was their living quarters and mess that were attacked, removing them even further from the "engagement." This raises the question of whether military personnel are legitimate targets under all conditions or only when engaged in war declared by a legitimate authority. On the other hand, bin Laden might argue that war had been declared in his *fatwa* and the soldiers of the USS Cole were instruments of the state engaged in military actions against the Muslim community. Was this an act of war? Maybe. It was an act of force by a political entity for the purpose of achieving a political end, but only if we allow for war by non-state actors and if you can ascertain an engagement. The engagement does not necessarily have to occur at the time of the bombing, but if the bombing can be seen as a "salvo" in an on-going conflict, the engagement exists. At fist blush, this conclusion seems to legalize the act. If we can determine that the tactic was illegal, however, we slip into the gray area between terrorism and guerrilla warfare, or least toward a characterization of the act as illegal.

The issue becomes clearer in cases like the attacks on the World Trade Center. In these cases, the tactics are certainly illegal by international convention—they are criminal—but more importantly, the targets are abnormal. While civilians have been considered legitimate targets in other periods of history, they are not today. So, if we want to apply some moral and criminal standard to the act, then terrorist attacks that are abnormal in terms of both target and tactic are far more heinous than those that are abnormal only in terms of one or the other. VNSA are not immune to this distinction, which may figure heavily into strategy development.

Returning to the original question, were the nineteen American airmen from Khobar Towers victims of crime or casualties of war? The question poses a false dichotomy. They were both. And the same goes for any victim or casualty of war involving terrorism. Terrorism is simultaneously an act of war and a crime by the very nature of target, most importantly, but also the tactic. To put it more directly, terrorism is criminal war. Indeed, it is this conjunction of crime and war that has come to be known as the grey area of informal war.

Closing

Returning to our opening vignette, the recent Chechen wars bear resemblance to the Caucasian wars of the mid-nineteenth century when Imam Shamil and his Murid warriors fought a limited war of attrition against the tsar's army, relying on tactics that shocked the Russians and brought into question their Clausewitzian assumptions about warfare. As an example, when an initial column of six hundred Russian soldiers pressed the imam's mountain holdout, Akhulgo, they were picked off by sharpshooters in conventional fashion.[82] The second column retreated under a hailstorm of boulders, reflecting a surprising asymmetry in weaponry but not in tactics. As the third column marched toward the village entrance, prepared as they were for guns and rocks, women and children lunged toward them wielding daggers. Surviving soldiers were

> struck by both the ferocity of the attack and the commitment to death. Women would snatch a soldier as they fell over the precipice, happy to perish if they might swap life for life. The Russians also remembered that the bodies of dead children were thrown against them.[83]

It was this final attack, asymmetric in nearly every conceivable quality, that forced the Russians to retreat until another day. They had confronted a VNSA that employed the full spectrum of collective violence as part of a total war for survival.

Operational asymmetry is only one of several implications of informal war that demand appreciation and investigation. Among others, the impact on and continued relevance of international law is one of the most important at the environmental level. The body of international customs and laws that govern war was initially inadequate for informal war, particularly when it involved terrorism. Informal war is often waged outside the system against the system, and therefore the rules of the system do not always apply. The legal difficulties surrounding informal war came to a head over the status of Taliban and al Qaida detainees at Guantanamo Bay. At the time, the United States concluded that the Taliban captives were entitled to the "Geneva Test" to determine if they were POWs, since Afghanistan was a signatory to the Geneva Conventions. Of course, they failed because they did not meet the four requirements for combatant status as outlined in Article 4 of the third Geneva Convention: commanded by one responsible for their conduct; have fixed and distinctive sign that is recognizable at a distance; bear arms openly; and follow the laws of war.[84] The al Qaida captives did not even get the test because they were not agents of the state, and thus remained detainees.

Historically, war has been the circumstance of states, and international law is the law of states. Informal war is with states and non-state actors, and with the few exceptions of a new body of laws pertaining to state responsibilities

regarding terrorism and organized crime, there is a paucity of law placing any
responsibilities on VNSA or guiding the conduct of informal war. Even if we
were to extend the existing laws of war to al Qaida, it rejects the system on
which these very laws are predicated. Nonetheless, the process of changing
international law to tackle war with non-state actors is already underway.
President George W. Bush asserted that the United States was at war in his
September 20, 2001, address to Congress, and Congress moved quickly to pass
a joint resolution supporting the use of force. The absence of a formal declaration of war is of little consequence, particularly when one considers that
the United States has used military force more than 220 times in its history
and only declared war 5 times. The process of creating new customary international law continued with invocation of the collective defense protocols of
the NATO Treaty and through the unanimous passing of UN Security Council resolution 1377, which asserted that any act of international terrorism is a
direct threat to peace and security.[85]

Where do we go from here? One option is to allow the evolutionary process to
continue with new customary law being established on the fly. A way to get ahead
of the curve is to call for a fifth Geneva Convention to deal with informal war.
Regardless of the approach, we strongly recommend that the process be ecu-
menical. International law will gain legitimacy if it embraces legal thought outside the western tradition. Specifically, there is real value in exploring the integration of the body of classical Islamic law or *sharia* that deals with international
law, known as *siyar*. *Siyar* governs both the justice of and in war and notably does
so without reference to the nation-state. If we are concerned about POW treatment, then it is worth considering that *siyar* sets forth standards of treatment that
rival the Geneva Conventions.[86] Absent any effort along these lines, significant
aspects of informal war will continue to be fought outside the law.

Another implication has to do with strategies for fighting informal wars,
which is the focus of our next chapter. One way of fighting asymmetry is with
law enforcement. This approach, which has dominated nation-state response
to terrorism prior to September 11, 2001, relies on investigation, forensics,
prosecution, and incarceration. It has proven effective when dealing with
TCOs, and given the system similarities among VNSA, it should also be applied to other groups including ethno-political groups and militant religious
movements. In fact, the integration of criminal and counter-intelligence practices with military action is already underway. But crime fighting is only marginally effective on its own. Dealing with crime domestically is hard enough
where a robust law enforcement and judicial system exists. The international
system is even less potent, suffering from voluntary participation, a weak Interpol, and an embryonic international criminal court. High profile cases like
Carlos the Jackal or Ramzi Youssuf notwithstanding, terrorists are incredibly
hard to arrest. And when arrested, convicting with proof beyond a reasonable

doubt is difficult, due to the high standards of proof, complications involving classified intelligence, and many other reasons. Of the two Libyans tried in The Netherlands for the Pan Am 103 bombing, Al-Amin Kalifa Fahima was released due to a combination of these reasons.

Warfighting is at the opposite end of the response spectrum. Certainly evidence must be marshaled for initiating a war, but the requirements for evidence, or intelligence, in the context of a firefight are considerably less. Warfighting is not about collecting evidence for prosecution, but collecting intelligence for disruption and ultimately termination. As demonstrated in Afghanistan, the innovative and agile integration of special operations and precision airpower is particularly effective in dealing with fixed targets, like the training camps in the Khowst area and massed forces, like al Qaida's 55th Arab Brigade near Mazar-i-Sharif. Warfighting, however, can be too blunt an instrument to deal with the asymmetry of the threat, particularly when networked cells base operations out of apartments in cities of allied countries, such as Hamburg, Germany.

An effective counter-VNSA military strategy must therefore blend the two capabilities, which occurs at an organizational level between agencies and at the operational level between forces. At the intersection between warfighting and crime fighting is intelligence. Knowledge is the key to fighting asymmetry. Of course, the full spectrum of response options can only be effectively engaged when the informal war is recognized and understood in the terms described here. But even when the war is recognized, we are reminded of the various constraints that may suggest a response short of warfighting. In addition to its bluntness, the use of military forces may be prohibited by domestic law (*posse comitatus* in the United States) or treaty, by moral limits such as a failure to meet the standards of just war theory, or by political considerations. In fact, under certain political circumstances, it may not be in the state's interest to use the rhetoric of war at all. The specific response should be engaged based on principles and strategies tailored to an open system. The major elements of such a strategy are the focus of our next chapter.

Notes

1. For an insightful, readable account of arguably the greatest Muslim warrior of the nineteenth century, Imam Shamil, and a modern travelogue reflecting on the current war in Chechnya, read Nicholas Griffin, *Caucasus: Mountain Men and Holy Wars* (New York: St. Martin's Press, 2001).

2. Robert J. Bunker edits a new, useful volume on the character of warfare involving VNSA in *Non-State Threats and Future Wars* (Portland, OR: Frank Cass, 2003).

3. Carl von Clausewitz, *On War: General Carl Von Clausewitz,* trans. Colonel J. J. Graham, 8th ed. (London, UK: Routledge and Kegan Paul, 1966), 25.

4. Steven Metz, *Armed Conflict in the 21st Century: The Information Revolution and Post-Modern Warfare* (Carlisle, PA: Strategic Studies Institute, April 2000), 48.

5. Charles Tilly, *The Politics of Collective Violence* (Cambridge, UK: Cambridge University Press, 2003), 3.

6. While other dimensions for categorizing collective violence exist, including lethality, duration, and others, Tilly argues, and we agree, that this approach: 1) identifies "significant, coherent variations in relevant combinations of outcomes and causal mechanisms"; 2) locates "clusters of collective violence within which similar causes operate"; and 3) helps explain "variation with respect" to the other possible dimensions, such as scale, duration, destructiveness, etc. Ibid., 14.

7. Ibid., 13.

8. Ibid.

9. Ibid., 14–16.

10. Ibid., 15.

11. Ibid., 172.

12. Ibid.

13. Ibid., 14–15.

14. Ibid., 14.

15. Ibid., 84.

16. Ibid., 103.

17. Adapted from Ted Robert Gurr, *Why Men Rebel* (Princeton, NJ: Princeton University Press, 1970), 11.

18. Tilly, *Politics*, 104.

19. Ibid., 104.

20. Carl von Clausewitz, *On War*, ed. and trans. Michael Howard and Peter Paret (Princeton, NJ: Princeton University Press, 1984), 75.

21. Ibid.

22. Donald Hanle, *Terrorism: The Newest Face of Warfare* (Washington, DC: Pergamon-Brassey's, 1989), 52.

23. Clausewitz, *On War*, 87.

24. Hanle, *Terrorism*, 52.

25. Clausewitz, *On War: General*, vol. 3, 122–23.

26. Hanle, *Terrorism*, 52.

27. The idea of war as a self-fulfilling act comes principally from John Keegan and is thoroughly examined in his seminal work *A History of Warfare* (New York: Vintage Books, 1993).

28. Keegan, *A History*, 3.

29. Ibid.

30. Two books in particular provide remarkable insight to non-political motives to violence. Dr. Willard Gaylin, *Hatred: The Psychological Descent into Violence* (New York: Public Affairs, 2003), helps understand the psychological attachment of terrorists to their victim population and the passions that underlie their acts of violence. *In Waging War Without Warriors: The Changing Culture of Military Conflict* (Boulder, CO: Lynne Rienner Publishers, 2002), Christopher Coker offers an intriguing discussion of the march toward post–human warfare and the demise of the warrior, who rarely fought for the advancement of state policy.

31. The *fatwa* is reprinted in part and analyzed by Bernard Lewis, *The Crisis of Islam: Holy War and Unholy Terror* (New York: Modern Library, 2003), xxvii.

32. Transcript of interview with Mullah Omar conducted by BBC. Thursday, November 15, 2001, 10:31 GMT. Available at news.bbc.co.uk/hi/english/world/south_asia/newsid_1657000/1657368.stm.

33. Michael Ignatieff, "It's War—But It Doesn't Have to be Dirty," *The Guardian*, October 1, 2001. Accessed on November 22, 2003. Available at www.guardian.co.uk/Archive/Article/0,4273,4267406,00.html.

34. Discussed by Donald M. Snow and Eugene Brown in *International Relations: The Changing Contours of Power* (New York: Longman, 2000), 46.

35. Edward J. Villacres and Christopher Bassford, "Reclaiming the Clausewitzian Trinity." Reproduced at www.clausewitz.com/CWZHOME/Trinity/TRININTR.htm with permission of *Parameters*, Autumn 1995. Accessed on December 10, 2003.

36. Christopher Bassford, "Teaching the Clausewitzian Trinity." Available on the Clausewitz homepage edited by Bassford at www.clausewitz.com/CWZHOME/Trinity/TrinityTeachingNote.htm. Accessed on December 10, 2003.

37. Harry G. Summers Jr., *On Strategy: A Critical Analysis of the Vietnam War*, 4th ed. (Novato, CA: Presidio Press, 1982), 5.

38. Keegan, *A History*, 5.

39. Martin van Creveld, *The Transformation of War* (New York: The Free Press, 1991), 57.

40. W. Michael Reisman and Chris T. Antoniou, eds., *The Laws of War: A Comprehensive Collection of Primary Documents on International Laws Governing Armed Conflict* (New York: Vintage Books, 1994), 40.

41. Gerard W. Gawalt, "America and the Barbary Pirates: An International Battle Against an Unconventional Foe." Available in the *Thomas Jefferson Papers* at memory.loc.gov/ammem/mtjhtml/mtjhome.html. Accessed on March 17, 2001.

42. Ibid.

43. Clausewitz, *On War*, 201

44. Ibid.

45. Ibid., 52.

46. Ibid., 197–99.

47. Clausewitz, *On War: General*, vol. 1, 1.

48. Montgomery C. Meigs, "Unorthodox Thoughts about Asymmetric Warfare," *Parameters* 33, no. 2 (Summer 2003), 4.

49 Steven Metz and Douglas V. Johnson II, *Asymmetry and U.S. Military Strategy: Definition, Background, and Strategic Concepts* (Carlisle, PA: Strategic Studies Institute, U.S. Army War College, January 2001), 5–6.

50. The indirect approach is explained in B. H. Liddell Hart's classic study, *Strategy* (New York: Signet, 1967).

51. "Rocket strikes 'militarily insignificant,'" CNN, November 21, 2003. Accessed on November 22, 2003. Available from *CNN on-line* at: www.cnn.com/2003/WORLD/meast/11/21/sprj.irq.main/index.html.

52. Hanle, *Terrorism*, 157.

53. Ibid., 62.

54. Ibid.

55. Ibid.

56. Ibid., 57.

57. Ibid., 59.

58. Ibid.

59. Keegan, *A History*, 29.

60. Hanle, *Terrorism*, 61.

61. Ibid.

62. Ibid., 30.

63. Ibid.

64. Ibid., 19.

65. Ibid., 52.

66. Bard E. O'Neill, *Insurgency and Terrorism: Inside Modern Revolutionary Warfare* (Washington, DC: Brassey's, Inc., 1990), 24.

67. Quoted from Max Boot in his excellent study of U.S. involvement in small wars during its history, *The Savage Wars of Peace: Small Wars and the Rise of American Power* (New York: Basic Books, 2002), 112.

68. Joint Publication 1-02, *Department of Defense Dictionary of Military and Associated Terms* (Washington, DC: US Department of Defense, April 12, 2001, as amended through December 17, 2003), 227

69. O'Neill, *Insurgency*, 25.

70. Among the many histories of guerrilla warfare, we recommend: Robert B. Asprey, *War in the Shadows: The Guerrilla in History* (New York: William Morrow and Company, 1994); Walter Laqueur, *Guerrilla Warfare: A Historical and Critical Study* (New Brunswick, NJ: Transaction Publishers, 1998).

71. O'Neill is quoting from Mao's *On Guerrilla Warfare* (New York: Fredrick A. Praeger, 1962) in *Insurgency*, 25.

72. Air Force Major Patricia D. Hoffman provides an excellent summary of the history and key elements of guerrilla warfare in her School of Advanced Air and Space Power Studies thesis, *Seeking Shadows In The Sky: The Strategy Of Air Guerrilla* (Air University, Maxwell Air Force Base, AL, June 2000), 18.

73. Brian Jenkins first introduced the idea of "terrorism is theater" in "International Terrorism: A New Mode of Conflict" in David Carlton and Carlo Schaerf, eds., *International Terrorism and World Security* (London, UK: Croom Helm, 1975), 16.

74. Ibid., 13.

75. Ibid., 38.

76. Ibid.

77. For a listing of the key terrorism conventions, see the United Nations website available at: untreaty.un.org/English/Terrorism.asp. Available as of January 10, 2004.

78. Bruce Hoffman, *Inside Terrorism*, (New York: Columbia University Press, 1998), 43.

79. Ibid., 107.

80. Ibid., 118.

81. Ibid.

82. Griffin, *Caucasus*, 21.

83. Ibid.

84. Reisman, *The Laws of War,* 179.

85. Text of the resolution is available from the United Nations at: ods-dds-ny.un.org/doc/UNDOC/GEN/N01/633/01/PDF/N0163301.pdf?OpenElement. Available on January 10, 2004.

86. For further discussion of Islamic law pertaining to war, see Troy S. Thomas, "Prisoner's of War in Islam: A Legal Inquiry," *The Muslim World* 87, no. 1(January 1997).

7

Countering Violent Non-State Actors

Pedro entered the police complex through the unlocked door on the south-west side of the rusty corrugated tin structure that housed the infirmary; the small bomb he carried with him had been manufactured by three experts in bomb-making, themselves recently recruited by the People's Revolutionary Army (ERP). Three hours after Pedro left the bomb in the corner of the room immediately next to the patient's ward, it detonated, killing two people and injuring three others. The response was as draconian as Pedro could have hoped: the Argentina Anticommunist Alliance (AAA) sprang into action, drag-netting the entire south side of Buenos Aires. Along the way, the AAA "accidentally" killed eight innocent people (although Pedro knew that in reality, the corrupt Alliance was using the dragnet as cover to settle gang debts and collect on protection rackets). Pleasantly, at the next ERP meeting, there were twice as many young men present as compared to the previous month. Two of them had lost parents in the Alliance dragnet. Pedro knew that they would soon fall under the sway of the charismatic inner circle of neo-Trotskyites who managed the ERP . . . only three years ago, he was just like them, orphaned by an out of control and corrupt police force. The government was so stupid, Pedro thought, as Comrade Garcia opened the meeting with a flamboyant reading from Trotsky's treatise "Terrorism and Communism." They just didn't understand how things worked—how things "hung together." Marx certainly did.

IN THIS EXAMPLE, AND COUNTLESS OTHERS, a government's blunt response often contributes to the VNSA's ability to develop negative entropy while also enhancing the performance of key functions like recruitment. A more nuanced, and we argue more effective, strategy is armed with the increased insight into the structure and function of VNSA afforded by a systems approach to VNSA ontogeny, allowing the formulation of a more comprehensive effects-based counter-VNSA (C-VNSA) strategy. This strategy will address VNSA vulnerabilities across its life cycle, in terms of organization/environment interfaces and functions; in other words, some parts of our C-VNSA strategy will focus on boundary relations, while other aspects of it will focus on the "internal physiology" of a prototypical VNSA and how we can disrupt that physiology to maximum effect.

Successfully countering VNSAs across the geo-political landscape is complicated by a host of factors, including but certainly not limited to the dynamic, adaptive character of the threat and the difficulty of developing and implementing a coherent strategy that engenders measurable, operational success. The vulnerabilities examined in previous chapters set the stage for a C-VNSA strategy that goes beyond coercion to the defeat of the enemy. Moreover, understanding indicators of organizational change during a life cycle may enable a preemptory defeat before the VNSA reaches maturity. Rather than concentrating on countering the specific tactics of terrorism and guerrilla warfare, or unique armed groups such as the Chechen resistance, this strategy has universal application due to its innovative emphasis on disrupting congruence among organizational functions—something all VNSA display and must have to survive.

Our strategy is developed in two parts. The first examines coercion, and more specifically deterrence, as a means of compelling VNSA behavior. To this end, we introduce the concept of ecological deterrence, which further blurs the line separating deterrence and compellence and argues for an expanded conception of deterrence that acknowledges the organic and developmental nature of VNSA. Coercion allows the VNSA to survive, or at least be transformed into a non-violent organization. When total system failure is the goal, our C-VNSA strategy conquers a VNSA by: (1) denying the negative entropy, or stores of energy, required to survive attack; and (2) disrupting congruence, or fit, among sub-systems to achieve system failure. Importantly, our approach allows for measuring success by assessing changes in VNSA effectiveness. Thus armed, prospects improve for inter- and intra-governmental collaboration, intelligence collection and analysis, and successful execution of a multi-faceted, effects-based strategy.

Coerce

Coercion is the use or threatened use of force to induce an adversary to act in a different manner than planned.[1] Under this umbrella, conventional deterrence centers on preventing an action that has yet to occur, while the second pillar of coercion, compellence, involves efforts to reverse an action that has already occurred, or to change a current behavior.[2] Coercion takes us to the cusp of war, but stops short of warfighting. The adversary group may retain the capacity for organized violence, but chooses not to develop or use it.[3] Our interest is in deterrence strategies that dissuade VNSA from embracing collective violence in the first place. This is closely related, and some cases barely distinguishable, from compellence strategies that would induce VNSA to abandon their reliance on collective violence once they have embraced its use. The former—dissuading VNSA from embracing collective violence—is far preferable to dealing with them once such a decision is made. For example, we are more concerned in this first section with deterring the Masai tribe of Tanzania from taking up arms against the government than we are with tactics for defeating the Maoist rebels of Nepal in open battle. We are more interested in compelling the Kurdistan Worker's Party (PKK) to abandon terrorist attacks than we are with an operational plan for destroying the infrastructure of the Abu Sayyaf.

A successful deterrence strategy must account for the challenges posed by the range of VNSA types and their unique character. It is our purpose to examine the conventional formulation of deterrence in light of these challenges. Essentially, we assert that traditional deterrence is only relevant under a highly ordered set of conditions that apply to the formally organized, mature VNSA. The life cycle concept also acknowledges the non-rational or affective factors that compel organizational behavior. Recognizing that emotive dynamics are always relevant to the decision making of VNSA, particularly during gestation and growth, is essential to crafting effective strategy. Traditional, rationality-based deterrence may still have a role to play throughout the life cycle; however, a broader environmental shaping or prevention strategy subsumes it. The result is ecological deterrence, which expands our deterrence toolkit to include affective and rational as well as diachronic and synchronic interventions. We apply ecological deterrence to create a strategy matrix that crosses the life cycle with a three-prong strategy of shaping, denial, and punishment.

The form of organization our adversaries adopt will determine whether traditional conceptions of deterrence will be effective in helping us formulate strategies to deal with them and will thus affect whether we adopt a broader theory of deterrence. Before critically reviewing the "received view" about deterrence (which we call "Traditional Rational Choice theory," or TRC), it will be useful to give our project context by distinguishing between narrow and broad conceptions of deterrence, and narrow and broad conceptions of psychology.

Narrow and Broad

A *narrow* conception of deterrence has an essential psychological component, where psychology is construed in the slimmest sense possible. Narrow deterrence revolves around preventing action by influencing another actor's psychology directly. *Broad* deterrence, on the other hand, revolves around preventing action by either direct *or* indirect influence on psychology, where indirect is given a very liberal reading. Narrow conceptions of deterrence will be more likely to leverage rational actor assumptions, whereas broader conceptions will consider other aspects of the psychology of action, as well as environmental factors that are only indirectly—through a longer causal chain—related to psychological concerns.

Narrow and broad conceptions of deterrence go hand in hand with narrow and broad conceptions of psychology. Narrow psychology focuses only on traditional "folk psychological" concerns—that is, it considers only beliefs, desires, and attitudes to be the objects of psychology proper. In its most constrained form, this school of thought focuses only on *rational* folk psychology, a small subset of possible belief/desire relationships. Narrow psychology contrasts with broad psychology, which consists in considering *all* those states of the mind/brain information processing system that influence action, be they conscious or not, be they rational or not, be they distributed across an organization or not—they must only involve, either directly or indirectly, *some aspect* of information processing.[4]

Proper consideration of the life cycle of VNSA forces us to adopt the broadest possible stance with regard to both these "conceptual cuts"; a broad conception of deterrence in conjunction with a broad conception of psychology allows us to deal with both the rational and irrational aspects of decision making, whether they be in organizations or individuals, and it gives us the most possible "causal traction" as we attempt to prevent VNSA action. We call this conjunction *ecological deterrence.* Understanding why ecological deterrence is desirable for formulating deterrence strategy requires that we examine the assumptions of the classic picture.

Rational Choice

TRC theory makes several assumptions regarding an agent's psychology. Some of these assumptions include that the agent (1) has a well ordered and transitive utility function; (2) possesses full or perfect information, or some subset thereof that can be modeled using the assumptions of bounded rationality; (3) is a "perfect reasoner" who has a reliable method of identifying the relevant premises in argument-driven choices and uses rational rules of inference when working from these premises so as to reach a conclusion regarding what to do; and (4) has well-nigh unlimited time to reason.[5] While these assumptions have received minor modification over the years (for instance, via Daniel Kahneman and Amos Tversky's "prospect theory," which is based on TRC assumptions but just changes the utility function based on whether the item being threatened is a gain or a loss),[6] their core has remained more or less constant since being explicitly formulated by game theorists early in the Cold War. However, these assumptions are realistic only under certain conditions: they cohere best with the information processing characteristics of a large formal organization or of human beings in tightly constrained circumstances, such as those that characterize a classic post–Westphalian nation-state. They do not cohere well with the characteristics of fledgling non-state actors, nor with the vagaries of human psychology in the broadest terms. Bluntly, they fail to capture a large portion of human information processing that is relevant to deterrence strategy.[7] Given that VNSA are dynamic open systems that do not fall in line with the characteristics of large tightly structured and rule governed formal organizations, human "molar level" psychological processes will be even more important than in the classic picture, as these processes will be more likely to influence the action of the VNSA. For example, "filtering out" the irrationality of a single person in a large formal organization is difficult enough, but such filtering may be more difficult in a typical terrorist cell of three people where individuals can expect to operate more often in isolation from organizational mechanisms.

Exceptions

As other theorists have pointed out, molar level psychological processes do not always conform to the normative predictions of the TRC model. Pertinent, although not exhaustive, examples of exceptions include heuristics and biases, ecological rationality, fast and frugal heuristics, metaphor and analogy, the storytelling mind, "hot" emotional cognition, and the dynamic nature of cognitive states. We discuss these briefly in turn, keeping in mind that they apply to VNSA because such organizations are composed of people, and all people are subject to these psychological phenomena.

Humans often take cognitive short cuts that do not conform to TRC theory.[8] These include such phenomena as *anchoring*, where the first external suggestion for a potential answer to a question influences the range of answers given by a subject ("Is the Mississippi River longer or shorter than 500 miles?" or, more pertinently, "Would you have the United States station more or less than ten thousand troops in your country?"). Another example is the *availability heuristic*, where our judgments about relative frequency can be skewed by the availability of events to our memory ("Which is more common: the letter 'k' beginning a word, or the letter 'k' occurring as the third letter in a word?" or, "Which is more common: terrorist incidents that involve crashing airplanes into buildings, or terrorist incidents that involve the use of bridges?"). The *representativeness heuristic* says that we judge the probability of events based on the extent that they represent the features of their parent populations, even when this leads to irrational conclusions. For example, "Linda is 31, single, outspoken, and very bright. She majored in philosophy in college. As a student, she was deeply concerned with discrimination and other social issues, and participated in anti nuclear demonstrations." Which statement is more likely? (a.) Linda is a bank teller, or (b.) Linda is a bank teller and active in the feminist movement. Most people say "b," even though the conjunction of two statements *can't* be more likely than the probability of either of them taken singly.[9]

The ecological rationality program, explored by Gerd Gigerenzer, states that in certain cases the mind's ability to leverage structure present in the environment so as to achieve reasonable conclusions can be affected by the format in which the information is delivered.[10] An example here includes the fact that whether or not probabilistic events are expressed in natural frequencies ("Ten out of every one thousand women have breast cancer," "Ten out of every one thousand Palestinians is a terrorist") or in terms of base rates ("The probability that one of these women has breast cancer is 1 percent," "The probability that one of these Palestinians is a terrorist is 1 percent") makes a huge difference in whether or not we can reason successfully from these premises. This gives us reason to doubt that human cognition works in the strictly formal manner of TRC.

The "fast and frugal heuristics" agenda, also developed by Gigerenzer, notes that cognitively successful outcomes can be achieved even by mental processes that are not classically rational; as he states, "the major thrust of the theory is that it replaces the canon of classical rationality with simple, plausible psychological mechanisms of inference—mechanisms that a mind can actually carry out under limited time and knowledge."[11] Being able to manipulate the inferences that *actually* occur is critical for deterrence theory. Examples of fast and frugal heuristics include "take the best," where, when given a forced choice between two alternatives, you assume that the answer you recognize is probably the answer to the question.

Reasoning by metaphor and analogy argues that our most complex mental tasks are usually carried out not by the "classical mechanics" of the TRC, but rather by a set of analogy making and metaphor mapping abilities that form the core of human cognition.[12] Reasoning by analogy and metaphor can often lead to the same conclusions as a TRC style deduction, but does so more quickly and cleanly; on the other hand, they can also lead to critical mistakes, perhaps dangerous ones (a self-referential example: treating the human mind "as a machine"—itself a metaphor—can both enlighten and mislead us about the nature of human cognition).

The story-telling mind is a research program that combines metaphor and analogy into an exploration of the powerful grip narrative has on human cognition; narratives can restructure our mental spaces in ways that profoundly impact our reasoning ability, and yet that cannot necessarily be captured by TRC assumptions (think of the grip that the "Jihad versus McWorld"[13] narrative has on al Qaida and how this affects the way they think about the future).[14] As Mark Turner notes, "Story is a basic principle of mind. Most of our experience, our knowledge, and our thinking is organized as stories."[15]

The "hot mind" and affective/limbic considerations point out that reasoning itself is shot through with emotional and affective considerations, some of which operate subconsciously but nonetheless do more to affect the course of our reasoning than explicit arguments and premises do. Humans are emotional as well as rational creatures, and action occurs only when beliefs are conjoined with desires—the type of actions we want to deter lie at the crossroads of reason and emotion; "somatic markers"[16] (what Antonio Damasio calls those mental structures that tie together emotional reactions and gut feelings with judgment and decision making) are crucial for fully understanding the complexities of decision making, both by individual humans, and by humans who find themselves in an organization.

The diachronic (changing over time) nature of human cognition has been the focus of recent work in dynamic systems approaches to human reasoning. Dynamic systems theory first pointed to the time laden complexities of human thought.[17] TRC assumes that reasoning takes place in a synchronic "timeless realm," unaffected by the dynamic complexities of the cognitive system; the inference I draw today from the same set of premises should be like the inference I draw tomorrow from the same set of premises. But, alas, it is not: time matters as a component of our model of human cognition, and we should expand the assumptions of our deterrence theory to deal with the diachronic nature of decision making, as well as to comport with the diachronic nature of the organic growth and development of organizations.[18]

Ecological Deterrence

Ecological deterrence pushes for a broad conception of deterrence (and hence can easily accommodate these phenomena that traditional rational choice driven deterrence theory has problems coping with) insofar as any intervention that will eventually influence some aspect of VNSA information processing so as to prevent action is a deterrent action and deserves to be labeled as such. We also argue for a broad conception of psychology, as a rational actor focus preludes consideration of the psychology of the VNSA over all phases of its life cycle and mistakenly focuses only on a mature organization (and only a certain kind of mature organization at that—a large formal organization where the environment of action is highly constrained and specified).

Other traditional "conceptual cuts" that can be made when talking deterrence are pertinent as well and can be accommodated using ecological deterrence. General deterrence versus immediate deterrence still matters. We have to adjust our strategy appropriately if we are looking to deter all species of VNSA (militant religious movements) from acting versus deterring a particular specimen of a VNSA (Hamas) from performing a particular action. Denial is still pertinent, although our position is that denial of goal achievement is a TRC move appropriate mostly in the mature phase of VNSA development; we need to think of denial along the lines of "species-specific" goals. That is, any move we can make that can disrupt the eventual goals of the mature form of the VNSA in question should be thought of as disruptive deterrence; similarly for punishment. All these conceptual cuts have a place in our theory of deterrence. However, they need to be augmented by general environmental considerations. As any social psychologist and organizational theorist can tell you, the structure of the environment can have a dramatic impact on information processing. A broad conception of deterrence thus demands another conceptual cut: that of environmental shaping, which we define as actions taken to shape the environment so as to preclude the continued emergence of the organizational structures necessary to act on goals and intentions. This arises naturally as a result of taking ecological deterrence seriously.

Deterrence Strategy *or it just expands the modes and uses of a relatively basic tool kit.*

The application of ecological deterrence concepts to deterrent strategy can vastly expand the number of tools we have in our deterrence toolkit. It is instructive that TRC theorists have festooned rational choice theory with qualifications and assumptions; this is praiseworthy, but the limiting conditions required to make the normative model actually predictive are an indication that we should cast our conceptual net more widely. Moreover, the types of "creatures" we are trying to catch with our nets have changed, which means we need to modify both the form and matter of these nets. In general, then, our deterrent strategy should meet the following criteria:

(1) It should be able to "capture" the successes of TRC theory as a subset of its domain;
(2) It should be driven by the biological metaphors discussed in the "life cycle" section of this book (gestation, growth, maturity, transformation);
(3) It should be structured according to the useful conceptual divisions to be made between aspects of deterrence (general vs. immediate, denial vs. punishment, affective vs. rational considerations);

(4) It should be supplemented with a recognition that the VNSA organism emerges from and interacts with an environment and that such an environment can be shaped so as to prevent the VNSA from maturing or so as to perform a kind of transformational "genetic engineering" whereby we shift the VNSA's nature so that it becomes a peaceful movement;

(5) Our deterrent strategy should be tested against empirically valid success measures; this means we have to be able to model the VNSA/ environment interface so as to support counterfactual prediction (i.e., "*if* we hadn't intervened in this way, *then* the non-state would have become violent").

Driven by the recognition that instrumental rationality may be a characteristic of some mature VNSA but may not characterize the VNSA at all points in its life cycle (nor at any point for certain VNSA), our strategy should be a function of at least three things: whether we are focusing on shaping, denial, or punishment; what stage of the life cycle a given species of VNSA is in; and whether we are aiming at general or immediate deterrence. Figure 7.1 displays these relations. We know which tool to use from our toolkit depending on where we are in the matrix.

Early in a VNSA's ontogeny, deterrent strategies that appeal to the affective component of cognition will most likely be more effective, whereas interventions at a mature stage for many VNSA can usefully leverage rational actor assumptions. The matrix is not intended to be binary; that is, at every step in the determination of deterrent strategy there will be both affective and rational components. We are merely emphasizing that at certain stages one approach may be more effective in a wider range of circumstances than the other.

FIGURE 7.1
Ecological Deterrence Strategy

Traditional rational strategies involve appealing to the utility functions of the organization and actors involved so as to affect their decision-making calculus. These strategies include policy changes, the threat of incarceration, counter-mobilization, counter-insurgency operations, and the like. Affective interventions, on the other hand, will not be driven by rational actor considerations but will instead appeal to the heuristics and biases embedded in human cognition; to the power of myth, narrative, metaphor, and storytelling to affect human world views; and may very well involve using "sub-cortical" emotional systems to impact action via a-rational or irrational means.

Since affective interventions are more unusual than rational interventions, they require more discussion; examples include traditional psychological operations, myth creation, alternative exemplar cultivation, metaphor shifts, and manipulation of identities. Traditional psychological operations (the use of multiple media, including radio, television, print, and computers, to affect the psychology of the target) often have as their goal the manipulation of sub-cortical systems, either by creating an irrational fear of certain actions or by drawing on somatic markers already laid down by previous experience to encourage defection and withdrawal from plans of action. It is interesting that research indicates that people are more vulnerable to certain kinds of cognitive illusions if their lives are laced with "positive affect";[19] it may very well be that a coordinated strategy will thus also include the creation of feelings of well-being so that other affective strategies that appeal to heuristics and biases can be effective. In addition, positive psychological operations may have the effect of disrupting a critical aspect of the VNSA life cycle, recruitment, as disaffection and dissatisfaction are key elements in creating an at-risk population. Psychological operations often produce change by indirectly manipulating some of the other affective strategies we discuss, such as myth creation.

Myth creation involves the weaving together of the narrative elements of a story with facts about past and present situations so as to create an emotionally compelling background that very often directly influences the susceptibility of a population to manipulation by "myth mongers." The fanatical devotion shown by al Qaida operatives stems in large part not from any rational deliberative process but rather from the success Osama bin Laden and others have had in fashioning a coherent and appealing foundational myth. The events of September 11, 2001, can be thought of as the punch line of a chapter in an epic that sets "the warriors of God" against an "infidel West." This myth did not propagate itself via rational actor channels but instead was indoctrinated via a multi-pronged effort on the part of fundamentalist strains of Islam (such as Saudi Arabia's Wahhabis). Successful myth creation may very well leverage the heuristics and biases listed earlier (it certainly takes advantage of the availability heuristic, as this heuristic probably undergirds human propensity to form stereotypes).[20]

Myth creation usually involves the effective use of narrative. As we formulate an "affective strategy," we should keep the elements of a narrative in mind, for it is only by disrupting the story that you can interfere with myth creation. Good stories need protagonists, antagonists, tests for the protagonist, a promise of redemption, and a supporting cast of characters (at the very least). Disrupting al Qaida's foundational myth may involve undermining the belief that we are the antagonists in the narrative bin Laden is constructing. We can either undermine the foundational myth being used to drive VNSA development, or we can construct an alternative myth that is a "better story" than the one being offered by the myth mongers. Examples of myth creation in action include the stories told by the rulers of Plato's ideal city (the "Republic") that were designed to motivate members of the different classes,[21] or the foundational myths that supported the violent actions of *both* the Hutus and the Tutsis during the Rwandan massacres of 1994.[22]

Closely related to myth-making is the strategy of creating alternative exemplars. Members of an at-risk population often become at risk because of a failure to identify with a member of a *non-violent* non-state actor or a member of the *government*. VNSA identity entrepreneurs can exploit existing ethnic, racial, economic, or social political differences by elevating someone who shares the same characteristics as the exploited class to a position of prestige or power. Members of the at-risk group then come to identify with that exemplar and may feel compelled to adopt the violent strategies advocated by the exemplar's VNSA. Creating alternative exemplars who do not advocate violence or who can show the way toward a non-violent solution to the issues that are fueling VNSA emergence can go a long way toward interrupting the VNSA life cycle. Alternative exemplar creation may involve symbolic acts on the part of the government that tap those elements of hot cognition and heuristics and biases mentioned earlier. An example of the alternative exemplar creation strategy in action is the praise and warm endorsement heaped upon John Garang, the leader of the Sudanese guerrilla faction of the Sudanese People's Liberation Army (SPLA), during his visit to Washington just before Christmas of 1995; such endorsement was critical for the recruitment and logistics boost the SPLA received that enabled Garang's forces to recapture crucial cities in southern Sudan soon thereafter.[23] In this case, we encouraged the growth of a VNSA by cultivating an exemplar saliently different from the leaders of the Sudanese regime.

An alternate affective strategy includes fomenting a metaphor shift that impacts the way in which at risk populations or members of a VNSA frame their actions. Given the power of metaphor to shape human thought, it should come as no surprise that shifting metaphors people use to frame worldviews and guide decisions could cause a change in their reasoning about the situation. For example, to convince someone that "young human" is a more appropriate metaphor for an unborn embryo than "cluster of cells" (or vice-versa) may very well change their stand on the issue of abortion.[24] Shifting metaphors requires making connections between the way people presently view a situation or issue and the way you would like them to frame the situation or issue.[25] The common refrain, "one man's terrorist is another man's freedom fighter," is a simple example of metaphor shift. Even the patriotic revolutionaries participating in the Boston Tea Party were viewed as criminals and dangerous insurrectionists by many of their fellow colonialists.

Manipulation of existing identities (be they national, tribal, ethnic, etc.) is another affective strategy.[26] This does not necessarily require creating new foundational myths or alternate exemplars; instead, skillful use of existing cleavages can decrease a VNSA's stock of negative entropy. This is the "flip side" of the identity entrepreneur's efforts that are often part of the genesis and growth of VNSA. For example, the Masai warriors in Tanzania have skillfully manipulated existing identity cleavages so as to elevate the *warrior* aspect of Masai culture over other aspects (*pastoral herder* or *Tanzanian citizen*). This involved the creation of camps for young Masai; following their circumcision ritual, Masai males attend the camp and learn compelling stories about ancient Masai warriors while cultivating their hunting and combat skills.[27] The Tanzanian government, if it wished, could exploit *other* aspects of Masai history, including the fact that their lineage includes an important pastoral element, so as to de-emphasize the violent aspects of Masai culture to ensure that they remain peaceful.[28]

Critically, the strategy matrix we have formulated points out that interventions that are effective at one point in VNSA development may be ineffective at another, and vice versa. The diachronic nature of VNSA development and of the information processing that takes place at each stage is reflected in the changing efficacy of particular strategies and in the varying ratio of affective to rational strategy elements as you move to the right on the matrix. Taking organizational theory and extended psychology seriously means coming to grips with the fact that the same intervention at different points in time can have dramatically different effects. TRC requires that our assumptions about the state of beliefs, desires, and attitudes be held fixed, as this is the only way rational inference can occur (the first order predicate calculus is "a-temporal"—that is, all the computations that take place within it at any given point are assumed to be at hand immediately). Ecological deterrence leverages diachronic rather than merely synchronic assumptions about the effects of intervention. While such a task is beyond the scope of the current study, ideally, we would "flesh out" strategy matrices for each of the types of VNSA confronted. Particular strategies embedded in these matrices would be tested against the empirical data for reliability and could then serve as cues for decision makers to work from when formulating the general shape of a deterrent strategy.

Conquer

Should coercion fail, outright destruction of VNSA may be the only viable option.[29] Achieving this objective requires a C-VNSA strategy that takes into account the super-system, system, and sub-system aspects of such actors, all married to the life cycle account of their ontogeny. In this section, we offer an analysis of general principles for C-VNSA strategy, a compendium of desired effects, and a set of strategic options that arise from the fusion of these principles and effects. The two pillars of this strategy are: (1) denying the negative entropy, or stores of energy, required by the VNSA to survive crisis and/or attack; and (2) disrupting congruence, or fit, among sub-systems to induce system failure, either immediately or over time.

The desired effects depend on whether our goal is coercion or defeat. For coercion, the measure of merit would be the actual change in behavior. For defeat, the measure of merit is the total failure of the VNSA system. In reality, behavioral changes will not be clear and defeat a distant and sometimes elusive goal. Nonetheless, we can measure progress in our C-VNSA campaign as a function of VNSA system characteristics and performance. At the system level, we should be pursuing effects of positive entropy, increased uncertainty and incongruence—all essential to crippling a system. In terms of performance, systems theory helps as well by directing attention to an input metric of resource utilization, an output metric of goal attainment, and a conversion metric of process efficiency. Thus, we can think about input effects broadly as inefficient resource utilization, which can be further broken down into effects such as dysfunctional stakeholder associations, reduced recruitment, and resource disruption. Conversion effects relate to sub-system performance, such as poor decision-making, misperception, disrupted communications, or importantly to incongruence, a breakdown in role behaviors. An output effect, where assessment traditionally focuses, includes failed operations, reduced quality products, and a general failure to achieve desired changes in policy or defeat of an enemy.

Operational Art

Military theorists often guide operations using principles of war. These are general principles that have withstood the test of time and which can often serve as a useful guide for developing and shaping strategy and operations. Traditionally, there are nine principles, ranging from mass to economy of force to surprise.[30] Some of these traditional principles will have analogues in our systems-tutored view of VNSA, while others will not; concepts on offer here are not necessarily intended to transcend the traditional principles of war, but rather works in concert with them to produce maximum effect on the VNSA system. As a prelude to a more comprehensive discussion, we offer the following operational concepts to keep in mind when formulating a strategy to confront VNSA.

Leverage diachronic effects

Much of the time, military planners seek systemic effects to manifest themselves immediately upon intervention into the system. In this sense, much of military strategy focuses (understandably) on *direct* effects: effects that manifest themselves simultaneously, or nearly simultaneously, when action is taken. However, open systems and the VNSA that develop within them present opportunities for *indirect* interventions; these are interventions whose impact is often not felt until far later in the developmental cycle. The beauty of indirect effects is that, owing to the feedback loops present in the system, they can offer a huge ratio between the cost of the intervention and its impact upon the system.

Much has been made in the literature on chaos theory of the "butterfly effect," wherein sensitive dependence upon initial conditions entails that a butterfly flapping its wings in China can cause a tornado in Oklahoma a year later.[31] In chaotic systems, this means that certain indirect interventions have generally unpredictable consequences; in an open system, however, regularities in causal relations between sub-systems mean that we can often *forecast* what impact an indirect intervention may have on the mediate end state of the system. For example, injecting a small amount of thalidomide into a baby's blood stream can have horrific large-scale developmental impact in the long run. The impact manifests itself reliably; "thalidomide babies," as the United States found in the 1960s when experimentation with this sedative used to treat nausea in pregnant women reached its peak, usually grow misshapen arms and legs.

In a VNSA, disabling or destroying identity entrepreneur influence may delay or even prevent VNSA ontogeny. For example, preliminary computer modeling of the situation in Peru in 1975 (as discussed in the technical appendix to this book) indicates that had Abimael Guzman not been on the scene serving as the lightning rod for efforts to organize a Maoist resistance to the Peruvian government, the Sendero Luminoso might not have developed at all (although the environmental preconditions that cause population disaffection would still have been present).[32] At this stage in Sendero's development, a single well-timed intervention could have dramatically altered the course of Sendero Luminoso development.

Seek "synergy minus one" interventions

Complex systems usually manifest synergy; they produce effects that one would not have otherwise expected from a mere additive summation of the parts of the complex system. For instance, gathering a critical mass of plutonium together does not merely produce yet more radioactivity—instead, a high energy explosion results. In much the same way, well constructed VNSA are often able to leverage synergy to have impacts disproportionate to their size: when you gather together multiple intelligent disaffected Japanese youth and place them in the same room with a charismatic leader and certain pieces of chemical weapons technology, you do not merely get a group of intelligent disaffected Japanese youth in the same room as a charismatic leader and chemical weapons technology; rather, you get Aum Shinrikyo and the consequent nerve gas attack upon Tokyo's central subway system . . . indeed, it was the confluence of the first two components of the system (Shoko Ashara, the leader of Aum Shinrikyo, and disaffected Japanese youth) that led to the system seeking out the third component (a nerve gas production and delivery system).[33]

Synergetic systems are troublesome to deal with; however, this synergetic strength is also their Achilles' heel: generally, the removal of even *one* component of the synergetic complex disables the complex entirely. The mere conjunction of Ashara and intelligent disaffected Japanese youth does *not* produce a nerve gas attack; all three components of the system must be in place. Disabling synergetic sub-systems by removing or neutralizing just one of the causal factors is called a "synergy minus one strategy."[34] Those wishing to combat complex systems would do well to seek out the sub-systems that leverage synergetic effects and focus on disabling just one of the functions contributing to the production of the synergy.

Note that not all functions are synergetic; many will not be, but will instead impact the system in only a linear fashion. For example, reducing al Qaida's training capacity by half may only halve the number of attacks they conduct at best (or they may conduct the same number of attacks but with less skill); any synergistic effects from this function of the production sub-system will be very long term in nature (for example, halving the number of successful attacks will eventually probably lessen recruitment rates, and this will lead to fewer attacks, and so on; absent intervention by the cognitive sub-system, the VNSA could eventually disappear). Ascertaining which functions contribute synergistically to system output is a challenge for intelligence analysts, model builders, and VNSA experts. Once those sub-systems have been identified, their parts should be disabled.

Disrupt well-connected nodes

Certain sub-systems and functions will be critical for system effectiveness, whereas others will not. Generally, critical sub-systems will lie at the nexus of multiple inputs and outputs. Our brains, for instance, are well-connected nodes

Advertise & propagate the Irgun's terror attacks, you undermine the Haganah's effective political and diplomatic support fronts, which, in turn, destroys the Irgun's cover to perpetrate their conversion products.

in the human system: they receive multiple inputs from the remainder of the body and in turn have multiple outputs to it. Attacking these well-connected nodes can have a dramatic effect on system efficacy. You will be much more likely to paralyze me by attacking my brain than by attacking my hand; indeed, even a semi-successful assault upon my frontal lobe will impact my functioning *much* more than an entirely successful assault on both my arms.

In a VNSA, well-connected nodes include critical leadership posts, financial centers, staging areas for difficult-to-acquire technologies and skills, and certain intelligence functions. For example, the skills brought to the table by the financier for al Qaida's operations in Europe, Muhammad Galeb Kalaje Zouaydi, were critical during the growth stages; disrupting the influence he had on the system might have had a cascading effect on the growth of al Qaida's cell structure on the continent. Or consider Colombia's actions against FARC-related drug suppliers in the Medellin and Cali drug cartels: when they discovered that the Colombian judicial system could not bring the cartels to justice, the Colombian Congress eventually lifted a law that was preventing extradition of captured cartel members to the United States for trial. Once key leaders of the Cali cartel were captured and extradited, Colombia saw some limited success in their war on narco-terrorism.[35]

Leverage feedback loops

Some sub-systems will be recurrently connected to other sub-systems; others will not. For a sub-system to be recurrently connected, its function(s) must provide causal input into another function, and that function must, in turn, provide causal input back into the previous sub-system. Interventions that affect the status of these sub-systems will have cascading effects on the system as a whole. An example from aviation may help: beginning flyers are subject to correction/over-correction cycles. An initial mistake in flight path results in an overcorrection in the opposite direction, which in turn results in an over-correction back, and so on. In the worst of cases, these oscillations increase until the pilot loses control of the aircraft, possibly overstressing the airframe or even crashing altogether.

In a VNSA, effective manipulation of the intelligence apparatus of the VNSA can cascade; for instance, suppose that Hezbollah believes (wrongly) that Israeli commandos in the process of training with blank ammunition will be vulnerable to a midnight strike; when the commandos overcome the Hezbollah force, Hezbollah may contemplate a retaliatory action; this retaliatory action will, in turn, be vulnerable to the exact same manipulation that the presence of the mole on the Hezbollah planning staff made possible in the first place (the Israelis have, in essence, gotten permanently inside Hezbollah's decision cycle).[36] Absent intervention by someone who suspects an intelligence agent on the staff, Hezbollah could enter a death spiral relatively quickly. Over-stressing the defensive cognitive sub-system of a VNSA can have a similar effect. Put a terrorist organization in a difficult position by feeding noise into its intelligence and counterintelligence functions; being in this difficult position, in turn, makes good intelligence all the more important, which (again, in turn) magnifies the impact that the noise will have on the system. Arguably, something akin to this happened with factions of the IRA in the late 1970s.[37]

Increase entropy

One way in which organizations attempt to isolate themselves from rapid environmental change and environmental disorder is by accumulating negative entropy. For example, a terrorist organization that relies on suicide bombing needs a steady stream of recruits in order to execute its agenda; if recruits dry up, the group can decrease the impact this lack of resources has on it by drawing upon a reserve stock of recruits. In much the same way that some amount of body fat is useful to survive a famine period, a stock of negative entropy enables a VNSA to weather poor environments. Philosopher David Weissman makes this point at the abstract level:

> Systems are complex, because each embodies a network of relations that are spatial, temporal, and causal. The new complex is sustained—stabilized—because the energetic bonds within it have established a particular equilibrium, one that will sustain this thing's integrity until some greater energy is used to destroy it, or until energy within the system dissipates.[38]

Critically, a knockout blow can only be delivered to an organization if its key stocks of negative entropy are already disrupted. Attacking stocks of energy may not directly impact the short-term ability of the VNSA to export its product (terrorist bombers, active cells, etc.), but it will set up the necessary conditions needed for a VNSA to die when it is attacked directly. For instance, owing to our inability to interdict al Qaida's stock of negative entropy in the form of autonomous cells operating in continental Europe, any knockout blow we deal to the operational arm will be short-lived; so long as al Qaida has fat to draw upon, starvation will not succeed on its own.

If a VNSA has rich connections to varied environments in which it can find plentiful input resources, possessing stocks of negative entropy may not be as crucial. For instance, in the war in Afghanistan, the availability of safe havens just across the Pakistani border, with plenty of sympathizers willing to supply shelter, food, and other resources, decreased al Qaida's need to possess organic stores of energy as it weathered the coalition assault. Failed or failing states can serve as safe havens where VNSA can retreat to survive even when they lack fat. Environmental shaping and good governance emerge as critical strategies yet again in the war on terrorism.

Disrupt boundary relationships

Organizations need input to survive. Disrupting critical inputs, especially at developmentally important phases of the organization's life cycle, can stunt the organization's growth or possibly even shift it into an entirely different developmental pathway. In much the same way that vitamin D deficiencies in young children cause rickets that in turn affect the overall development of their muscular skeletal system, so can critical deficiencies create brittleness in a VNSA. Scurvy, caused by a lack of vitamin C, killed many a British sailor until the Navy realized that sucking on lemons and limes would provide the critical missing vitamin (this is how they earned the nickname "Limeys"). A good model of VNSA ontogeny would provide policymakers with insight into critical variables. At least in the gestation and growth phase, a large population of disaffected youth seems to be a requirement for a healthy terrorist organization. Lack of disaffection may cause the organization to be especially brittle—amenable to breakage around critical cut points. For instance, November 17, a radical leftist Greek terrorist organization, while a relatively healthy VNSA, nonetheless has a tiny membership (probably no more than 25 members). The recent decline in November 17 activity is directly attributable to Greek government action designed to boost popular support for the antiterrorist campaign, including appealing to Greek patriotism (as Greece played host for the 2004 Olympic Games) as well as to the fact that the members of November 17 are just getting old (and have failed to recruit new members).[39] By attacking the boundary layer between November 17 and the environment in which they thrive, Greece has successfully reduced this VNSA's ability to export its product, so that bombings and related violent activity have been on the decline.

Weissman drives home the point about the importance of environmental input for sustaining a system:

> Every system has an inside and an outside. Each is a relationship of parts with an internal equilibrium and relations to those things outside from which the system draws material, energy, or information. The inside is constituted of the parts in their reciprocal relatedness. Energy or information is cycled through these bonds, so that every dynamic relation to things outside a system is mediated by its material properties and architecture, or by that interpretation of the outside created by this agent's synthesis of the available information. . . . This is its distinguishing privacy and integrity, but also its vulnerability. For each, stability is generated and sustained in the nourishing sea from which it derives energy and substance.[40]

While VNSA are made more robust by certain environments, others also make them weaker. Environmental shaping is a critical part of any deterrent, compellance, coercion, or disruption strategy.

Pay attention to life history[41]

The fact that VNSA have a life cycle is important, as it opens the door for VNSA to adopt different "life history strategies" (either rationally or through the accidental combination of luck and appropriate environmental exigencies). In population ecology, life history traits are traits that affect basic reproductive and survival schedules of organisms (such as size at birth, number of offspring, longevity, stage-specific growth rate, etc.). There are trade-offs among these components of life history (otherwise, for example, organisms would be produced large at birth and keep producing many large offspring in perpetuity). Of course, given that production of large offspring requires more energy and a longer gestation period, producing large offspring most often means that fewer offspring can be produced. Different VNSA can leverage different trade-offs between these structural features; combating VNSA effectively can be aided by diagnosing whether or not they'll pursue two strategies in particular that organisms in nature have adopted.

Ecologists have identified two general strategies that organisms can use from the life history perspective: *r* versus *K* selection. Table 7.1 shows the attributes of organisms that pursue an "r-selected" strategy versus those that pursue a "K-selected" strategy (the r and K refer to the values of the variables that will be maximized in the standard logistic equation governing population growth).

TABLE 7.1
Life History Selection Strategy

Attribute	r selection	K selection
Mortality	Variable	Constant
	Unpredictable	Predictable
Population Size	Variable	Constant
	Below carrying capacity	Close to carrying capacity
Competition	Variable	Usually strong
	Often weak	
Selection Favors	Rapid development	Slow development
	Early reproduction	Delayed reproduction
	Small body size	Large body size
	Semelparity	Iteroparity
Length of Life	Usually shorter	Usually longer
Leads to	High productivity	High efficiency

Let's walk through one row of this table to ensure its meaning is clear. Reading right from the "selection favors" label (which simply means that there will be environmental selection pressures that encourage these traits), we can see that VNSA, whether by accident or by design, which pursue an r-selected strategy will be more likely to have parts (such as cells) that develop rapidly, which fission early, which are small, and which will probably only produce offspring cells once ("semelparity" is the biological term for organisms that reproduce only once, but that produce large numbers of offspring when they do). Certain aspects of al Qaida appear to have adopted an r-selected strategy. On the other hand, reading further right from "selection favors," we can see that K-selected organisms, such as the IRA, will have a slower development cycle (but will have more "sticking power" once they've developed), will delay reproduction until an offspring organization can be ensured of survival, will have a large organizational structure, and will have the capacity to reproduce more often ("iteroparity," as contrasted with semelparity).

If we can determine whether a VNSA will pursue an r- or K-selected strategy throughout its life, we can gain important clues as to how it might progress throughout its life cycle. For instance, a cell-like structure that proliferates quickly is more like an r-selected life history. We could also expect that it will have high productivity (e.g., it will eventually engage in violent action) but will not be especially efficient at generating new cells itself (it is not efficient at resource conversion). The mortality for a cell is unpredictable; because it is so small, when it is detected, it can be destroyed with relative ease as compared to a large and complex organization. This can also influence strategy; for example, direct arrests may stop an r-selected VNSA, especially if the maintenance sub-system is rusty, whereas in a K-selected VNSA, chances are that new recruits will handily offset arrests and a more effective strategy might focus on other points of weakness. These similarities are merely suggestive, of course; but it may very well be that similar functional structures drive similar life history traits for both organisms and VNSA organizations in many cases.

Increase uncertainty

If organizations are to cope with and adapt to their environment, especially in the mature phase of their life cycle, they must bring to bear some cognitive capacity. Learning is a hallmark of a mature organization, and is an important function of the cognitive sub-system. In turbulent environments, the organization must spend valuable time (expend energy) looking for resources in its environment. If such resources are unpredictable, the organization has to spend more time worrying about building up a stock of negative entropy . . . it will forage more and spend less time actually *producing* a product. Increasing uncertainty will send a VNSA into a cognitive tailspin akin to what hu-

But remember pg. 114, "Conversions DO NOT have to occur for a VNSA to survive." Therefore, attacking the Cognitive sub-system must be primarily disruptive to the Support and Maintenance sub-systems, not just Conversion.

mans experience in the face of sensory overload. Decision-making under uncertainty is more difficult, generally, than decision-making in stable environments, and may also cause heuristics and biases to manifest themselves in a way that makes the organization more subject to coercion. This is a strategy advocated by those sensitive to "netwar-centric" conceptions of the war on terrorism. At the extreme, an uncertainty-based strategy could create an analogue to "allostatic overload" in a human, where stress and fear disrupt the normal endocrine maintenance processes, thus accelerating wear and tear on tissues and boosting the chances of physio-pathology such as angst and social dysfunction (the analogs in organizational theory would be breakdown of role-specific functions and a decrease in organizational cohesion).[42]

Establishing roles and task-specialization is crucial to the function of any complex org. Increasing uncertainty will cause certain functional sub-systems Implement across the system *to try to operate outside their specialization and fail, disrupting the org. as a*

Even if the appropriate inputs do make their way into the organization, such *whole* inputs still must be reorganized by the system to be useful. Inputs must be processed into outputs. To confront outputs (in the case where the outputs are armed personnel ready to commit acts of violence) directly is to engage in a force-on-force, and often defensive, confrontation with the VNSA; this is effective in some circumstances but not in others and can play into the hands of an enemy that is planning on leveraging force asymmetries in its favor. A more effective way to disrupt the cycle would be to interdict the inputs (via environmental shaping). But even the process itself is amenable to disruption. To ensure our strategy achieves its desired effects, we need to look across the system, considering inputs, processes, and outputs and their interrelationships.

Beginning with the input side of the input/processing/output equation, we offer a brief list of strategies for attacking inputs:

(1) *Environmental Shaping.* Ascertain critical environmental variables influencing VNSA ontogeny. Shape the environment by removing those variables or making them harder to find. For example, if a VNSA is recruiting personnel from a disaffected population, take action to address the sources of disaffection. When fighting VNSA, states should take care to notice the relationships between the actions they take to counter such organizations and the environmental variables that serve as input to conversion processes. A lack of awareness in this area can cause a policy to backfire, as discussed in the reinforcing actions and niche construction sections earlier in the book. For example, consider the case of Argentina's response to the Trotskyite People's Revolutionary Army (ERP) in the mid-1970s. Rather than considering how a peasant population might react to a draconian government response to a terrorist threat, the Peron government formed a vigilante police force, the

Alianza Anticommunista Argentina (AAA). The AAA was undisciplined but nonetheless was granted a license to kill; their harsh actions,
used to settle grudges more often than to counter suspected communist terrorists, were entirely overlooked, and this did much to feed local
toleration for the ERP. Human Rights Watch estimates that the numbers of people who were illegally detained, tortured, or killed by the
AAA is into the thousands, but despite this not a single AAA member
has ever been arrested.[43]

(2) *Financial Interdiction.* Interdict financial input into the organization.
Busting money laundering networks and cracking down on the international flow of dirty money has been an effective input-oriented
strategy for multiple countries dealing with terrorism, including the
United States in its struggle against al Qaida and the UK in its struggle against the IRA. The fungibility of cash makes it the preferred
medium of exchange for most VNSA, so focusing on it can be an effective long-term strategy. However, VNSA have shown some considerable skill at continuously finding creative alternative sources of
funds (such as cigarette smuggling and coupon schemes) as well as an
ability to move away from money to various forms of barter, such as
illegal commodity trading in diamonds and drugs, to get their resources. As such, financial interdiction will be effective in dampening
VNSA activity and decreasing VNSA efficiency but should not be considered a stand-alone silver-bullet C-VNSA strategy.

(3) *Diaspora Disruption.* Diasporas who have fled a nation-state because of
an actual or perceived wrong are sometimes involved in supporting
VNSA, which attack the nation state or its interest. As Robin Cohen
noted in 1997, "Diasporas as a social form have predated the nation-
state, lived uneasily within it, and now may, in significant respects,
transcend and succeed it."[44] The roots of violence identified earlier feed
the ability of Diasporas to influence the environment in which VNSA
operate: "Diasporas draw strength and increased viability from
[changes in global structures and processes.] In particular, the role of
the media and modern means of communication in mobilizing and
facilitating Diaspora politics cannot be underestimated. Second, the
economic dimension of globalization is part and parcel of Diasporas'
economic relations with their homeland and with other parts of the
Diaspora."[45] If a well entrenched Diaspora is providing significant
input, be it moral, material, or manpower related, it may be necessary
to disrupt the connections between the Diaspora and the VNSA; this
can be done using a counter-narrative strategy or traditional law enforcement mechanisms. It may also involve addressing any bona fide
grievances the Diaspora may have.[46] Diaspora disruption amounts to a

special case of dissociating stakeholder associations, preventing VNSA from having "willing customers" who can sustain their activities and define their agenda.

(4) *Counter-narratives.* VNSA often sustain their input of recruits by telling a compelling story that helps the potential recruit frame the world in the terms the VNSA would like (for example, as a battle of the infidel West against the righteous Muslim world). Counter-narrative strategies seek to disrupt the flow of recruits by reframing the story in a way that defuses the motivation to join the VNSA. For example, rather than being a battle of infidels against the righteous, perhaps the story is better framed in terms of those who would keep a nation downtrodden economically versus those who want to develop a better standard of living. In order to win the "story war," we will have to strengthen our research on public opinion, develop a rapid media response capability, prioritize public diplomacy in the foreign policy process, empower ambassadors and others to be storytellers, create "presence posts" outside of foreign capitals, better utilize the media in the Arab world, bolster radio programs and create new outlets and media, support outside partners, cultivate foreign leaders, sustain foreign exchange programs, and engage ethnic and religious groups involved in VNSA prosperity to communicate the counter-message.[47] As philosopher and systems theorist David Weissman notes, "every system has a developmental history. Each is generated as antecedent stabilities interact or evolve: they are transformed, eventuating in this new complex, or they give up matter and energy, thereby supplying material sufficient to establish it. . . . Some stabilities are conscious of their histories, telling stories about them, reenacting parts of them. These are developmental histories defended as traditions."[48] To disrupt the ability of the cognitive sub-system to maintain cohesion on the part of its followers already in the organization, and to prevent it from reaching into a disaffected population so as to import manpower, is just to interfere in the developmental history of an organization.

(5) *Identity Gerrymandering.* Some VNSA thrive on cleavages created by race, class, ethnicity, or religious background. Identity entrepreneurs exploit existing cleavages to increase recruitment. A gerrymandering strategy would seek to alleviate the sources of such cleavages, either by taking material steps to reduce the disparity between the groups or by otherwise alleviating the tension driving recruitment. For example, if Catholics really do earn less than other Christians when wages are controlled, perhaps the British government could alleviate recruitment into the IRA by addressing the income disparity through a public benefits program. *or, assimilation of the entire identity is not necessary, only assimilation of the boundaries where cleavages exist*

Disrupting the *process* portion of the equation would involve intervening into any of the sub-systems: support, maintenance, cognitive, and conversion. Even if interventions into a particular sub-system are not successful, disruption can be achieved by boosting *incongruity* (literally, "lack of fit") between successfully functioning sub-systems. If the support sub-system cannot successfully feed into the conversion sub-system, this is functionally equivalent to entirely disabling the support sub-system itself. Support-related disruptions include convincing stakeholders not to materially or morally support the VNSA, interdicting recruitment efforts, and otherwise stifling resource acquisition. Cognitive-related disruptions include targeting key VNSA leadership or decreasing the span of control such leaders have within the organization, targeting intelligence units to drop an organization back to single-loop learning, and interdicting flows of information. Conversion related disruptions include intervening to prevent VNSA from actually carrying out violent actions. Maintenance related disruptions would involve sabotaging the ability of a VNSA to socialize its members or interfering with the rewards and sanctions system (possibly by beating the VNSA at its own game: cultivate an alternate attractive identity replete with even greater rewards).

Output strategies include as a subset traditional force-on-force interventions and confrontations. Owing to the asymmetrical nature of VNSA warfare, this will sometimes be successful, other times not. Force-on-force interventions will be more successful early in VNSA ontogeny, before the group has an effective training mechanism in place and before group identity has congealed to produce a cohesive fighting force. Conversely, this could have undesirable consequences, as the world audience may not see such an early act of aggression as necessary; indeed, hitting a VNSA in such an early state of its ontogeny may be to act before anyone else perceives a threat—thus marking the attacker as more dangerous than the young VNSA. Perversely, force-on-force confrontations are perhaps the most studied of the interventions we've discussed, so we will not belabor the literature.[49] However, there are other output-related strategies besides confronting the guerrillas and terrorists that emerge from the "business end" of VNSA, as VNSA produce other products besides men with guns. They also manufacture all the products necessary to sustain the inputs they need to accomplish stakeholder goals. This may include drugs, sex slaves, smuggled weapons, and the like. An output-based strategy can seek to displace important VNSA output by providing substitutes. For example, if a VNSA is boosting popular support by providing social services, the government could one-up the organization by providing the same services more cheaply and efficiently. If the VNSA is outputting drugs in order to provide a steady stream of capital so as to fund a weapons of mass destruction research program, a government could undercut the black market by legalizing certain drugs with due consideration of socio-economic consequences. VNSA have more outputs than suicide bombers, and a more comprehensive examination of those outputs and the role they play in sustaining VNSA metabolism might reveal new confrontational policy options.

Ideally, for every VNSA we seek to coerce or destroy, a matrix will be built that lists inputs, processes, and outputs for all the major sub-systems of support, maintenance, cognitive, and conversion. We could then "personalize" strategy around a group's particular signature across this matrix. After matching instruments of state power to life cycle vulnerabilities, with the requisite sensitivity to the principles discussed here and with careful attention to the dynamics of the system we are about to intervene upon, we might discover a whole new suite of tools that can be used to coerce or destroy VNSA. "War" as such might not even be a necessity.

Closing

The marrying of ecology to open systems theory promotes a fundamental shift in our thinking on coercion, which should be founded in an interdisciplinary approach to assessing the dynamic nature of the VNSA threat. Ultimately, it should involve rethinking the intelligence architecture we use to support deterrence indications and warning (I&W). Ideally, we will modify our intelligence apparatus, keying it to identify the conditions that engender VNSA growth with a reliable set of I&W markers cued to critical life cycle transitions. Such a system, informed by the open systems theory and life cycle considerations surfaced in this paper, will enable us to better predict *what kinds* of VNSA would emerge and *when*. This capacity will be critical in formulating an effective strategy.

This chapter has made several important conceptual contributions to coercion theory and practice. We have: focused on VNSA, doing so within a systems theoretic framework; discussed the importance of environmental shaping strategies for deterrence theory; called for an expanded conception of both deterrence and rationality that includes the multiple aspects of information processing that takes place in VNSA as well as affective considerations; articulated systems-tutored operational concepts for defeating VNSA; and outlined specific cross-system strategies for achieving system failure. Nonetheless, there is much that remains to be done, including more closely exploring the links between the system in which VNSA develop and how this affects critical life cycle transitions; discussing the tools we use to assess life cycle status; and researching specific environmental shaping strategies as well as new affective and rational strategy elements.

When disruption or defeat is the mission, this analysis should add multiple dimensions to a strategy that sometimes focuses too much on the product of the system and not enough on the system itself. To disrupt the importation of energy, shape the environment and attack the environment/organization boundary. To destroy throughput, have a process-oriented attack plan. To attack export, meet the product head on before it has been fully deployed. To interfere with the cyclic pattern of activities, interfere with internal activities that are critical, well-connected, or consist of exponential feedback loops. Attack negative entropy by disrupting or destroying critical stores. Disrupt the feedback and coding process by engaging in counter-intelligence and influence operations designed to increase uncertainty and disrupt communication. Destroy homeostasis by attacking critical nodes and disrupting system congruity. While doing these things, keep in mind our newly formulated concepts of operational art for countering VNSAs, as they should inform all actions whether directed at input, conversions, or output. Our inter-disciplinary application of open systems theory provides a powerful framework for diagnosing adversaries, shaping their development and structuring an effects-based strategy for coercion and conquering. It is a global approach to a global challenge.

Notes

1. This definition is adopted from *Airpower as a Coercive Instrument*, Daniel L. Byman, Matthew C. Waxman, and Eric Lawson, eds. (Santa Monica, CA: RAND, Project Air Force, 1999), 10. They drew upon the seminal works in this field by Thomas Schelling, *Arms and Influence* (New Haven, CT: Yale University Press, 1966), and Alexander George and William E. Simons, eds., *The Limits of Coercive Diplomacy* (Boulder, CO: Westview Press, 1971).

2. Byman, *Airpower*, 10.

3. Robert A. Pape, *Bombing to Win* (Ithaca, NY: Cornell University Press, 1996), 13.

4. For an introduction to the different senses in which one can use the term "psychological state," see George Botterill and Peter Carruthers, *The Philosophy of Psychology* (New York, NY: Cambridge University Press, 1999), 12–48. The conception of cognition that views it as "computation across representations," i.e., as information processing, is a standard one in the cognitive sciences.

5. The list of assumptions varies from author to author; this list is a compilation of several standard recitations. For an example, see Ariel Rubinstein, *Modeling Bounded Rationality* (Cambridge, MA: The MIT Press, 1998), 7–10, who lists these foundational assumptions: knowledge of the problem, clear preferences, ability to optimize, indifference to logically equivalent descriptions of alternatives and choices. Compare also with page 4 of Martin J. Osborne and Ariel Rubinstein, *A Course in Game Theory* (Cambridge, MA: MIT Press, 1994).

6. See, for example, David Kahneman and Amos Tversky, "Prospect Theory: An Analysis of Decisions Under Risk," *Econometrica* 47 (1979): 313–27.

7. While we are, to our knowledge, the first to surface some of the considerations mentioned in this paper, criticisms of deterrence theory that rely on criticisms of the shortcoming of rational choice theory are not new. See Frank C. Zagare's summary (and rebuttal) in "Rationality and Deterrence," *World Politics* 42, no. 2 (January, 1990): 238–60. See also Robert Jervis et al.'s classic, *Psy-*

chology and Deterrence (Baltimore, MD: The Johns Hopkins University Press, 1985), which is in need of updating given the rapid progress in the field of judgment and decision-making.

8. See their classic collection: D. Kahneman, P. Slovic, and A. Tversky, eds., *Judgment under Uncertainty: Heuristics and Biases* (New York: Cambridge University Press, 1982). For a general reference, see Terry Connolly et al., eds., *Judgment and Decision Making: An Interdisciplinary Reader* (New York: Cambridge University Press, 2000).

9. See Kahneman et al., *Judgment under Uncertainty*, as well as D. Kahneman and A. Tversky, "Choices, Values and Frames," *American Psychologist* 39 (1984): 341–50, and also their recent book of the same title (New York: Cambridge University Press, 2000). For critical review of that book, see Philip Tetlock and Barbara Mellers, "The Great Rationality Debate," *Psychological Science* 13, no. 1 (January 2002): 94–99.

10. See Gerd Gigerenzer, *Adaptive Thinking: Rationality in the Real World* (New York: Oxford University Press, 2000).

11. Ibid., 170.

12. Classic works here include George Lakoff and Mark Johnson, *Metaphors We Live By* (Chicago, IL: The University of Chicago Press, 1980); Dedre Gentner, Keith Holyoak, and Boicho Kokinov, *The Analogical Mind: Perspectives from Cognitive Science* (Cambridge, MA: The MIT Press, 2001); and Gilles Fauconnier and Mark Turner, *The Way We Think: Conceptual Blending and the Mind's Hidden Complexities* (New York: Basic Books, 2002).

13. This is the structuring metaphor of Benjamin Barber's "clash of the world views" book, *Jihad vs. McWorld: How Globalism and Tribalism Are Reshaping the World* (New York: Ballantine Books, 1996).

14. Mark Turner, *The Literary Mind* (New York, NY: Oxford University Press, 1998).

15. Ibid.

16. See Antonio Damasio, *Descartes' Error: Emotion, Reason, and the Human Brain* (New York, NY: G. P. Putnam and Sons, 1994).

17. A classic work here is Robert Port and Timothy Van Gelder, eds., *Mind as Motion: Explorations in the Dynamics of Cognition* (Cambridge, MA: The MIT Press, 1995). See also Alicia Juarrero, *Dynamics in Action: Intentional Behavior as a Complex System* (Cambridge, MA: The MIT Press, 1999).

18. On the biological side of the house, it is well known that the exact same interventions at different points in an organism's growth and development can have dramatically different impacts on outcomes (this is called "heterochrony"). See, e.g., John Gerhart and Marc Kirschner, eds., *Cells, Embryos, and Evolution* (Malden, MA: Blackwell Science, 1997).

19. Joseph Forgas, "Affect, Cognition, and Interpersonal Behavior: The Mediating Role of Processing Strategies," as printed in Forgas, ed., *Handbook of Affect and Social Cognition* (Mahwah, NJ: Lawrence Erlbaum Associates, Inc., 2001).

20. G. Wendt and P. Vlek, eds. *Utility, Probability, and Decision Making* (Boston, MA: D.Reidel Publishers, 1973).

21. See Book Four of Plato's *Republic*, trans. Robin Waterfield (New York: Oxford University Press, 1993).

22. For more about these myths, see Ryszard Kapuscinski, *The Shadow of the Sun* (New York: Vintage Books, 2001). Owing to the (mostly fabricated!) "early history" of the region, the Tutsis were viewed as being pastoral patrons (read: rulers) who presided over their clients (read: slaves), the Hutu agriculturalists. Under colonial rule by both the Germans and the Belgians, this foundational myth was reinforced, with separate identity cards being issued for both peoples. The Belgians even went so far as to argue that the Tutsi were, racially speaking, more closely related to white people, and were hence a superior race, putting in place a quite different but nonetheless related foundational myth. Needless to say, these myths played a large part in the violence that erupted in 1994.

23. See Bill Berkeley, *The Graves are Not Yet Full: Race, Tribe and Power in the Heart of Africa* (New York: Basic Books, 2001), 224–25.

24. See Paul Churchland's *Toward a Cognitive Neurobiology of the Moral Virtues,* as reprinted in Joao Branquinho, ed., *The Foundations of Cognitive Science* (New York: Oxford University Press, 2001).

25. See Fauconnier and Turner, *The Way We Think,* for more advice here regarding how to enable these "frame shifts."

26. Daniel Byman has an excellent discussion of this process in his book *Keeping the Peace: Lasting Solutions to Ethnic Conflicts* (Baltimore, MD: The Johns Hopkins University Press, 2002), 100–124.

27. As the authors discovered during various interviews with Masai in the Serengeti of Tanzania in the summer of 2003.

28. Various interviews, Masai nationals in Tanzania, June 2002. For more background on Tanzania's history, as well as detail on the Rwandan situation, see Taisier Ali and Robert Matthews, eds., *Civil Wars in Africa: Roots and Resolution* (Montreal, Canada: McGill Queen's University Press, 1999).

29. From the U.S. perspective, as one example of a state goal, the U.S. national security objective is "stop[ping] terrorist attacks against the United States, its citizens, its interests, and our friends and allies around the world and ultimately, to create an international environment inhospitable to terrorists and all those who support them." See the White House's *National Strategy for Combating Terrorism,* February 2003, 11.

30. According to *Army Field Manual FM 3 Operations,* the nine principles of war are mass, objective, offensive, surprise, economy of force, maneuver, unity of command, security, and simplicity.

31. For an accessible account of the butterfly effect, and chaos theory in general, see James Gleick's popularly acclaimed *Chaos: Making a New Science* (New York: Viking, 1987).

32. This is only a tentative result, as the model constructed by Jake Bartolomei and William D. Casebeer has been subjected to only preliminary validation and verification (although it has successfully retrofitted the growth curve for Peru's Sendero Luminoso).

33. See Ian Lesser, et al., *Countering the New Terrorism* (Santa Monica, CA: RAND Corporation, 1999). The sarin attack killed a dozen people and wounded 3,976 others. Aum Shinrikyo had plans to launch a similar attack upon the United States.

34. This language is taken from Peter Corning's book *Nature's Magic: Synergy in Evolution and the Fate of Humankind,* (New York: Cambridge University Press, 2003).

35. See p. 137 of James Zackrison's essay "Colombia" from *Combating Terrorism: Strategies of Ten Countries,* ed. Yonah Alexander (Ann Arbor, MI: University of Michigan Press, 2002).

36. For an excellent discussion of the OODA Loop concept of Colonel John Boyd, see *John Boyd and John Warden: Air Power's Quest for Strategic Paralysis,* by David S. Fadok (Maxwell Air Force Base, AL: Air University Press, 1995). Also, Robert Coram, *Boyd: The Fighter Pilot Who Changed the Art of War* (New York: Little, Brown and Company, 2002).

37. See David J. Whittaker, *The Terrorism Reader* (New York: Routledge, 2001).

38. David Weissman, *A Social Ontology* (New Haven, CT: Yale University, 2000), 312.

39. See the Council on Foreign Relations terrorism information website at www.terrorismanswers.org/groups/rps.html. Accessed on January 9, 2004.

40. Weissman, *A Social Ontology,* 313.

41. Most of the information in this section, including the table, is adapted from John H. Vandermeer and Deborah E. Golberg's excellent *Population Ecology: First Principles* (Princeton, NJ: Princeton University Press, 2003), 39.

42. See Jay Schulkin, *Rethinking Homeostasis: Allostatic Regulation in Physiology and Pathophysiology* (Cambridge, MA: MIT Press, 2003).

43. See the 2001 *Human Rights Watch Report on Argentina*, available online at www.hrw.org/reports/2001/argentina/argen1201-11.htm as of January 10, 2004.

44. Robin Cohen, *Global Diasporas: an Introduction* (London, UK: UCL Press, 1997), 520.

45. Daphne Josselin and William Wallace, eds., *Non State Actors in World Politics* (New York, NY: Palgrave, 2001), 222.

46. See the essays in *The Battle for Hearts and Mind: Using Soft Power to Undermine Terrorist Networks*, ed. Alexander T. J. Lennon (Cambridge, MA: MIT Press, 2003).

47. See "Winning the War of Ideas" by Antony J. Blinken for much more detail (as printed in Lennon's *The Battle for Hearts and Minds*).

48. Ibid., 313.

49. For a concise historical review of successful force on force interventions, see Alexander's excellent edited volume *Combating Terrorism: Strategies of Ten Countries.*

8

Beyond Warlords

Osama bin Laden collapsed against the limestone cavern he had been using as shelter for the past two months (ever since the latest Pakistani offensive had ferreted out the remainder of his supporters in the Waziristan region of the northwest Paki frontier). He had just been told by his key financier that the latest coalition efforts to crack down on the money laundering operation financing al Qaida's training camps in northern Sudan had severely constricted the funds needed to continue operations. More gravely, the last of the base's active cells in Germany and the United States had been discovered, owing in part to sharper allied intelligence and to a radical new technology that disrupted cell phone use in a targeted fashion. Perhaps most importantly, the Baker Peace Plan was making headway in resolving the Israeli/Palestinian dispute (indeed, the Israelis had actually started to dismantle the security wall); combined with resurgent Jordanian and Syrian economic growth, and with the overwhelming success of the U.S.-led "Marshall Plan for the 'Stans," new recruits into the organization had diminished to a barely sustainable trickle. With no stores of money, no cells left in reserve, no mechanism for obtaining new weapons, no process for training new recruits, no means of maintaining popular support, and no reservoir of disaffected youth to draw from, al Qaida was breathing its last. It was about to cease to exist as a viable organization. Bin Laden had sensed that his charisma—and his ability to exert nominal control over others in al Qaida by encouraging or admonishing them—was on the wane, probably terminally. "How did we let this happen?" bin Laden asked, noticing and focusing determinedly on an especially deep crevice in the cave wall. "Arab League support for the peace plan did not help, nor the economic growth in the region brought on by economic liberalization," his financier responded. "It is Allah's will," bin Laden replied, involuntarily taking a sud-

den series of sharp deep breaths. Maybe a different approach than terrorism to dealing with the West would have been more effective, bin Laden
thought to himself; but it made no difference now, as he could tell by the
sharp pain in his chest that soon he would be receiving his celestial reward
of seventy-two virgin houris . . . or so his world-view told him. He'd soon
find out if his world-view was right. The black pocket in the back of the
crevice expanded suddenly, filling his entire visual field. And then a giant
hit him in the chest.

CONFRONTING VIOLENT NON-STATE ACTORS is no easy task, but is instead a
challenge that must be undertaken with the appropriate combination of
intellectual determination and cognitive humility. Learning to tackle the challenge posed by resurgent VNSA is not optional. Globalization and the concomitant erosion of the Westphalian status quo has changed (and is changing)
the international security environment irrevocably, and the growing preva-
lence of VNSA in transnational conflict ensures they will remain a fixture in
the world's political ecology for some time to come.

In this book, we have offered a framework for thinking about VNSA systematically. This framework implies, in turn, a set of strategies for preventing
their development, deterring them when they do gestate, and finally for disrupting their integrity across all phases of their life cycles. A brief review of the
territory we have surveyed in the past seven chapters sets the stage here for a
summary of our proposed counter-VNSA strategy; this will inform a "White
Paper for Blue Strategists," where we urge a re-thinking of the war on terror.
Finally, we conclude by briefly discussing an agenda for future inquiry driven
by our open-systems world-view, noting how our research program has the
ability to resolve some troublesome anomalies plaguing our current confrontational paradigm.

Core Concepts

Recall that the initial territory we explored was that of the *super-system*: the
international environment that gives rise to VNSA. Some of the *inputs* into
this super-system included such things as resource scarcity, demographic
pressures, socio-economic deprivation, organized crime and corruption,
and multiple identity cleavages. Against a *background* of globalization, failures of governance on the part of the state (and activity by industrious identity entrepreneurs and myth mongers) can serve as *conversions*, transforming these inputs into the *outputs* of nascent armed groups. Actions (or
failures to act) on the part of the state, combined with niche construction
activities on the fledgling VNSA's part, can encourage the growth of the
young organization, enhancing the inputs that move it through its ontogeny,

effectively foregrounding the background conditions that favored VNSA genesis to begin with.

At the level of the *system*, we were most concerned with the organizational structure exhibited by VNSA and its associated functions: once a VNSA has appeared, what inputs, processes, and outputs enable it to engage in the activities needed to sustain its life and progress through its development? Ultimately, VNSA organizations can take the form of religious movements, ethnopolitical groups, warlords with militias, transnational criminal organizations, eco-warriors, tribes, and clans, and ideological and interest-driven groups. Despite the unique characteristics of each discussed herein, there are important commonalities. All these groups follow life cycles, moving from genesis through growth to maturity and, ultimately, transformation. Asking the question "what are the inputs, conversions, and outputs at the organizational level?" necessarily forces us next into a functional analysis.

At various parts of the life cycle, different sub-systems and associated function are brought on line so as to engender organizational growth and allow the organization to develop goals and take steps to achieve them. *Support, maintenance, cognitive,* and *conversion* sub-systems, all active at maturity, ensure ongoing organizational survival and mission accomplishment. Hovering at the nexus of all these sub-systems is organizational *culture.*

The support sub-system procures VNSA inputs and disposes of outputs; functions include recruitment, resource acquisition, and stakeholder associations. The maintenance sub-system serves as a kind of clutch between task demands and human needs so as to maintain the organization coherence; its functions include socialization and role-related rewards and sanctions. The cognitive sub-system serves the managerial and adaptive role for the organization. Cognitive-related activities thus include learning, strategy development, and organizational control, which includes traditional structural considerations as well as communication means. Finally, the conversion sub-system transforms energy and material into outputs; functions include operations, training, and production. The relative importance of each sub-system varies across the life cycle of the organization.

After discussing some of the legal and ethical issues related to VNSA decisions to engage in terrorist activity, our discussion led naturally to considerations of *coercion* and ultimately the *conquering* of undesirable violent non-state actors. We argued that VNSA can be deterred, especially if we are willing to broaden our notion of what deterrence (and the human psychology that underpins it) consists in. Early in the VNSA life cycle, affective considerations are more likely to hold sway, while traditional rational actor considerations can effectively deter later in the life cycle. *Ecological deterrence* thus couples ideas regarding the importance of environmental shaping with affective and rational considerations: a more full understanding of deterrence related psychology allows us to see how we can shape VNSA cognition across its life span.

Should coercion fail, system disruption might become a necessity. Defeating VNSA requires formulation of a comprehensive *counter-VNSA strategy*. A robust C-VNSA strategy requires consideration of all three levels of interaction, married to a life cycle account of the VNSA's development. New *operational concepts* (leverage diachronic effects, seek "synergy minus one" interventions, disrupt well-connected nodes, leverage feedback loops, increase entropy, disrupt environment/system interfaces, pay attention to life history analysis, increase uncertainty, implement across the system, and disrupt congruence) help guide our thinking. In the broadest terms, open-systems theory then encourages us to *assess* the effectiveness of our C-VNSA actions in terms of input metrics (how well is the VSNA using resources?), conversion metrics (how efficient is the conversion process?), and output metrics (are VNSA goals being obtained?).

Synchronization

The VNSA is a dynamic enemy that employs asymmetric means. Hence, our C-VNSA strategy will itself need to be dynamic. A mantra we would do well to repeat as we formulate grand C-VNSA strategy is "time, location, application." *When* will the instruments of state power be brought against the VNSA? *Where* in the environment or organization? To what end are they *applied*, and what tool will best achieve that end? Essentially, our goal must be to synchronize, or orchestrate in time, space, and action, a systems-based diagnosis and strategy for VNSA.

Keeping these three questions in mind enables us to build a time-phased C-VNSA strategy. A time-phased plan for all the resources that will be brought to bear across the VNSA life cycle would be invaluable. Certain instruments of state power will be most appropriate to *preventing* VNSA genesis (by addressing root causes and disrupting the connection between the international ecology and transformative processes). Others will be most effective at *slowing* or *shaping* VNSA growth once genesis has already occurred (by pruning back critical inputs, dampening reinforcing actions, and disabling nascent VNSA sub-systems). Still others will be most effective at *disrupting* mature VNSA, using the operational concepts and the strategy and tactics implied by them (perhaps by disrupting congruence while simultaneously increasing organizational entropy). Some instruments of state power will be most effective at encouraging the *transformation* of VNSA into non-violent actors (be that by co-optation, negotiated settlement, or destruction).

Understanding the synergetic relationships between actions that intervene upon the system earlier and the effects produced later is admittedly very difficult. As we discuss later in the appendix, good models of this process are problematic to build, although the task is possible using a structured, systems-based computer modeling approach. In any case, whether it be via qualitative or quantitative methods, we need to plot inputs into and interventions upon the system against VNSA life cycles, ascertaining our action's effectiveness at helping us achieve our desired end-state (be it prevention, deterrence, coercion, or disruption and destruction).

The importance of leveraging multiple instruments of state power (including soft power) should be obvious. A "military only" response to the VNSA problem would hamstring our C-VNSA strategy. Numerous instruments of state power (ranging from economic aid to transnational education reform to conflict resolution to alternate identity cultivation to targeted special operations to international police cooperation to more traditional military force-on-force confrontations), applied at the right time at the right level of the system, will have maximal impact. A counterterrorism strategy driven primarily by output considerations, either force-on-force or security-style confrontations of existing VNSA, lacks balance. To address the system only at the level of output or by confronting only one aspect of the multiple functions is to unnecessarily limit the full range of options we have for confronting VNSA. For this reason, we offer the following white paper for blue strategists.

White Paper for Blue Strategists

To ensure that we consider the full range of policy options available for confronting VNSA, we offer the following list of bullets. None (of course) is a "magic" bullet, but taken together, we think they provide a coherent and workable alternative to a C-VNSA strategy sometimes hobbled by a failure to think *system*atically about the nature of violent non-state organizations.

(1) *Force-on-force confrontations are only a small part of the "confrontational equation."* VNSA embrace asymmetric warfare: the forces they field are non-traditional, striking in ways that maximize the effect they can produce on far larger forces while using only minimal resources. Confronting a VNSA force with yet another force (e.g., using soldiers to stop suicide bombers) can work, in the short term; but to have this as the primary or only aspect of your C-VNSA strategy is to play directly to the strengths of asymmetric confrontations (this is why VNSA chose this tactic to begin with). We must be more asymmetric than our VNSA adversaries, and that involves coalition members striking in ways that maximize the effect *they* can produce using only minimal resources.

Secretary of Defense Donald Rumsfeld expressed much this senti-
ment in a portion of the infamous two-page memo to his staff (including the chairman of the Joint Chiefs of Staff, General Richard
Myers, and Deputy Secretary of Defense Paul Wolfowitz) that was
leaked to USA Today on October 22, 2002:

> Does the United States need to fashion a broad, integrated plan to
> stop the next generation of terrorists? The United States is putting
> relatively little effort into a long-range plan, but we are putting a
> great deal of effort into trying to stop terrorists. The cost-benefit
> ratio is against us! Our cost is billions against the terrorists' costs
> of millions.[1]

(2) *VNSA can be deterred.* VNSA are often thought to be irrational. For that
reason, critics contend, it's impossible to deter VNSA . . . they can only
be destroyed. However, an open systems perspective on VNSA development reveals multiple opportunities we have to influence VNSA ontogeny in a way that uses proximate psychological mechanisms to preclude action contrary to our interests. Broaden our notion of
deterrence and of psychology, and use those expanded notions to deter
VNSA when they can be deterred.

(3) *We should all become ecologists.* A critical insight for C-VNSA strategy is
that webs of environments, interactions, and processes both contribute
to and constitute VNSA growth. Those involved in formulating counterterrorism strategy need to be experts in these webs of structured interactive relationships. We could do worse than taking our cues from
those who manage eco-systems such as foresters, farmers, and artificial
life theorists. Or, as UCLA research fellow Raphael Sagarin maintains,

> The real challenge is to apply evolutionary thinking to homeland
> security in a more structured, broad-based manner. Evolutionary
> biologists, ecologists, and paleontologists understand better than
> anyone the evolutionary successes and failures of genes and
> species and what it takes to survive in the natural world. Officials
> prosecuting the war on terrorism should bring experts on evolu-
> tion into the discussion.[2]

The members of the military profession involved in combating terrorism should, at the end of the day, be part of a transformed cadre of military professionals, possessing a very different set of skills not traditionally associated with the warrior profession: this is not our
grandfather's security environment. Biology, rather than physics, might
be the operative structuring metaphor.

(4) *VNSA are not monolithic, nor do they exist in splendid isolation.* VNSA do not spring onto the international scene fully formed and made of solid granite. They develop over time, and as they do so, they articulate parts that have functions. VNSA are (thankfully) neither *hermetically* nor *hermeneutically* sealed. They exist as part of an open system and the parts of a VNSA are constantly exchanging matter and energy with that system; more, the meanings VNSA leadership use to reinforce group and role-specific identity are not water-tight. Undermine a VNSA's "story," and you go a long way toward winning the hermeneutic struggle. VNSA are not granite-like rocks that can only be crushed. Instead, they are more like extremely porous stones—pour in the right kind of liquid at the right temperature, let it sit overnight, and the rock disintegrates from the inside, slowly falling apart.

(5) *Confrontation happens in many ways.* There are multiple paths toward successful confrontation with VNSA and the environments that generate them. We should not think of the war on terrorism as consisting only in armed struggle. Rather, aspects of this war may be more like the "war" on illiteracy—war-like in the sense that we take (or ought to take) the root causes of illiteracy very seriously and struggle mightily against them, but not war-like in the sense that we shoot bullets at people who can't read. Effective use of the multiple instruments of state power is not to shrink from confrontation nor to handle VNSA with kid gloves; rather, it is to boost our ability to successfully shape the international security environment in a maximally efficacious manner.

(6) *Effective, possibly non-traditional, intelligence is critical.* Doing this all well is an intelligence-intensive enterprise. Much of our intelligence, especially military intelligence, is geared toward traditional battlefield-style warfare. The sources and methods used to gather this intelligence will be useful, but perhaps more useful will be improved *warning analysis* and *forecasting* related to the root causes and transformative processes discussed in the first third of the book. Moreover, *social intelligence* is required to avoid mirror-imaging and to gain insight into our adversary's mindset, operational code, and cultural underpinnings. Much of this intelligence will be open-source, but will be manpower intensive and require a rich conceptual infrastructure in order to organize effectively. Actionable intelligence needs to be placed in boxes that bear a clear connection to policy and strategy; open-systems theory does some of this work for us.

We don't mean to imply that none of these points is factored into our current national security posture; on the contrary, seeds of them can be found scattered throughout our national security apparatus. Rather, our contention is that (in the main), we have *tended* toward output confrontations, ignored deterrent options, undervalued ecological insights, treated VNSA monolithically and without due regard to their meaning-laden nature, defaulted to a narrow sense of confrontation rather than a broad sense, and not focused effectively on the appropriate intelligence tools. Moreover, our expertise is centered on specific groups, thus demanding a policy so nuanced that it lacks the cohesion required to synchronize the instruments of power. This is understandable, given the lack of a comprehensive framework for thinking about such organizations. If we are to overcome some of our disappointments with the results obtained thus far in our war on terror, though, we would do well to embrace systems thinking.

Research Agenda: Where To Now?

In this book, we have visually scanned the visible portion of the VNSA iceberg, touching only its tip. Our brief survey, and attempt to formulate a synoptic theory of VNSA, unearths myriad research programs and questions that beg for further exploration if we are to truly understand this security challenge. Here are some of our suggestions regarding where, corporately, we ought to go next:

(1) *Use the open systems approach to structure our thinking about VNSA.* Currently, there exists no unifying paradigm that allows us to think and speak coherently about VNSA. While there are some advantages to having a piecemeal approach to a topic, there are considerable benefits to be gained by structuring conversations across milieu using a common vocabulary. Our guess is that we can gain even deeper insight into many phenomena already well discussed in the VNSA literature by rethinking some positions in light of open-systems theory. The conceptual system we use to make sense of the world affects our ability to cope with it (compare the raw capacity of any five-year-old with that of any twenty-year-old), and the strength of open systems concepts as applied to terrorist groups lies in the explanatory unification and increased insight that results from using them. With insight comes the ability to *control* a system. Piecemeal approaches are useful, especially at the beginning of inquiry, but on the other hand nothing beats theoretical unification for increased prediction, control, and influence (and we'd like to do all these things for many VNSA).

(2) *Validate factual assumptions about the state of the environment.* Have we appropriately identified the aspects of the international environment that are conducive to VNSA formation? Can we more precisely state the

relationship between globalization and the rise of non-state actors? What other types of state failure contribute to VNSA genesis? Are there other interesting respects in which VNSA can construct environmental niches, or in which states can engage in niche destruction? These are all open questions. Our assumptions, while plausible and reflecting a broad consensus in the literature, nonetheless require further exploration to boost our confidence level and to gain insight into the web of ecological relations that is the international environment.

(3) *Validate our initial take on multi-level relationships.* VNSA are very complex dynamic systems. While the general concepts we've used to discuss parts and relationships are sound, they require further investigation. Many relationships between system variables have not been explored in any detail (the general shapes of the curves that define those relationships are not even known in many cases, as we haven't thought to frame questions in this way). Moreover, our initial cut on functions may have overlooked other patterns of activity that contribute to a VNSA's prosperity. Much of the iceberg remains unexplored.

(4) *Boost rigor; drive quantitative analyses.* Some of our insights are driven by case-study based analyses. These are useful, but have their shortcomings. Ideally, some relationships, which we discuss in qualitative terms, could be expressed rigorously in a quantitative manner. This would allow us to more thoroughly "reverse engineer" terrorist organizations, working backwards from observed strategy and tactics to infer interior system structure and relationships. Possessing this capacity is important for the articulation of a good C-VNSA strategy.

(5) *Develop species-specific functional architectures.* VNSA are alike in the critical respects (in much the same way that people are alike in the critical respects, which is why it is possible to have a science of medicine); however, there are probably species-specific differences in functional architecture that space considerations have prevented us from exploring in any detail. For example, certain types of VNSA (e.g., religious movements) will leverage charismatic identity entrepreneurs for their continued influence more so than others (e.g., crime networks). This may result in crucial differences in the authority and maintenance subsystems. Knowledge of these differences will be critical for driving C-VNSA strategy formulation.

(6) *Develop the allied intelligence tools and architecture required to validate the model and use it effectively.* To exhaustively validate some of the assertions made in our book will require a more theory-driven intelligence architecture than is in place at the national level currently. There is a fundamental shortage of methodologists in the intelligence community. We are not collecting against some of the variables and rela-

tionships necessary to gain full insight into the VNSA system. Our framework offers insight that will allow us to drive indications and warning decks, for instance; identifying VNSA signatures and growth profiles will cue us to potential areas of concern. The quality of our warning and threat estimates could increase if the thinking about them were structured in this way. Systems insights may drive more effective forecasting tools. Ideally, they could even allow us to answer Secretary of Defense Donald Rumsfeld's demand for a way to know whether we are winning the war on terror.[3] Developing the intelligence tools and architecture that make the most sense for confronting VNSA given our framework is extremely important.

(7) *Put computational bite into the theory.* We've stressed the dynamic nature of the VNSA threat, and how our strategy should be sensitive to diachronic concerns. One way in which these arguments could be made more rigorous and useful is to translate them into workable computer models that allow analysts to accomplish forecasting, engage in stem and branch decision analysis, and stress test strategic options *in silico* before trying them on for size in real life. This is, in part, the task of the technical appendix, but a great deal of work remains if the theory is to be translated into workable computer models.

Much else remains to be done, as we have only scratched the surface in this text. Nonetheless, the work we've accomplished thus far has allowed us to address some of the issues that have plagued reductionist approaches to VNSA; in this sense, open-systems analysis of violent non-state groups is a *progressive* research program, capable of solving some of the anomalies that traditional approaches leave untouched.

Paradigm Shift: Resolving Anomalies, Securing Progress

The philosopher and sociologist of science Thomas Kuhn is famous for articulating the idea of a paradigm shift.[4] Kuhn postulated that all science is conducted with the boundaries of a paradigm: fundamental assumptions about what we should count as real and how we come to possess knowledge about those things. From paradigms fall such items as testing procedures, methodological considerations, and vocabularies. Eventually, paradigms may enter a crisis stage because of their inability to resolve anomalies. For instance, the Newtonian paradigm eventually entered crisis because of its inability to explain multiple stellar phenomena, including the precession of Mercury. When a new paradigm emerges that explains away the anomalies that the paradigm in crisis could not, it is oft-times adopted, becoming the new and normal way of doing science. Progress occurs by the successive replacement of failing paradigms with more expansive explanatorily fecund paradigms.[5]

Current approaches to VNSA understanding have multiple anomalies. Defense decision-makers have complained that we have no comprehensive understanding of terrorism as a phenomenon; we have no way of knowing whether or not we are winning the war on it; ultimately, critics say, we are on unsure ground as we confront what could eventually become an existential challenge to our way of life. The way we best solve these anomalies and deal with the complexity before us, is by shifting to a more comprehensive framework that gives us the tools, methods, and vocabulary we need to be able to make sense of them. That new paradigm is the one we have articulated in the past eight chapters: the open-systems framework can unify disparate approaches to VNSA, providing us with comprehensive insight into how we can both effectively confront them across their entire life-cycle and measure whether or not our confrontation is effective.

There is much at stake. The success of our national security posture rides on whether or not we are willing to think creatively and "outside of the box" about violent non-state actors. Nothing less is acceptable if we are to successfully confront a dynamic and growing threat to international security: warlords rising.

Notes

1. See the original article in *USA Today* of 22 October 2003 available at www.usatoday.com/news/washington/executive/rumsfeld-memo.htm as of January 10, 2004, or the excellent summary of the incident from *Slate Online Magazine* at slate.msn.com/id/2090250/ available as of January 10, 2004.

2. See his "Adapt or Die: What Charles Darwin can teach Tom Ridge about homeland security," *Foreign Policy* (September/October 2003): 68–69.

3. Ibid. Rumsfeld asks: "Today, we lack metrics to know if we are winning or losing the global war on terror. Are we capturing, killing or deterring and dissuading more terrorists every day than the madrassas and the radical clerics are recruiting, training and deploying against us?"

4. Thomas Kuhn, *The Structure of Scientific Revolutions* (Chicago, IL: The University of Chicago Press, 1962).

5. For technical reasons regarding the incommensurability of vocabularies between paradigms, Kuhn is sometimes cast as a skeptic regarding the idea of scientific progress. We can set aside this concern for present purposes. Even if paradigms *are* problem-driven, and our problems *change* from epoch to epoch, it still remains the case that solving the VNSA problem is critical currently.

Appendix

Modeling VNSA: Growth Dynamics of Peru's Sendero Luminoso

with Jason E. Bartolomei

OUR BOOK EMPHASIZES THE IMPORTANCE of open-systems approaches for a comprehensive understanding of VNSA. In the concluding chapter, we discussed the importance of formulating systems-level computer models that may enable us to forecast VNSA growth and formation, and that also give us leverage for effects-based operations and planning. In this appendix, we apply tools from systems engineering to turn our *qualitative* systems-level mental models of VNSA into *quantitative* computer models. By using a systems engineering approach, policy-makers will be able to expand the number and quality of their mental models surrounding reasoning about how VNSA develop so as to gain deeper insights into the complexity of the system. The technical tools introduced in this appendix are not the primary focus of our book, so our treatment will be brief; however, they complement the framework so very well that discussing them in this appendix is natural.[1]

Modeling is an art, and so there are some very slight variations between structures discussed in the book and those leveraged in the model. This is not troublesome, as there is more than one way to skin the functional cat; other models with functional architectures more tightly wrapped around the qualitative understanding detailed in this book (and which co-evolved with our modeling process) may prove yet more effective. Let a million flowers bloom . . . so long as they aren't poppies in Afghanistan.

Developing the Structure of a VNSA Architecture

Systems engineering consists of an array of heuristic tools that are used within an iterative process to solve a defined problem; for example, to understand how the parts of a plumbing system interact, we would repeatedly apply a version of the steps we recommend below until reaching sufficient understanding of the system for our purposes (this may be a very complex and deep understanding if we are redesigning a bathroom from the ground up, or a relatively shallow understanding if we are merely fixing a leaky faucet). To better understand VNSA structure and processes, we implemented the following steps:

Step 1: Identify VNSA Stakeholders
Step 2: Define Stakeholder Objectives
Step 3: Identify Activities to Achieve Objectives
Step 4: Identify Agents Responsible for Activities
Step 5: Define Measures of Performance for Activities
Step 6: Identify System Drivers
Step 7: Highlight the Causality within the System

This process provides a rigorous methodology for efficiently identifying the system boundary (where do we start?) and the critical system variables (what are the important things?). Once the system variables are defined, they can be organized into a system causal matrix structure, which highlights the causal nature between variables, and which is then relatively easy to transform into a systems level computer model. We will discuss each of these steps in slightly more detail.

VNSA Stakeholders

The process for moving from a qualitative understanding to a quantitative model began by identifying the stakeholder associations, which are a function of the support sub-system. The stakeholders are individuals and organizations that drive the requirements of the system. Performing a stakeholder analysis is similar to the customer/market analysis required in traditional systems engineering and product development. Chapter 4 details specific methods for mapping the stakeholder associations of a VNSA. For typical VNSA, these stakeholders might include sympathetic state leaders, religious leaders, VNSA leaders and identity entrepreneurs, and a vulnerable population which the VNSA is trying to influence. The success of the VNSA hinges on its ability to meet the stakeholder requirements; if VNSA can't gather the appropriate human inputs, for example, then in the absence of negative entropy (such as stores of recruits waiting in the wings) the organization will eventually collapse.

Defining the Stakeholder Objectives through Functional Analysis

The behavior of any system is based on the structure of the system and the causal relationships between the variables within the system. For VNSA, the stakeholders drive the causal relationships between many of the system variables (for example, if a sympathetic state leader demands that a VNSA commit terrorist acts if it is to receive continued funding and support, this will spur the development of certain relationships and processes). Therefore, an understanding of the stakeholder's objectives (their vital interests) is necessary to gain insight into the causal structure driving the system behaviors.

In many cases, the stakeholder objectives are easily determined. For instance, Sendero Luminoso leaders are quite vocal about their desires to overthrow the government.[2] Other times, stakeholder interests are less obvious—the Senderistas were less vocal concerning their desire for wealth and their desires to strengthen their stake in the drug trade. Despite these difficulties, we can work backwards from the actions of the stakeholder to reasonably infer what objectives they are pursuing so as to maximize our chances of correctly identifying vital interests. Engineers often struggle with similar issues when reengineering products designed by other companies ("What were they thinking when they put the power switch on the computer here rather than there? What did they hope to achieve?").

A common methodology employed by engineers to tackle this problem is to perform a functional analysis of existing products. The goal of the functional analysis is to clearly identify the functions of the parts of a physical system. Once the functions for each part are identified, the engineer can *re*engineer the system so as to (hopefully) improve it. Generally, the functions can be arranged hierarchically. Based on the hierarchy, the objectives of the system can be inferred even in the absence of *specific* knowledge about the intention of the designers.

VNSA Activities Defined and Classified

In the largest sense, VNSA have as their goal the imposition of their will on others; as discussed in the text, based on the overall objective of IMPOSING WILL, a mature VNSA will develop multiple subfunctions, with many layers of systems and sub-systems that are performing multitudes of activities. Although the methodology enables us to fully decompose the entire system, in this appendix we will only develop the *attract people* function—a VNSA must be able to recruit if it is to sustain itself (in the framework developed earlier in the book, this would be a major function of the support sub-system). There are many other functions a full-blown VNSA must implement, as our text made clear; a comprehensive model would include sketches of those functions also.

Identify VNSA Agents

For each of the activities identified, an agent or multiple agents of the organization must be responsible for the execution of the activities. Paul Davis and Brian Jenkins present the different types of agents found within a VNSA in their excellent book *Deterrence and Influence in Counterterrorism: A Component in the War on al Qaeda*.[3] These include the following: top leaders, lieutenants, foot soldiers, and recruiters, among others.

Sendero Luminoso (SL hereafter) had multiple agents responsible for recruitment activities to include all of these forms of actors. For example, Abimael Guzman, the founder of the Sendero and himself a university philosophy professor, recruited heavily at San Marcos University in Lima and at his home institution of the University of San Cristobal de Huamanga (in Ayacucho) during the early stages of SL's development. As the organization grew, SL foot soldiers comprised of Peruvian peasants were able to attract people by leveraging peasant dissatisfaction with the state of their environment and the Peruvian government's responses to it (recall the reinforcing actions and niche construction discussions in the main text).

VNSA Activity Measures of Performance

Once the activities and the agents are identified, the next questions include: How do we measure whether the agents are successfully achieving their objectives? What are the most important external indicators of the VNSA's organization health and effectiveness? How might the VNSA know when they are meeting their goals?

For the *attract people* function and supporting activities, we determined that two indicators seemed most logical: total number of VNSA members and total number of VNSA sympathizers. In most cases, the general population of a country does not fill out registration cards for their local VNSA, nor do they volunteer information about their level of sympathy for the VNSA. In the real world, it would require significant human intelligence to determine these measures. For the SL, we looked to historical data presented by David Scott Palmer from 1970–1992.[4]

In addition, other measures of performance for other critical functions and supporting actions might include: VNSA Cash Reserves and Arms Supplies for an *acquire material* function (part of the support sub-system) and the number of acts of terror for the *commit terror* functions (part of the conversion sub-system). For SL, the identification of these variables is important when modeling recruitment, since these variables likely directly affect the identity entrepreneur's ability to influence the population (recall that the identity entrepreneur is the person or persons, like Guzman, who exploits existing identity cleavages in order to mobilize a disaffected population).

Identifying the VNSA's measures of performance serves two major functions. First, clearly articulating the measures of performance can be helpful in driving the intelligence requirements in the surveillance of a particular VNSA, as discussed in chapter eight. In addition, it is important to understand the effectiveness of the VNSA in the execution of activities not only for intelligence and policy effectiveness assessments but also because these activities directly affect other variables of the system that influence VNSA ability to recruit. For example, the larger the VNSA membership, the greater the identity entrepreneur's indirect influence on the population, and also the greater the VNSA's ability to collect intelligence (in support of the cognitive sub-system). The measure of the identity entrepreneur's influence on the population is a good example of an endogenous variable that is affected and affects other variables within the system. The next step of the process requires a through analysis of the system to identify both the endogenous and exogenous variables with the system.

VNSA System Drivers

We call these internal ("endogenous") and external ("exogenous") variables the VNSA system drivers. These are the variables that directly affect the VNSA's ability to execute activities and conversely can be affected by VNSA's (or state's) reinforcing actions. For example, population disaffection is a critical system driver that positively influences the VNSA's ability to attract people. Using the open-systems assumptions presented in the book, we believe VNSA grow and develop at the intersection of environmental conditions and group psychology; certain environmental variables contribute to the conditions that make VNSA genesis possible. For a VNSA, the system drivers will be the environmental and psychological variables that are influencing the system's key states.

For recruitment, many important environmental variables influence the disaffection of the VNSA's target population. To fully decompose the variables that contribute to population disaffection, we reviewed the literature and relied on expert opinion. We classified the variables into four distinct categories as follows: Maslow variables, Camus variables, Smith variables, and Dewey variables. The Maslow classification represents variables that relate to a population's fundamental needs being met. Maslow variables include food and water availability, infant mortality rate, level of medical care, etc. Recall the discussion of the relationship between these variables and identity formation in chapter three. Camus variables, named after the existential philosopher Albert Camus, include variables that deal with the spiritual and moral fabric of a population (for example, is the population identity such that people are likely to resort to violence to resolve disputes?). Dewey variables, after the philosopher of pragmatism and democracy John Dewey, consist of social factors like freedom of movement, freedom of speech, etc. Smith variables represent the system economic variables. All of the variables listed above are external to the VNSA and are considered inputs into the system. Exogenous factors are sometimes independent of the VNSA activities; in some cases, it is difficult for the VNSA to influence these variables with reinforcing actions. In other cases, VNSA will expend efforts in niche construction, which will earn it some influence in otherwise external variables; in other words, the VNSA will attempt to turn exogenous variables into endogenous ones.

Examples of endogenous system drivers for the recruitment activities of the VNSA are the variables associated with the role of the identity entrepreneur. For example, in order for the identity entrepreneur to exercise his ability to convert a VNSA sympathizer into a full-fledged member of the VNSA, he must be able to influence society—that ability to influence is a function of the developing cognitive sub-system in the VNSA. The measure of this ability is hence an endogenous variable that lies within the VNSA and positively affects the VNSA's ability to accomplish its functions. In addition, endogenous variables are factors that the VNSA can more easily affect, as they are ofttimes directly within the organization's control.

Highlight the Causality within the System

The next step of the process is to highlight the causal relations that exist between variables. A common systems-thinking methodology for capturing these causal relations is through the use of causal-loop diagrams. Systems engineers and the product development community when developing complex engineering systems have used an alternative method of capturing these relationships through the use of matrices. Matrices have many advantages: they are generally very orderly and efficiently determined, they organize the variables in a structured format, and they enable analysts to quickly determine the boundaries of the system (this can be a taxing effort otherwise).

To determine the causal relations for VNSA, we employed a tailored version of common systems engineering/design matrices designed explicitly for tackling a non-engineering system. We call this tool a System Causal Matrix.

VNSA System Causal Matrix

A System Causal Matrix is a matrix that captures the entirety of variables uncovered through the analysis of steps 1–6 of the process presented above. These variables are organized into the format listed in figure A.1. The matrix in the top left-hand corner captures the Stakeholders and the Stakeholder Objectives into an inter-relational matrix. This is an important matrix because each stakeholder has objectives supported by the VNSA, and all activities performed by the VNSA flow from these objectives.

The next matrix organizes the hierarchal relationships between the objectives of the system. The highest order objectives and the supporting objectives from the functional analysis described above are placed into the intra-relational matrix. The next matrix is the matrix that correlates the activities and the objectives which those activities support. Moving to the right in figure A.1, the next matrix highlights agent/activity relationship by showing which agents are responsible for the VNSA activities. Next, the VNSA activities and the system drivers are captured in the inter-relational matrix. This is the first causal matrix, where causal relationships between variables are defined. For example, Level of Disaffected Population is a system driver that positively influences the VNSA's ability to cultivate sympathizers. The next matrix connects the VNSA activities with the Measures of Performance for each activity. Each activity should have at least one Measure of Performance.

As we move clockwise around the right-hand side of the diagram, the lower-right hand matrix highlights the causal relationship between Measures of Performance and the System Drivers. This matrix captures the reinforcing actions the VNSA has on the system drivers. The intrarelational matrix on the left represents the causal relationships between the systems drivers.

The unique arrangement of the system causal matrix not only organizes the variables, but also captures the feedback relationships within the system. These feedback relationships can be organized into a tabular "system causal matrix," which lists the variables within the system and their positive and negative feedback relationships to one another.

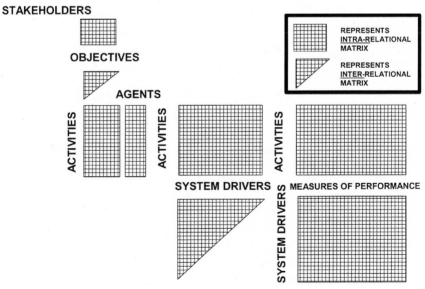

FIGURE A.1
System Causal Matrix

VNSA Policy Architecture Analysis:
Moving from the Matrix to a Systems-level Model

After accomplishing these steps, the policy analyst has a choice that can be satisfied with the insight gained into the system merely by asking and possibly answering these questions. The qualitative insights gained by framing policy problems in this way can be very helpful. Or, the analyst could decide to move from the answers to these questions to a high-level systems dynamics model of the system; in other words, our technique can be used to translate qualitative theories about the nature of the system into quantitative theories and then to models. These models can be quickly built using inexpensive commercially available software such as Stella VIII.

If they decide to model the system mathematically and develop a systems-level simulation of the system the analyst must perform the following steps, which we will discuss only briefly:

Step 8:   Determine the Nature of the Causal Relations Mathematically
Step 9:   Develop Systems-level Model for the System
Step 10: Perform Validation/Verification of the Model

Systems-level Model Using Stella VIII

Because VNSA development occurs over time (as we were at pains to note in the main text), we decided to use a system dynamics approach to create a systems-level model. The first step in this process is to translate the variables defined in the matrix into a "stock and flow" structure based on the causal relationships highlighted in the matrix and the nature of the variables (for example, we may have a stock of $1,000 that flows out at the rate of $20 an hour as we buy ammunition for weapons, while money flows in at a rate of $22 an hour from payments from druglords for protecting their coca crops). Owing to our specific focus on the growth of VNSA and related recruitment activities, we first started by trying to understand the conversion of the general population into sympathizers, and the ability of the VNSA to convert sympathizers into full-blown VNSA members.

Based on our qualitative understanding, population disaffection is a major factor affecting growth and recruitment rates. So we first determined the mathematical nature of these relationships so they can be captured in the model. Smith variables include a free market index, trade, unemployment, general infrastructure, information infrastructure, and excessive governance index. Maslow variables include mean education level, infant mortality rate, basic consumables, medical care, social capital, crime rate, and police malefi-cence. Camus variables include index of religious worship sites, cultural homogeneity, propensity to use violence, and value of life indexes. Dewey variables include freedom of speech, press, movement, and government liberalism.

One advantage of using a system-dynamics approach is the flexibility (inherent in the software and the process) to easily change assumptions and relationships between variables. In many cases, we had dissenting opinions about certain relationships between variables. It was effortless to change the assumptions and test the hypotheses quickly with the systems-level model.

After determining how the general population is converted into sympathizers because of the level of disaffection, the next portion of the model to be tackled was the ability of the VNSA to convert the sympathizer into an actual VNSA member. Based on the relationships uncovered by the matrix, we knew that this was a function of the identity entrepreneur's effectiveness. His effectiveness results from (among other things) his inherent charisma, his finances, and his ability to commit terror, which directly impacts his ability to recruit. Figure A.2 illustrates the stock and flow structure of the system by graphically highlighting the variables which contribute to the causal chain. The modeling package used in our exercise allows you to construct these systems of stocks and flows relatively quickly and easily. Once the critical variable relationships are defined with data and/or expert opinion it is time to run the model to test its ability to recreate history.

Validation/Verification of SIMulation Sendero Luminoso

Despite the multiple studies performed on SL, the data available for the important variables uncovered through employing the methodology was quite anemic. In fact, only a few of the variables affecting population disaffection were available in comprehensive and reliable time series (such as infant mortality rates). Thus, we were forced to rely on the opinion of experts for many of the inputs. In addition, David Scott Palmer's historical report on SL cited earlier (p. 228) had valuable information including multiple data points on SL membership, acts of terror, and number of deaths. He had only one data point for SL sympathizers and very rough estimates of SL finances, however. Our goal was to make the best assumptions possible and try to recreate the growth of SL membership from 1970–1992 both in terms of actual cadre members and sympathizers.

Using the best assumptions available, we were able to recreate the curves for VNSA membership growth as shown in figures A.3 and A.4, hitting the number of SL sympathizers in 1992 very closely. Despite our success in matching the shape and value of the growth curve, it is far more accurate to describe this model as a rough forecasting tool rather than as having strict predictive value. Overfitting is a constant concern (solved in this case by jackknifing the data[5]), and while it may be possible to develop good forecasts in

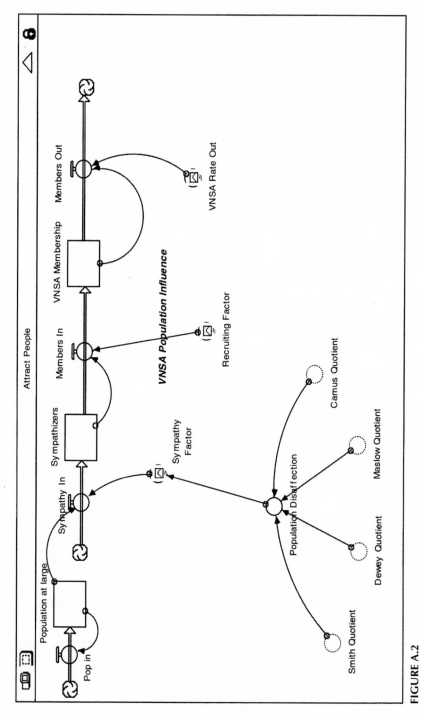

FIGURE A.2
Example of Sub-System Analysis: "Attract People"

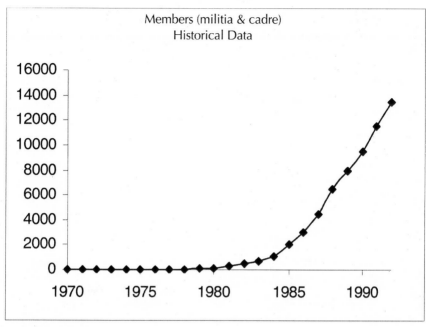

FIGURE A.3
Sendero Membership, Real World

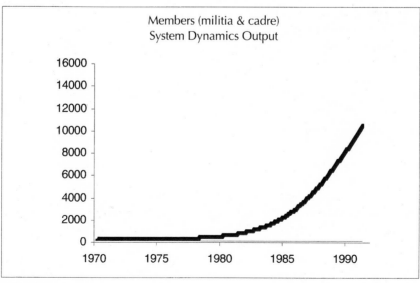

FIGURE A.4
Sendero Membership, as Modeled

some tightly constrained circumstances, we are more comfortable describing the process as an insight-generating tool and hip-pocket decision aid than as a process for producing predictive models.

VNSA Policy Architecture Synthesis

Now that we have built a system-level computer model, we can use it to help rethink policy options for influencing the system in question. The following steps (*Step 11: Use Model to Glean New Insights into the System* and *Step 12: Employ Other Analytical Tools to Gain Deeper Insight as Needed*) will help us flesh out a "policy architecture synthesis"—a plan similar to the one discussed in chapter 8 to guide us as we develop counter-VNSA strategy.

Use Model to Glean New Insights into the System

We can use our model to brainstorm policy options. For instance, the model forecasts that if we had been able to neutralize the influence Guzman had on the population, recruitment rates would have dropped to near zero (even though disaffection rates stay very high). On the other hand, if we had addressed environmental variables significantly (such as infant mortality rate or amount of trade), we might have nearly halved the size of SL over the course of its ontogeny. These forecasts are problematic, of course, given the nature of the modeling process (they are highly contingent on the quality of the time series data and on expert opinion); but they are very useful, nonetheless, for helping us brainstorm about alternate policy options and for making rough forecasts regarding possible futures. This modeling process can be used to derive computer simulations that can support stem and branch policy analysis (if I did this at this time, what might have happened?); they can also be used to ascertain regret curves (if I got this variable relationship wrong, how much would I regret that?), and that may be useful for helping us prioritize intelligence and policy priorities.

Employ Other Analytical Tools to Gain Deeper Insights as Needed

Once high-level systems modeling has been accomplished, a policy-maker can use more traditional analytical tools, such as agent-based models, to gain higher fidelity insight into the system. Our tool complements the other tools available to the modeler. This process is relatively cheap, easy, and low-fidelity. Higher confidence models can be gained by drilling down deeply using more traditional (and usually slower and more expensive) modeling methods.

Benefits of a Systems-level Model

The easy-to-use graphic interface on these programs makes it unproblematic for analysts and policymakers to use the quantitative system model to gain insight into the system, and possibly even to forecast the consequences of interventions into the system. At the very least, these models can be used for alternate futures analysis, or to drive a stems-and-branches style brainstorming session. They can also help policymakers decide where more time, effort, and other resources should be dedicated (e.g., "we need to conduct a discrete event analysis of the effect that population size and food availability has on regime desperateness").

The procedures we have argued for in this appendix are designed to make such high level systems-level exploratory modeling quick and easy for the analyst or policymaker. This can be a very valuable process as it may highlight additional policy options available, and is a necessary part of any good effects-based operation. They are a natural fit with the open-systems framework we've elaborated fully in this book, and could be a crucial tool in helping us effectively confront VNSAs.

Notes

1. Jason Bartolomei, William Casebeer, and Troy Thomas, *Modeling Violent Non-State Actors: A Summary of Concepts and Methods*, Institute for Information Technology Applications, Research Publication 4, Information Series, November 2004, U.S. Air Force Academy, Colorado.

2. Refer, for example, to chapter 15 of Gustavo Gorriti's, *The Shining Path: A History of the Millenarian War in Peru* (Chapel Hill, NC: University of North Carolina Press, 1999). Guzman's plans for replacing the government of Peru with a Maoist regime are made explicit in great detail.

3. Paul Davis and Brian Jenkins, *Deterrence and Influence in Counterterrorism: A Component in the War on al Qaeda* (Santa Monica, CA: RAND Corporation, 2002), 15.

4. See David Scott Palmer, "The Revolutionary Terrorism of Peru's Shining Path," printed in *Terrorism in Context*, ed. Martha Crenshaw (University Park, PA: The Pennsylvania State University Press, 1995). Palmer is careful to place large error bars on the estimates we use in the text.

5. Jackknifing is a technique where a given dataset is split in half, with one half the dataset used to build the model and the other half used to test the model. This technique can be used both to combat overfitting and to build and test models where data is difficult to obtain or where multiple controlled experiments cannot be conducted.

Selected Bibliography

Alexander, Yonah. *Combating Terrorism: Strategies of Ten Countries*. Ann Arbor, MI: University of Michigan Press, 2002.

Ali, Abdullah Yusuf, trans. *The Meaning of the Glorious Qur'an*. London: Nadim and CO, 1976.

Ali, Maulana M. *The Religion of Islam*. Lahore, Pakistan: The Ahmadiyya Anjuman Isha'at Islam, 1983.

Ali, Taisier, and Robert Matthews, ed. *Civil Wars in Africa: Roots and Resolution*. Montreal: McGill Queen's University Press, 1999.

Argyris, Chris, and Donald Schon. *Organizational Learning II: Theory, Method and Practice*. Reading, MA: Addison Wesley Publishing Company, 1996.

Arquilla, John, and David Ronfeldt. *Networks and Netwars*. Santa Monica, CA: RAND Corporation, 2001.

Arquilla, John, and David Rondfedt, eds. *In Athena's Camp: Preparing for Conflict in the Information Age*. Santa Monica, CA: RAND, 1997.

Asprey, Robert B. *War in the Shadows: The Guerrilla in History*. New York: William Morrow and Company, 1994.

Barber, Benjamin. *Jihad vs. McWorld: How Globalism and Tribalism Are Reshaping the World*. New York: Ballantine Books, 1996.

Barth, Frederick. *Ethnic Groups and Boundaries: The Social Organization of Culture Difference*. Boston: Little and Brown, 1969.

Bennigsen, Alexandre. "Islam in Retrospect." *Central Asian Survey*. 1989, vol. 8.

Bennigsen, Alexandre, and S. Enders Wimbush. *Muslims of the Soviet Empire*. Bloomington: Indiana University Press, 1986.

Bergen, Peter L. *Holy War, Inc.: Inside the Secret World of Osama bin Laden*. New York: The Free Press, 2001.

Berkeley, Bill. *The Graves are Not Yet Full: Race, Tribe and Power in the Heart of Africa*. New York: Basic Books, 2001.

Betts, Richard. *Conflict after the Cold War: Arguments on Causes of War and Peace*. Upper Saddle River, NJ: Allyn and Bacon Publishers, 1994.

Boot, Max. *The Savage Wars of Peace: Small Wars and the Rise of American Power*. New York: Basic Books, 2002.

Botterill, George, and Peter Carruthers. *The Philosophy of Psychology.* New York: Cambridge University Press, 1999.

Bowden, Mark. *Killing Pablo: The Hunt for the World's Greatest Outlaw.* New York: Penguin, 2001.

Branquinho, Joao, ed. *The Foundations of Cognitive Science.* New York: Oxford University Press, 2001.

Brown, Lester R. "Redefining National Security." *Worldwatch Paper* 14. October 1977.

Bunker, Robert J., ed. *Non-State Threats and Future Wars.* Portland, OR: Frank Cass, 2003.

Burles, Mark. *Chinese Policy Toward Russia and the Central Asian Republics.* Santa Monica, CA: RAND Corporation, 1999.

Buzan, Barry. *People, States and Fear: An Agenda for International Security Studies in the Post–Cold War Era.* Boulder, CO: Lynne Rienner Publishers, 1991.

Byman, Daniel. *Keeping the Peace: Lasting Solutions to Ethnic Conflicts.* Baltimore: The Johns Hopkins University Press, 2002.

Byman, Daniel L., Peter Chalk, Bruce Hoffman, William Rosenau, and David Brannan. *Trends in Outside Support for Insurgent Movements.* Santa Monica, CA: RAND, 2001.

Byman, Daniel L., Matthew C. Waxman, and Eric Lawson, eds. *Airpower as a Coercive Instrument.* Santa Monica, CA: RAND Corporation, 1999.

Caponera, Dante A. *Principles of Water Law and Administration: National and International.* Rotterdam, NE: Brookfield Press, May 1992.

Carlton, David, and Carlo Schaerf, eds. *International Terrorism and World Security.* London: Croom Helm, 1975.

Catanzaro, Raimondo. *Men of Respect: A Social History of the Sicilian Mafia.* New York: The Free Press, July 1992.

Clausewitz, Carl von. *On War.* Edited and translated by Michael Howard and Peter Paret. Princeton, NJ: Princeton University Press, 1984.

Clausewitz, Carl von. *On War: General Carl Von Clausewitz.* Volume 1. Translated by Colonel J. J. Graham. London: Routledge and Kegan Paul, 1966.

Coker, Christopher. *Waging War Without Warriors: The Changing Culture of Military Conflict.* Boulder, CO: Lynne Rienner Publishers, 2002.

Connolly, Terry, et al., eds. *Judgment and Decision Making: An Interdisciplinary Reader.* New York: Cambridge University Press, 2000.

Corning, Peter. *Nature's Magic: Synergy in Evolution and the Fate of Humankind.* New York: Cambridge University Press, 2003.

Crenshaw, Martha. "Theories of Terrorism: Instrumental and Organizational Approaches." In *Inside Terrorist Organizations*, ed. David Rapoport. Portland, OR: Frank Cass Publishers, January 2001.

Cummings, Thomas G., and Christopher G. Worley. *Organization Development and Change.* Cincinnati, OH: South Western College Publishing, 1997.

Daft, Richard L. *Organization Theory and Design.* Mason, OH: Thomson South-western, 2004.

Damasio, Antonio. *Descartes' Error: Emotion, Reason, and the Human Brain.* New York: G. P. Putnam and Sons, 1994.

Davis, Anthony. "Xinjiang Learns to Live with Resurgent Islam." *Jane's Intelligence Review*, September 1996.

Eshel, David. "The Rise and Fall of the Al Aqsa Martyrs Brigades." *Jane's Intelligence Review*, June 2002, vol. 14, no. 6.

Fauconnier, Gilles, and Mark Turner. *The Way We Think: Conceptual Blending and the Mind's Hidden Complexities.* New York: Basic Books, 2002.

Fierman, William. *Soviet Central Asia: The Failed Transformation.* Boulder, CO: Westview Press, 1991.

Fiorentini, Gianluca, and Sam Peltzman, eds., *The Economics of Organized Crime.* Cambridge, UK: Cambridge University Press, 1995.

Gambetta, Diego. *The Sicilian Mafia: The Business of Private Protection.* Boston: Harvard University Press, 1996.

Gaylin, Willard, Dr. *Hatred: The Psychological Descent into Violence.* New York: Public Affairs, 2003.

Gentner, Dedre, Keith Holyoak, and Boicho Kokinov. *The Analogical Mind: Perspectives from Cognitive Science.* Cambridge, MA: The MIT Press, 2001.

George, Alexander, and William E. Simons, eds. *The Limits of Coercive Diplomacy.* Boulder, CO: Westview Press, 1971.

Gerhart, John, and Marc Kirschner, eds. *Cells, Embryos, and Evolution: Toward a Cellular and Developmental Understanding of Phenotypic Variation and Evolutionary Adaptability.* Malden, MA: Blackwell Science, 1997.

Gigerenzer, Gerd. *Adaptive Thinking: Rationality in the Real World.* New York: Oxford University Press, 2000.

Gleick, James. *Chaos: Making a New Science.* New York, NY: Viking, 1987.

Gleick, Peter, ed. *Water in Crisis. A Guide to the World Fresh Water Resources.* New York: Oxford, 1993.

Gochman, Charles, and Alan Sabrosky, ed. *Prisoners of War: Nation-States in the Modern Era.* Lexington, MA: Lexington Books, May 1990.

Gorriti, Gustavo. *The Shining Path: A History of the Millenarian War in Peru.* Chapel Hill: The University of North Carolina Press, 1999.

Griffin, Nicholas. *Caucasus: Mountain Men and Holy Wars.* New York: St. Martin's Press, 2001.

Gunaratna, Rohan. *Inside Al Qaeda: Global Network of Terror.* New York: Columbia University Press, 2002.

Gurr, Ted Robert. *Why Men Rebel.* Princeton, NJ: Princeton University Press, 1970.

Haghayeghi, Mehrdad. *Islam and Politics in Central Asia.* New York: St. Martin's Press. 1996.

Hanle, Donald. *Terrorism: The Newest Face of Warfare.* Washington, DC: Pergamon-Brassey's, 1989.

Harrison, Michael I., and Arie Shirom. *Organizational Diagnosis and Assessment: Bridging Theory and Practice.* Thousand Oaks, CA: Sage Publications, 1999.

Hart, B. H. Liddell. *Strategy.* New York: Signet, 1967.

Hatch, Mary Jo. *Organization Theory: Modern, Symbolic, and Postmodern Perspectives.* Oxford, UK: Oxford University Press, 1997.

Hendrickson, Anne. *The "Youth Bulge": Defining the Next Generation of Young Men as a Threat to the Future.* Population and Development Program, Hampshire College. No. 19, Winter 2003.

Hoffer, Eric. *The True Believe: Thoughts on the Nature of Mass Movements.* New York: Harper and Row, 1951.

Hoffman, Bruce. *Inside Terrorism.* New York: Columbia University Press, 1998.

Hoffman, Bruce, and Ian Lesser. *Countering the New Terrorism.* Santa Monica, CA: RAND Corporation, 1999.

Homer-Dixon, Thomas F. "Environmental Scarcity and Violent Conflict." *Scientific American.* February 1993.

Huntington, Samuel. *Clash of Civilizations and the Remaking of World Order.* New York: Simon and Schuster, 1996.

Janzen, Leslie, and Alpa Patel. *The Economic Impact of Non-State Actors on National Failure.* Annapolis, MD: U.S. Naval Academy, 2001.

Jawahar, I. M., and Gary L. McLaughlin. "Toward a Descriptive Stakeholder Theory: An Organizational Life Cycle Approach." *The Academy of Management Review.* Briarcliff Manor, July 2001, vol. 26, issue 3.

Jervis, Robert, et al. *Psychology and Deterrence.* Baltimore: The Johns Hopkins University Press, 1985.

Joshua, Goldstein. *International Relations.* New York: HarperCollins College Publishers, 1996.

Juarrero, Alicia. *Dynamics in Action: Intentional Behavior as a Complex System.* Cambridge, MA: The MIT Press, 1999.

Kahneman, D., P. Slovic, and A. Tversky, eds. *Judgment under Uncertainty: Heuristics and Biases.* New York: Cambridge University Press, 1982.

Kakar, Sudhir. *The Colors of Violence: Cultural Identities, Religion, and Conflict.* Chicago, IL: University of Chicago Press, 1996.

Kaldor, Mary. *New and Old Wars: Organized Violence in a Global System.* Stanford, CA: Stanford University Press, 1999.

Kapuscinski, Ryszard. *The Shadow of the Sun.* New York: Vintage Books, 2001.

Katz, Daniel, and Robert L. Kahn. *The Social Psychology of Organizations.* New York: John Wiley & Sons, 1978.

Keegan, John. *A History of Warfare.* New York: Vintage Books, 1993.

Kegley, Charles W. Jr., and Eugene R. Wittkopf. *World Politics: Trend and Transformation.* New York: Bedford/St. Martins, 2001.

Kelly, Robert, Ko-lin Chin, and Rufus Schatzberg, eds. *Handbook of Organized Crime in the United States.* Westport, CT: Greenwood Press, 1994.

Khan, Mian R. A., *Islamic Jurisprudence.* Lahore, Pakistan: Sh. Mohammad Ashraf, 1978.

Kuhn, Thomas. *The Structure of Scientific Revolutions.* Chicago, IL: The University of Chicago Press, 1962.

Kurlansky, Mark. *The Basque History of the World.* New York: Penguin Books, 1999.

Lakoff, George, and Mark Johnson. *Metaphors We Live By.* Chicago, IL: The University of Chicago Press, 1980.

Laland, Kevin, and John Odling-Smee. "Niche Construction, Biological Evolution and Cultural Change," *Behavioral and Brain Sciences,* 23, 1, 2000.

Laqueur, Walter. *Guerrilla Warfare: A Historical & Critical Study.* New Brunswick, NJ: Transaction Publishers, 1998.

Lennon, Alexander T. J., ed. *The Battle for Hearts and Mind: Using Soft Power to Undermine Terrorist Networks.* Cambridge, MA: The MIT Press, 2003.

Lewis, Bernard. *The Crisis of Islam: Holy War and Unholy Terror.* New York: Modern Library, 2003.

Lubin, Nancy, Keith Martin, and Barnett R. Rubin. *Calming the Ferghana Valley: Development and Dialogue in the Heart of Central Asia.* (New York: Council for Foreign Relations—Ferghana Valley Working Group, 1999.

Mackinlay, John. "Defining Warlords." Published in *Monograph 46, Building Stability in Africa: Challenges for the New Millennium.* Peoria, South Africa: Institute for Security Studies, February 2000.

Makarenko, Tamara. "Terrorism and Religion Mask Drug Trafficking in Central Asia." *Jane's Intelligence Review.* November 2000, vol. 12, no. 11.

Mashenko, Alexi, and Martha Brill Olcott, eds. *Multidimensional Borders of Asia.* New York: Carnegie Endowment for International Peace, April 2000.

Matveeva, Anna, and Duncan Hiscock, eds. *The Causcus: Armed and Divided.* London: Saferworld, 2003.

Meigs, Montgomery C. "Unorthodox Thoughts about Asymmetric Warfare." *Parameters.* Summer 2003, vol. 33, no. 2.

Metz, Steven. *Armed Conflict in the 21st Century: The Information Revolution and Post-Modern Warfare.* Carlisle, PA: Strategic Studies Institute, April 2000.

Metz, Steven, and Douglas V. Johnson II. *Asymmetry and US Military Strategy: Definition, Background, and Strategic Concepts.* Carlisle, PA: Strategic Studies Institute: U.S. Army War College, January 2001.

Mintzberg, Henry. *The Design School: Reconsidering the Basic Premises of Strategic Management.* New York: John Wiley and Sons, 1990.

Nichiporuk, Brian. *The Security Dynamics of Demographic Factors.* Santa Monica, CA: RAND Corporation, 2000.

Norton, Augustus Richard. *Amal and the Shi'a: Struggle for the Soul of Lebanon.* Austin, TX: University of Texas Press, 1987.

Odling-Smee, F. J. "Niche Construction, Evolution and Culture." *The Companion Encyclopedia of Anthropology,* ed. by Tim Ingold. New York: Routledge, 1994.

Oliker, Olga, Thomas Szayna, and Sergej Mahnovski. *Potential Sources of Conflict in the Caspian Region.* Santa Monica, CA: RAND Corporation, March 2001.

O'Neill, Bard E. *Insurgency and Terrorism: Inside Modern Revolutionary Warfare.* Washington, DC: Brassey's, Inc., 1990.

O'Neill, Bard E. *Insurgency in the Modern World.* Boulder, CO: Westview Press, 1980.

Pape, Robert A. *Bombing to Win.* Ithaca, NY: Cornell University Press, 1996.

Peters, Rudolph. *Islam and Colonialism: The Doctrine of Jihad in Modern History.* New York: Mouton de Gruyter Publishers, 1984.

Plato. *Republic.* Translated by Robin Waterfield. New York: Oxford University Press, 1993.

Port, Robert, and Timothy Van Gelder, eds. *Mind as Motion: Explorations in the Dynamics of Cognition.* Cambridge, MA: The MIT Press, 1995.

Rabasa, Angel, and Peter Chalk. *Colombian Labyrinth: The Synergy of Drugs and Insurgency and its Implications for Regional Stability.* Santa Monica, CA: RAND, 2001.

Rapoport, David, ed. *Inside Terrorist Organizations.* London: Frank Cass Publishers, 2001.

Rashid, Ahmed. *The Resurgence of Central Asia: Islam or Nationalism.* Karachi, Pakistan: Oxford University Press, 1994.

Raskin, P., E. Hansen, Z. Zhu, and M. Iwra. "Simulation of Water Supply and Demand in the Aral Sea Region." *Water International,* vol. 17, 1992.

Reisman, W. Michael, and Chris T. Antoniou, eds. *The Laws of War: A Comprehensive Collection of Primary Documents on International Laws Governing Armed Conflict.* New York: Vintage Books, 1994.

Rubinstein, Ariel. *Modeling Bounded Rationality.* Cambridge, MA: The MIT Press, 1998.

Schelling, Thomas. *Arms and Influence.* New Haven, CT: Yale University Press, 1966.

Schulkin, Jay. *Rethinking Homeostasis: Allostatic Regulation in Physiology and Pathophysiology.* Cambridge, MA: The MIT Press, 2003.

Sears, David, et al., eds. *Oxford Handbook of Political Psychology.* New York: Oxford University Press, 2003.

Selznick, Philip, "Foundations of the Theory of Organization." *American Sociological Review* 13, 1948.

Shafritz, Jay M., and J. Steven Ott, ed. *Classics of Organization Theory.* Fort Worth, TX: Harcourt College Publishers, 2001.

Shultz, Richard H., and William J. Olson. *Ethnic and Religious Conflict: Emerging Threat to U.S. Security.* Washington, DC: National Strategy Information Center, 1994.

Simonsen, Clifford E., and Jeremy R. Spindlove. *Terrorism Today: The Past, the Players, the Future.* Upper Saddle River, NJ: Prentice Hall, 2000.

Singer, J. David, and Associates. *Explaining War.* Beverly Hills, CA: Sage, 1979.

Snow, Donald. *Uncivil Wars: International Security and the New Internal Conflicts.* Boulder, CO: Lynne Rienner Publishers, 1996.

Snow, Donald M., and Eugene Brown. *International Relations: The Changing Contours of Power.* New York: Longman, 2000.

Staub, Ervin. *The Psychology of Good and Evil: Why Children, Adults, and Groups Help and Harm Others.* New York: Cambridge University Press, 2003.

Summers, Harry G., Jr. *On Strategy: A Critical Analysis of the Vietnam War*. Novato, CA: Presidio Press, 1982.

Sykes, Gresham. *Criminology*. New York: Harcourt Brace Jovanovich, 1978.

Szayna, Thomas S., ed. *Identifying Potential Ethnic Conflict: Application of a Process Model*. Santa Monica, CA: RAND Corporation, 2000.

Thomas, Troy S. "Prisoner's of War in Islam: A Legal Inquiry." *The Muslim World*. January 1997, vol. 87, no. 1.

Tilly, Charles. *From Mobilization to Revolution*. New York: Random House, 1978.

Tilly, Charles. *The Politics of Collective Violence*. Cambridge, UK: Cambridge University Press, 2003.

van Creveld, Martin. *The Transformation of War*. New York: The Free Press, 1991.

Viotti, Paul R., and Mark V. Kauppi. *International Relations and World Politics: Security, Economy and Identity*. Upper Saddle River, NJ: Prentice Hall. 1997.

Wallace, William, and Daphene Josselin. *Non State Actors in World Politics*. New York: Palgrave, 2001.

Weiner, Myron. "Security, Stability and International Migration." *International Security*, vol. 17, no. 3, Winter 1992/1993.

Weissman, David. *A Social Ontology*. New Haven, CT: Yale University, 2000.

West-Eberhard, Mary Jane. *Developmental Plasticity and Evolution*. New York: Oxford, 2003.

Whittaker, David J. *The Terrorism Reader*. New York: Routledge, 2001.

Williams, Phil. "Transnational Criminal Organizations." In *In Athena's Camp: Preparing for Conflict in the Information Age*, ed. John Arguilla and David Ronfedt. Santa Monica, CA: RAND, 1997.

Index

militant religious movements, groups, and organizations, 8, 18, 80, 100, 105, 121–23, 133–42, 180, 192. *See also* Abu Sayyaf; Al Qaida; Al Aqsa Martry's Brigade; Christian Patriotic Union; Egyptian Islamic Jihad; Hezbollah; Islamic Army of Aden; Islamic Jihad; Islamic Movement of Uzbekistan; jihadist; Moro Islamic Liberation Front

Military operations, 173; Desert Fox, 107; Enduring Freedom, 112, 127, 141

Montaigne, Michel de, 4

Mintzberg, Henry, 109, 119

mobilization, 15, 17, 20, 35, 54, 57, 63, 66, 78–79, 143, 145, 194; identity, 25, 65, 74–79, 92, 96, 100, 117

model, 19, 20, 101; computer modeling, 11, 20, 21, 26, 32, 198, 199, 212, 218, 222, 223; rational choice model, 109, 118; systems model, 97, 143, 202

Moro Islamic Liberation Front (MILF), 8, 59. *See also* Philippines

Moro National Liberation Front (MNLF), 59. *See also* Philippines

Mufti (of Tashkent), 72. *See also* Uzbekistan

Mujahideen, 136, 170, 173. *See also* Afghanistan

multinational corporations, 25, 128

Muslim, 57–59, 64–68, 70, 71, 74, 77, 82, 84–85, 89, 111, 114, 136–39, 145, 154, 165, 178, 207

Muslim Brotherhood, 58, 87, 135, 154

myth creation, 79, 194–95, 215; foundational, 194–96, 211

Namangani, Juma, 140–41. *See also* Islamic Movement of Uzbekistan

narcotics, 40, 130, 133. *See also* drug trade

narrative, 190; rhetoric, 111, 134, 139, 143; story, 191, 194–95, 207, 220; storytelling mind, 189–90

nation, 65–67, 81, 144. *See also* ethnic groups, identity mobilization, tribe

National Liberation Army (ELN), 56, 117. *See also* Colombia

nation-building, 64, 143

nation-state, 2, 64–65, 80, 87, 94, 98, 158–59, 167, 180, 189, 206–207

negative entropy, 16–19, 86, 93–96, 98, 99, 102, 103, 105, 106, 108, 109, 113–17, 141,

148, 152, 158, 171, 174, 185, 186, 196, 197, 201, 204, 210, 226

network analysis, 103

Nevada-Semey Movement, 150

niche: construction, 16, 56, 80–86, 90, 115, 128, 205, 215, 222, 228, 230; destruction, 82, 222

Nigeria, 25, 136

Niyazov, Saparmurat, 28, 66–67, 144. *See also* Turkmenistan/Turkmenbashi

Northern Alliance, 36, 38, 125. *See also* Afghanistan

Ocalan, Abdullah, 79

Official Islam. *See* Islam

Oklahoma City, 134

Olcott, Martha Brill, 51, 69, 99, 131, 153

Omar, Mullah Mohammed, 165. *See also* Afghanistan

O'Neill, Bard E., 174, 183

open system, 2, 3, 12–14, 17, 18, 93, 95, 96, 109, 122, 151, 160, 175, 181, 189, 198, 209, 210, 215, 217, 219–20, 230; approach, 92, 221, 223, 225; framework, 54, 79, 92, 172, 224, 237. *See also* system

operational concepts, 197, 210, 217; attend to life history, 203–204, 217; diachronic effects, 187, 191, 196, 217, 223; disrupt boundary relations, 202–203, 217; disrupt well-connected nodes, 199–200, 217; implement across the system, 205–207, 217; increase entropy, 201–202, 217; increase uncertainty, 204–205, 217; leverage feedback loops, 200–201, 217; synergy minus one, 198–99, 217

Organization for Security and Cooperation in Europe (OSCE), 38

organizational theory, 16, 92, 98, 100, 120, 196, 205; classical theory, 92; formal organization, 92, 94–96, 104, 109, 111, 116; informal organization, 12, 92, 94, 97, 108, 111; mechanistic, 92, 97, 104, 109, 111; organic, 14, 111; progressive mechanization, 97–98; structural, 11, 92, 94, 97

organized crime, 15, 25, 32, 37–40, 42, 50, 61, 87, 94, 129, 131–33, 153, 176, 179, 215. *See also* Transnational Criminal Organizations

About the Authors

Troy S. Thomas is an Air Force officer assigned to the Joint Chiefs of Staff with professional experience in intelligence operations, defense policy, and academia. In addition to leading airmen in homeland defense missions and combat operations in the Middle East, Troy served as intelligence flight commander for the 1st Fighter Wing, a war planner in South Korea, an Assistant Professor of Political Science at the U.S. Air Force Academy, and a Fellow with the Center for Strategic Intelligence Research. A distinguished graduate from the Air Force Academy, he holds a MA in Government from the University of Texas, Austin, a MA in Organizational Management from George Washington University, and a MA in Operational Studies from the USMC School of Advanced Warfighting. Troy is a term member with the Council on Foreign Relations, a member of the Council for Emerging National Security Affairs, and Associate with the Institute for National Security Studies. Travel to over 38 countries informs his award-winning publications on leadership, conflict, intelligence, and Islam.

Steve Kiser is a Major in the United States Air Force and Commander of the 614th Space Intelligence Squadron. He has an MA in Asian Politics from the University of Hawai'i at Manoa and a PhD in Policy Analysis from the Pardee-RAND Graduate School in Santa Monica, CA. His dissertation modeled the financial infrastructure of the notional terrorist groups, testing the effectiveness of various U.S. and international policies aimed at disrupting those infrastructures. A career intelligence officer, Major Kiser has served in over a dozen countries around the world, including Saudi Arabia, Turkey, Uzbekistan, Republic of Korea, Panama and Peru. He also taught a variety of courses

'es Air Force Academy, including Terrorism and Political Vi-
ive Politics and International Relations. He is a term mem-
_ ⌐ouncil for Foreign Relations and the Pacific Council for International Programs.

Among other works, Major Kiser is the author of *Water: The Hydraulic Pa-
rameter of Conflict in the Middle East and North Africa*, and is the co-author of
Lords of the Silk Route: Violent Non-State Actors in Central Asia, as well as the
author of numerous articles, book chapters, and monographs on environmental security and non-state actors.

William D. Casebeer is a Major in the Air Force and an Air Force intelligence
officer with experience as a Southwest Asian political and military analyst.
Formerly an Associate Professor of Philosophy at the U.S. Air Force Academy,
Major Casebeer is currently studying Middle East affairs at the Naval Post-
graduate School, and has earned a BS in political science from the Air Force
Academy, an MA in Philosophy from the University of Arizona, and a PhD in
Cognitive Science and Philosophy at the University of California at San Diego
(where his thesis won the Council of Graduate School's campus-wide Out-
standing Dissertation Award). His critically praised book *Natural Ethical
Facts: Evolution, Connectionism, and Moral Cognition* was published by MIT
Press in 2003, and his work appears regularly in journals such as *Nature Re-
views Neuroscience, Biology and Philosophy, International Relations, The Journal of Moral Education, Strategic Insights*, etc. His research interests include the
naturalization of ethics, issues at the intersections of cognitive philosophy and
security issues, the psychology of terrorism, military ethics, and computer
simulations of social phenomena. Major Casebeer is a term member of the
Council on Foreign Relations, a fellow with the Pacific Council and the International Institute for Strategic Studies, and an Institute for National Security
Studies associate. His next book will explore the role military force plays in
culture change and democratization.